ECHOES FROM THE BLUFFS

Volume II

By:
The Green River Historic Preservation Commission
Green River, Wyoming

Echoes From the Bluffs: Volume II
© 2018 The Green River Historic Preservation Commission

All images are courtesy of the Sweetwater County
Historical Museum unless otherwise noted.

Cover design by Brigida R. Blasi

Originally published in 2004
2018 Reprint by
The Sweetwater County Museum Foundation
Green River, Wyoming
ISBN-13: 978-1725817357
ISBN-10: 1725817357

This book is dedicated to
Marna Jessen Grubb
for her tireless work in the preservation
and promotion of the history of the City of Green River.

As this book went to print, Marna was preparing to leave
Green River in order to move closer to her daughter and
family. Marna is one of Green River's finest local products,
having spent her entire life here. She served on the Green
River Historic Preservation Commission for fourteen years
and spearheaded many of its projects, including the
publication of this book.

During her time as Green River City Clerk she was also
responsible for installation of the historical photos and
artwork, which adorn the walls of City Hall.
She is the two-time winner of Green River's
Distinguished Citizen's Award.

Marna is one of those irreplaceable treasures and Green
River will be poorer for her departure.

Bon voyage, Marna, and best wishes
from your friends in Green River.

ECHOES FROM THE BLUFFS
Volume II

By:
The Green River Historic Preservation Commission
Green River, Wyoming

One of the objectives of the Green River Historic Preservation Commission is to capture the fascinating history of the Green River area and to preserve it for the enjoyment of generations to come. In November of 1991, the Commission began composing and publishing historical articles periodically in *The Green River Star* weekly newspaper under the heading of *Echoes from the Bluffs*.

In 1998, these articles from 1991 into 1998 were published into a book titled ECHOES FROM THE BLUFFS, Volume 1.

In 2004, the Echoes articles published in *The Green River Star* from 1998 into 2003 were gathered and published into this book titled ECHOES FROM THE BLUFFS, Volume 2. Volume 2 also contains information previously published in the Commission's brochure covering mayors since Green River was incorporated under the laws of the newly-formed State of Wyoming in 1891 to the present. Much time had been spent in researching these fine individuals. We hope you will enjoy this section also.

"Thank you" to *The Green River Star* for publishing our articles each month and for their encouragement and support.

THE GREEN RIVER
HISTORIC PRESERVATION COMMISSION

The five-member GREEN RIVER HISTORIC PRESERVATION COMMISSION was established by city ordinance in June of 1990 to preserve Green River history. Its members are appointed by the Governing Body of the City of Green River.

Current Commission members are Ruth Lauritzen, Marna Grubb, Terry Del Bene, Bill Thompson and Bill Duncan. Photo by Kathy Gilbert, *The Green River Star*

ECHOES FROM THE BLUFFS
Volume 2

CONTENTS
Articles originally published in *The Green River Star* 1998-2003

~ ~ ~ ~ ~ ~ ~ ~

GREEN RIVER MAYORS 1891 - 2003

POSTAL PROGRESS:
THE HISTORY OF GREEN RIVER'S FIRST FEDERAL BUILDING

By: Ruth Lauritzen

In 1997 a new property was added to the short list of Green River historic structures included on the National Register of Historic Places. The National Trust for Historic Preservation uses this program to recognize historical buildings that are significant in a community and which have undergone a minimum of external change and modernization. When the old Green River Post Office gained Register status on December 11, 1997, it joined just two other Green River properties on the Register, Expedition Island and the Brewery. The building represents a distinct type of construction and also tells much about the development of the town.

Architecturally speaking, the building is a well-preserved and unaltered example of Neoclassical design. This type of architecture was in common use for United States government buildings for many years and has its roots in ancient Greek design. Distinctive characteristics of this type of architecture are symmetrical placement of windows flanking a centrally-placed door, and the

The Green River Post Office was built in 1931 and was the town's first federal building. (Photo courtesy Sweetwater County Historical Museum)

use of a triangular pediment supported by columns.

From a historical perspective the Green River Post Office is also noteworthy. It was the first federally-constructed building in the city and its completion was an event that local citizens had worked for and anticipated for over twenty years. The town's post office had for years been housed in various business houses and storefronts in the downtown area. These accommodations, while at one time sufficient, had failed to grow with the town and by the early 1900s were considered sorely inadequate.

A building site at 3 East Flaming Gorge Way was purchased in 1910, but progress toward a building was slow. Many of the efforts and disappointments of the town are recorded in the local newspaper, *The Green River Star*. In a February 1916 article, Postmaster Elmer Ace, chairman of the post office committee, reported progress toward a new building. The Wyoming Congressional delegation was working for an appropriation. Representative Charles E. Winter had, on January 30th of that year, presented Bill 8648 to provide for the erection of a public building in Green River. However, nothing came from this early effort and Green River continued without its federal building.

The issue reappeared a few years later when on March 4, 1927, there was an article captioned, "Come on Green River Let's Get Federal Building". The city's need for the building was discussed in the monthly meeting of the American Legion. Unfortunately, telegrams from Senators John B. Kendrick and F.E. Warren directed to the Legion indicated that it would be impossible to provide appropriation for Green River in the near future.

However, two years later the news appeared brighter. On May 25, 1929 the Elliott Act, which authorized a massive public buildings construction program, was approved. This legislation provided for the construction of two public buildings in every state. The Wyoming delegation in Washington, D.C. selected Thermopolis and Green River in their recommendations to the Post Office Department. A *Star* article of March 1st reported that the outlook for the building was good. In a telegram received by William Yates of the Green River Community Club, F.E. Warren relayed that the Committee of Public Buildings had recommended to Congress an appropriation of $60,000 for a federal building in Green River.

Another year lapsed before a July 1930 item in the *Star* announced, "Green River Almost Certain of Federal Building Within Year". In spite of seemingly concrete evidence of the reality of the project, a published request for bids and a site survey, the skepticism of the locals can be seen in the phrasing of the article. It stated, "The plans, it is understood, are for an imposing structure that will add greatly to the beauty of the town, and it is sincerely hoped that at last there will be some material evidence produced that this much needed structure will be realized."

The news of the coming construction was not the only good news for the city at that time. In 1929 the Union Pacific had enlarged its yards and natural gas mains were serving the city. On May 2, 1930 it was reported that the population had reached 2,576, an 11% increase over 1920. An article of October 3rd reported that bank deposits were up and stated, "...the purported Depression said to have manifested itself in other parts of the country has apparently not materially affected business conditions here."

On November 28, 1930 the federal building seemed a step nearer when the *Star* reported that the building site had been ordered for clearance. Two structures were located on-site: an adobe building and the residence of the local superintendent of the Union Pacific Railway Company. The first was torn down while the second was moved to another lot on East First North (East Railroad Avenue).

It seemed that the years of high hopes and broken promises were soon to be at an end. As the year drew to a close, it was reported (December 12th) that the contracts for the post office would soon be let. Postmaster R.A. Hoover had been informed that the plans were being drawn.

In January 1931 construction bids were requested and excavation began on April 20, 1931, under the direction of Earl E. Garber of Bethlehem, Pennsylvania. Evers Brothers of Green River would complete the excavation work on the $75,000 building. A *Star* article of May 15th reported that excavation was nearly complete and the Evers Brothers would also complete the concrete work. "This structure", the article continued, "is going to be a most attractive feature, being just opposite the County Courthouse on the main Lincoln Highway, and judging from the drawing will be an architectural accomplishment that will be a great credit to the town."

On July 17th it was announced that the cornerstone for the new building would be laid the following Monday with impressive ceremonies. The event was no doubt of great importance and special interest to local citizens due to the years of effort involved in bringing the project to pass. The cornerstone ceremonies were presided over by the Masonic Grand Lodge of Wyoming and former Green River mayor and Masonic leader T.S. Taliaferro Jr. delivered an eloquent address to the hundreds of citizens gathered for the event.

Construction of the building was completed and hundreds of Green River citizens attended the dedication on April 29, 1932. The high school orchestra and several soloists provided music for the program. The *Star* commented that after many years of effort on the part of local citizens, "some of which have answered the Masters's call and have gone to their heavenly reward, Green River has at last realized the completion of one of the finest federal buildings that can be found in a town twice the population of Green River." An article of May 13th reported that the post office had moved into the federal building.

It is interesting to note that construction of the Green River Post Office building occurred not during Roosevelt's New Deal era as did many of the historic post offices in Wyoming, but under the early Depression intervention programs of Herbert Hoover's administration.

The building continued to serve as the Green River Post Office until 1981 when the new post office on the south side of town was brought into service. The old building was purchased by the City of Green River who leased it to Armando and Trudel Lopez who ran Trudel's Restaurante on the property. After Trudel's moved out, the building sat vacant for several years before a property swap between the city and Sweetwater County brought it under county ownership. The building was renovated and became the home of the Sweetwater County Historical Museum in November 2001.

A DOCTOR WHO MAKES HOUSE CALLS!

By: Marna Grubb

At the City of Green River's Boards and Commissions Appreciation Dinner held in May of 1998 at the Island Pavilion, William Close, MD, was guest speaker - and what a joy it was to hear of his "adventures"!

At the time, Dr. Close was a family physician practicing in the Big Piney, Wyoming area since 1977. At the age when most would have retired, Dr. Close was continuing to serve with sincere concern and compassion. His policy was "to see patients in **their homes** as often as necessary when they arrive at the end of their lives." He and his nurse did this together and often charged nothing for their calls.

In reading two of the books written by Dr. Close, *Ebola* and *A Doctor's Story,* one becomes aware of a humble, dedicated man who began as a "gung-ho surgeon" in New York City. He received his education at Harvard College and the Columbia College of Physicians and Surgeons, graduating with an MD in 1951. He had also served as a pilot in the U.S. Army Air Corps in France from 1942 to 1945.

God's guidance and a spirit of adventure called him to the Republic of Zaire in Africa in 1960. He had thought his stay in the Congo would be brief, but he became completely captivated by his work, his love for medicine and in helping others. He was in Africa for 16 years until 1976. During this time he had been the only surgeon in the 1500-bed Kinshasa General Hospital, Chief Doctor of the Congolese Army, Physician to the President of the Republic of Zaire and Director of Presidential Medical Services.

Looking back through the years, Dr. Close considered his most difficult years as moments in Africa. One such time was when his treatment of a young boy's leg had not gone well. With his feeling of responsibility, he nearly gave up surgery at that time.

Also his years in Africa were difficult in terms of his family. He and his wife, Bettine (Tine), married when they were 18. They have four children - Tina, Glennie, Alexander and Jessie. Glennie is actress Glenn Close.

Doctor Close is shown on the cover of one of several books he has authored. (Photo permission from Doctor Close)

While in Africa, Dr. Close found it difficult to get away and the children were attending school in Switzerland. Trying to balance family and career was difficult, if not impossible. Dr. Close had truly been blessed with a very supportive family during his endeavors to help people through medicine. Their love and respect for each other was most evident.

Dr. Close referred to the most memorable years of his career as those in Big Piney. He enjoyed his practice and spoke lovingly of the people in the area. He enjoyed the compassion and caring they exhibited for one another. "When they call," he said, "I go, because they do not call unless they really need help."

I wondered why he and his wife had decided to settle in the Big Piney area after his extensive travels. He explained that they had visited their daughter and grandchildren who were spending the summer in Jackson. Dr. Close and Tine felt they needed to find a place to "get off the world" for a while after leaving Africa.

Nothing around Jackson had seemed isolated enough until the real estate person took them into the mountains west of Big Piney. The ranch bordered Bridger National Forest, the wild flowers were abundant, and a cow moose and her calf were bedded down while a herd of antelope ran in the distance. They decided this was the place where they could quietly read, maybe write, and be with their dogs and an old horse.

Quoting from his book, "During the process of settling in, I went to the little clinic in Big Piney and told the nurse practitioner that I would be happy to come down from the ranch a couple mornings a week if she thought it would be helpful. Within a few months we were building a home near town, and the medical work had developed into a 24-hour-a-day, 7-days-per-week proposition.

Dr. Close had remained in touch with those responsible for medical services in the Congo where his responsibilities continued. He advised that most challenging had been the writing of his two books, and a third book had just been completed and was being prepared for publication.

He found it most rewarding to speak with students of medicine. Some of his speaking engagements had been for Columbia University, the University of Utah Medical School, the New York Surgical Society, the University of Virginia Medical School and the University of Colorado Medical School.

He received much satisfaction in leaving something to the young students of medicine. When meeting with these future doctors, he encouraged them to be more compassionate with their patients, to converse with them regarding their concerns and fears.

As quoted from *A Doctor's Story*, "Patients will always want and need technically competent physicians and surgeons who make time to listen and understand."

William "Beaver Dick" Leigh (standing) and his family. (William H. Jackson photo – courtesy Bill Thompson)

MOUNTAIN MEN, A RENDEZVOUS ON THE GREEN AND A BATTLE WITH THE BANNOCKS

By: Bill Thompson

My great-grandfather the Englishman Richard (Beaver Dick) Leigh was one of the last mountain men. He left the Mexican War and trapped for a time in the Salt Lake Valley. In the 1850s he came into the Teton area and described that range as "the beautifulist sight in the whole world." He married Jenny, a Shoshone from Chief Washakies' tribe. Leigh and the much older Jim Bridger were guides for the 1872 Hayden Expedition. In reward for his services as scout and guide in the Jackson and Teton region Jenny Lake and Leigh Lake were named in their honor. His beloved Jenny and his entire family died from Bea-inga-ta-se (Smallpox) during the Christmas of 1876. My daughter Jenny Leigh, although no blood relation, is her namesake. Leigh married Susan Tadpole, the daughter of Bannock Chief Pam Pigamea in 1879 (my great-grandmother).

The Bannocks ranged from their home base in present day Idaho through Utah, Colorado, Montana and Wyoming. Although the Bannocks were a small tribe in numbers, they were fiercely belligerent. But they got along well with the Shoshones in Wyoming. They would travel from Idaho through the Jackson region and visit their "cousins" in the Lander/Riverton area. Trading, games, contests and marriages took place there.

The trails of the original mountain men were luke warm when Leigh arrived in "his" valley. It was trapping from the 1820s through 1840s that furnished the stuff of legends and fact. As most of us know, mountain men hunted and trapped in the Rockies during the winter then met at a designated spot to trade furs for necessary supplies in the summer. This was the training ground for future guides to parties crossing the plains and mountains to California or Oregon. Osborne Russell was one such person. He spent the years 1834 through 1843 as a trapper in the Rocky Mountains. He relates of one such rendezvous in 1837 on the Green River in his "Journal of a Trapper or Nine Years in the Rocky Mountains."

Russell states that he found the hunting parties all assembled waiting for the arrival of supplies from the States. Here presented what might be termed a mixed multitude. The whites were chiefly Americans and Canadian French with some Dutch, Scotch, Irish, English, half-breed and full-blood Indians of nearly every tribe of the Rocky Mountains. He tells about some of gambling at cards, some playing the Indian Game of "hand" and others horse racing. Other small groups were under shady trees relating the events of the past year. He states that all were in good health for "sickness is a stranger seldom met with in these regions."

This quiet manner was interrupted when something new arose for their amusement. The Bannock Indians had for several years lived with whites on terms partly hostile, frequently stealing horses and traps and in one instance killed two white trappers. They had taken horses and traps from a party of French trappers who were hunting Bear River in April and "they were impudent enough to come with the village of sixty lodges and encamp within three miles of us in order to trade with the whites as usual, still having the stolen property in their possession and refusing to give it up."

On the 15th of June, while the men were out hunting buffalo, four or five whites and two Nez Perce Indians went to their village and took the stolen horses back to Osborne's camp. Around 3 p.m., 30 Bannocks armed with their weapons came riding at full gallop into the camp. They demanded the horses the Nez Perce had taken. But previously the Nez Perce numbering only six and not wishing to take on the Bannocks had given the horses to the whites for protection.

Nearly all the whites in camp were under arms. Some of the Bannocks learning of this started to leave. But one of the Bannocks rushed through the crowd, seized the bridle of the stolen horse Jim Bridger was holding and tried to drag it from him by force without heeding the cocked rifles that surrounded him. "He was a brave Indian but his bravery proved fatal." Two rifle balls whistled through his body. The others wheeled to run but 12 were shot from their horses. The camp mounted horses and pursued them. The village was plundered and destroyed. "We followed and fought them three days, when they begged us to let them go and promised to be good Indians in the future ..."

On July 5th a party arrived from the states with supplies. They were under the direction of Thomas Fitzpatrick accompanied by Captain William Stewart on another tour of the Rocky Mountains. Joy now ruled. There were letters from friends and relations, public papers and news of the day. Others got a blanket, a cotton shirt, or a few pints of coffee and sugar - at 2,000 percent profit to the traders. Sugar was $2 a pint, coffee the same, blankets $20 each, tobacco $2 a pound, alcohol $4 a pint, common cotton shirts $5 each. In return the trappers were paid $4 or $5 per pound for beaver.

Russell concludes that after a few days the bustle began to subside. The furs were done up in packs ready for transportation to the states.

Parties were formed for hunting the coming year. One, consisting of 110 men, was destined for the Blackfoot country under direction of L. B. Fontanelle and guided by Jim Bridger. "I started with five others to hunt the headwaters of the Yellowstone, Missouri and Big Horn Rivers, a portion of the country I was particularly fond of hunting."

YOUR HOME AND THE NATIONAL REGISTER OF HISTORIC PLACES

By: Terry A. Del Bene

You say you've got a nice older home? Would you like to show it off? Would you like to have some help in keeping it historic looking? Something you might wish to consider is getting your house on the National Register of Historic Places. There are literally hundreds of privately owned homes on the National Register at this time. The process to obtain listing need not be overly complex, time-consuming, expensive, or frustrating. In fact, there are several benefits to having your home listed. You can have one of those spiffy metal plaques attached to your home which identifies the property as being worthy of national recognition. You can get tax breaks for repair and maintenance of your historic home.

The National Register

The National Register is a compilation of sites, buildings, districts, structures, and objects which have been recorded, considered, and assessed, through a formal application process. Anyone can apply to have their property considered for inclusion within the National Register. The Register is intended to help in the preservation of properties significant to the Nation, the State, or the community. The first thing to keep in mind is that there are a lot of really nice homes and buildings in this nation Government and everything not all applications will result in listing.

Once on the Register, properties may be removed for a variety of reasons including: destruction of the property, alteration of the property, or loss of the qualities which made it eligible for inclusion within the Register.

As one might suspect if there is a Register someone has to keep it updated. This individual is called the Keeper. The Keeper (and her staff) review all the applications. In each application the Keeper is looking for several specific things. Remember, this is the Federal Government, and everything will have to be on the appropriate forms. Don't let that dissuade you from starting the effort. With a little help the forms are comprehensible and in no time at all you'll know things like the Keeper considers buildings and structures to be different things.

The Keeper Meditates Upon Your Request

The Keeper is required by law and regulation to assure that properties listed within the National Register meet the following criteria:

1) The property must meet one or more of the four criteria of evaluation (more than one for a property is better but not neccoary). The critcria are:

a) association with events which have made a significant contribution to the broad patterns of our history.

b) association with the lives of person significant in our past.

c) embodiment of the distinctive characteristics of a type, period, or method of construction, or that represent the work of a master or that possesses high artistic value.

d) that have yielded or may be likely to yield information important in prehistory or history.

Together these are quite a mouthful. Basically the Keeper will be looking to see if the building or structure was associated with important events, people, construction, art, design, or potential for historical research. Keep in mind that the importance need not be at a national level. The important event need not be the opening of the West but could be something of import to the community such as the founding of a town. The important people need not be Kit Carson, Mark Twain, or Butch Cassidy but could be a citizen of the community. The construction need not be designed by Frank Lloyd Wright but could use concrete blocks fabricated in Wyoming. The importance to research might be as simple as the property contains an intact privy or basement dating to the turn of the 19th Century.

2) The Keeper will need to determine if the property is more than 50 years old or meets exceptions to the 50-year-guideline. The guideline is a compromise as to what constitutes being old enough to be historic. Some of us are chagrinned to find out

that we have become historic or are not far from that magic designation. There are exceptions to this guideline and such properties as the Trinity Site (the place where the first atomic bomb was exploded) and a McDonald's restaurant (which was one of the last to still sport the golden arches) were put on the National Register before they hit 50. Such properties are put on the National Register because they had such overwhelming recognition in importance to history or our culture.

3) The Keeper will determine if the application is complete. This means the appropriate forms, maps, pictures, views of the State Historic Preservation Officer, etc. are included. If any of those components are missing the Keeper is more than happy to return the application for completion.

4) Something the Keeper is not officially looking for, but really affects the chances of getting on the National Register, is the hook. You have to make a case as to why your particular home is worthy of this national recognition.

Obviously if you're going through the application process you think it's a nifty place. Make sure those qualities jump out of the application and hit the Keeper on the nose. Remember the Keeper is looking at hundreds of applications each year. Your application might follow right on the heels of a dozen huge Pueblos in New Mexico, a Civil War Battlefield in Virginia, a steamship wreck in Missouri, or a plantation of one of the founding fathers. The Keeper is human and might wonder why a house in Green River should be considered with those stellar sites. We need to keep hammering on the importance of the property to the local community and history. Passion goes a long way in making the sale. I once saw a case where a Queen-Anne style home of little remark was placed on the register because Woodrow Wilson first bowled there (the property used to have clay bowling alleys in the back yard). I have to admit that I never really thought about President Wilson as the bowling president. However, the owner of the property did everything right and her passion for getting the listing won her the day.

Green River already has one National Register property, Expedition Island. We could easily have several others. Remember there are tax breaks and incentives for keeping such properties up. Show the world how proud we are of our homes.

GREEN RIVER:
THOMAS MORAN'S FIRST SKETCH OF THE WEST

By: Ruth Lauritzen

In the mid 1800s the trans-Mississippi west was known only to the Native Americans and a few intrepid souls such as mountain men, overland emigrants and early explorers. Indeed, some of the stories these people told were of a land so unusual and amazing that many easterners felt they must be outright lies. One of the first people to present visual evidence of these fantastic sites to the eastern public was landscape artist Thomas Moran. He painted the grand vistas and colors of the west in a style uniquely his own.

Moran was born in 1837 in Bolton, England. His family immigrated to the United States in 1844, taking up residence near Philadelphia. He served a short apprenticeship at an engraving firm, and began working with his brother Edward who was also an artist. In the 1860s the brothers went to England to study the work of famous British landscape artist J.M.W. Turner. This period of study undoubtedly influenced Moran as his later works were often compared to Turner's paintings.

Moran's rise to fame as a major artist began in 1871 when he was employed as a principal illustrator at *Scribner's Monthly*. That year the artist worked on illustrations for a series of articles in the magazine describing the experiences of a military expedition into the Yellowstone country the previous year. His drawings were based on descriptions and rough sketches provided by Nathaniel P. Langford who had accompanied the expedition, and his own artist's imagination.

As a result of this assignment he was seized with an intense desire to see for himself the wonders of Yellowstone. His opportunity came later that year when Langford again visited Yellowstone under an agreement with *Scribner's* to write another series of articles. Moran accompanied the writer to provide illustrations. The author and artist traveled in the company of the Hayden expedition, which was exploring the area for the United States government.

Long a Green River landmark, the Palisades were a favorite subject for Thomas Moran's paintings, and locally, a cool and shady picnic spot as shown in this 1920s photo. (Photo courtesy Sweetwater County Historical Museum)

Ferdinand V. Hayden was a surgeon by vocation, but a fine geologist and naturalist by avocation. Through the late 1860s and well into the 1870s he led numerous expeditions for the government in the American West. Also with the expedition was another soon-to-be famous artist, William Henry Jackson, renowned photographer of the westward movement. In addition to his sketching Moran worked extensively with Jackson on his photography.

Roughing it on the untamed frontier was a new experience for Moran. He had never ridden a horse before, nor slept outside and was known to have a delicate digestion with an intense dislike for fatty and fried foods. His desire to see Yellowstone outweighed any of these concerns and he bore up well under the conditions of the trip which included endless days in the saddle and camp food of bacon and fried bread.

In an article for *Appalachia* magazine in 1936, W.H. Jackson recalled that Moran "...made a picturesque appearance when mounted. The jaunty sombrero, long yellowish bead and portfolio under his arm marked the artistic type, with something of local color imparted by a rifle hung from the saddle horn."

Moran's "first sketch made in the West" was of the rock formations west of Green River currently known as Tollgate Rock and the Palisades. He was very intrigued with these massive geological formations. Using these sketches and others he made on subsequent trips, he produced many oil and watercolor paintings of the area during his artistic career. Each painting was different, but with one constant, the looming cliffs of the Green River valley. His final painting of the scene was made in 1918 when he was eighty-two.

Moran's work has sometimes been criticized as creating a romanticized and unrealistic view of the American West, however he has also been lauded as a major western American artist. He has been credited by some as the " Father of the National Parks". His large scale painting, "The Grand Canyon of the Yellowstone" impressed Congress with the beauties of the Yellowstone country and influenced them to designate it as the first National Park in the United States. This painting was purchased by Congress for $10,000 in 1872, becoming the first landscape in the Congressional Collection.

Thomas Moran died in 1926, leaving an impressive legacy to the art world. His importance to the promotion of the West is indicated by the fact that F.V. Hayden named Mount Moran, the largest of the three Grand Tetons, after his friend and colleague.

HEY MOM, WHAT DID YOU GUYS DO BEFORE TV?

By: Bill Duncan

Senator, what do you really think about the President and Monica? Well, Larry... Click!

And with that homer, the Rockies go down 17-0 in the bottom of the second ... Click!

Are you Hope, Kristen or Kari? I'm Stephano you fool! Click!

It's spandex around the middle with an 18 carat gold neck highlights and a silk bodice ... Click!

Remember how people used their "leisure" time before TV? Did parents hear the "I'm bored" cry as much? Barns needed shoveling out, water buckets needed carrying and darning or sewing was a necessity. Just listening to the radio was something one could do while doing something else - like homework. How far back would you like to go?

A little more than 60 years ago, Hard Times dances gave people a chance to get out and mingle without much cost. People enduring the depression could pay low admission, bring something for refreshments and dress in their daily work attire or worse without having to worry about wearing nice clothes. Folks could wear patched overalls, hard-worn shirts and old fashioned dresses to dance to schottisches, square dances, reels and polkas. Usually both music and food were donated.

The community hall at Farson and the old McKinnon School provided places for folks who were working hard and needed a socially acceptable way to let off steam. Some of the more energetic competed in Marathon Dances. Couples competed to see who could dance the longest. These highly publicized competitions gave prizes to whoever stayed on their feet the longest.

A decade or so later, girls threw one shoe into a pile on the middle of the dance floor. Boys scrambled into the pile and matched the shoe they recovered to its owner.

Music could be records or a movie projector showing a band playing. Hometown groups were popular. My grandmother accompanied my uncle's fiddle with chords from a portable pump organ. Another fellow joined them with his banjo or guitar.

Kids parked their cars around dark tennis courts at night and tuned their car radios to the same station for dance music.

Renowned big bands got off the train in Green River to play for dances on the Island.

A knock-knock-knock on the front door heralded the delivery of a May Basket on May 1 or the night before. Candy, a "special" piece of jewelry, some newly picked flowers or little keepsakes filled the baskets, which were usually homemade. Legend said that if the basket's receiver could catch the giver, then a kiss could be a reward. Of course that depended on who the giver was ... and how much the receiver wanted to kiss the giver. Dancing around Maypoles was popular with some Spring celebrations.

Spring brought lots of outdoor games. The quest for agates, cherries, steelies, clearies or boulders ruined knees on plenty of pants. Kids shot marbles out of big rings, into five holes or away from a line drawing in the dirt. Usually boys played marbles while the girls played variations of jacks. During the evening glow after the sun set, many Green River streets echoed with cans being kicked for Kick the Can. Hide and Seek or No Bears Are Out Tonight kept kids busy until it was too dark to play. Playground teachers organized more physical games like Red Rover or Red Light/Green Light.

I wonder what the kids who strapped on their roller skates and tightened them with a key would think of today's roller blades. Certainly the half pipes and paved parking lots are smoother and quicker than the old cement sidewalks. Many locals learned to skate in the Expedition Island building or the roller rink that's been turned into a storage facility.

During a break in the dancing, Box Socials provided fun, food, and raised money. Girls brought supper in a decorated box. Boys bought the pretty boxes because the real prize was eating with the girl who prepared that box. Of course the box maker was secret, but woe to the boy who couldn't buy his favorite girl's lunch.

Drive-in movies provided a great social opportunity for two or three decades. All one needed to do was wrangle a car, get a date, pay the money to get in and get parked next to the post with the speaker. Sometimes people actually put the speaker in the car and watched the movie. Tuesdays were dollar nights where I lived. Then we could cram as many kids as we could into the car and get in for a buck.

This social recount wouldn't be complete without remembering some of the mischief. Tipping over garbage cans (the 55-gallon drums that everyone burned rubbish in) or outhouses happened especially around Halloween. So did burning tires and hay bales in the middle of the street. Animals like pigeons and sheep found their way into schools. No newly wed couple's nuptials were complete until they had been "chivareed" and the groom wheeled the bride down the street in a wheelbarrow.

I'm sure our parents and grandparents heard the "I'm bored" question too. Mine countered with chores around the house, books to read or a shopping list. An ex-English teacher who now hangs around the senior citizens center used to say, "There are no bored people, just boring people."

I think I'll turn off my computer and go roll my hoop.

FIRST CAME THE STAGE

By: Ruth Lauritzen

Officially speaking, Green River began with the arrival of the railroad in 1868, but settlement in the area began six years before with the establishment of a stage station in 1862. The first stagecoach traffic rumbled across the continent in 1861 over the Oregon/California Trail route thirty miles north of Green River. However, the next year the coaches moved to a more southern trail due to the development of Denver, Colorado as a thriving commercial center and more importantly, the increasing danger of Indian attack on the northern plains.

The Central Overland Express stage station stands near the confluence of the Bitter Creek and the Green River. The site is located in the area of the Wyoming Game and Fish building on Astle Avenue. (Photo courtesy Sweetwater County Historical Museum)

The new line, the Central Overland Express, began in Atchison, Kansas and ended in Placerville, California for a total of 1,913 miles and seventeen days travel time. The track wended its way across Kansas and into Denver. From there it turned north to Wyoming where it crossed the southern part of the state, passing through both Green River and Rock Springs. It went on to Salt Lake City and continued south through central Nevada by way of Carson City and thence into Placerville, which was located in the "elbow" of California.

During its heyday the stage line was owned and run by Ben Holladay who was known as the "Stagecoach King". The logistical problems of running passenger and mail service over so many miles of trail through such remote areas were considerable. A speedy trip required good and frequently replaced horseflesh, sturdy coaches and some trail upkeep. Because it carried human cargo, the line also had to ship out supplies and personnel to provide meals.

The system devised by Holladay consisted of a series of stations spread across the route. A swing station was located every ten to fifteen miles to provide a change of animals. Such frequent substitution of animals was necessary because an average speed of eight miles an hour was required. About every fifty miles were the home stations where the driver was changed and passengers had a chance to stop for about forty minutes to eat a meal. This usually occurred about twice a day.

The quality and price of meals varied widely, depending on the location of the station. Closer to civilization, fifty cents could buy a dinner of two types of meat, potatoes, fresh vegetables, bread and butter, pie and coffee or tea. Further out in the wilderness a two-dollar fee purchased a handsome repast of fried salt pork, biscuits and bad coffee. According to many travelers, the worst food to be had was available between Denver and Salt Lake City due to the remote location of the stage stops. Green River, perhaps, provided better than many because of its proximity to good water. Hunting and fishing allowed for a greater variety of foods, and clean, clear water made a much better cup of coffee.

Some home stations were more important than others. The entire line was divided into divisions with certain home stations designated as the division headquarters. Green River was one such station. As such, the station was overseen by an agent and a steward who were in charge of distribution of supplies and livestock, hiring of personnel and resolution of disputes. The division headquarters were also home to the farrier and harness maker who had a separate team and outfit and traveled continually from station to station within the division to do necessary repairs and maintenance.

According to Frank A. Root, an employee of the stage line and author of *The Overland Stage to California*, the home stations were generally "...commodious buildings, arranged with sleeping rooms, dining-room, office, telegraph office, barn, etc." Because of its status as a division headquarters, the Green River Station complex would have also had storerooms for the division supplies. According to local historian Adrian Reynolds, these buildings were constructed of native sandstone and located approximately where the Wyoming Game and Fish building is on Astle Avenue.

This busy little outpost in the wilderness lost a great deal of its importance with the arrival of the railroad in 1868 and the shifting of development activity to the north side of the river. The buildings saw some continued use, but were eventually abandoned and razed. Because no built evidence of this settlement remains, it is easy to forget that the oldest buildings in Green River were not on the "old" north side of the river, but on the "new" south side.

RIVERVIEW CEMETERY

By: Marna Grubb

Webster defines the word cemetery as "a place for the burial of the dead; formerly, a churchyard or a catacomb; now, usually, a large park-like enclosure, laid out and kept for purposes of interment, put to sleep."

Green River's Riverview Cemetery is an area of which residents can be most proud. It is located on the hill above the city, east of Castle Rock. It reminds me of a plushy green oasis in the middle of the "desert."

Memories of many fine people came to mind as I toured the cemetery one day in 1998 with Allan Wilson, the City's cemetery caretaker. I was reliving Green River's history, and mine, as I passed by grave markers bearing names of former mayors, businessmen, my family doctors, relatives, friends, and acquaintances. I marveled at the variety of beautiful stones marking the spots of the many loved ones resting there.

Gate to Green River's Riverview Cemetery was purchased in 1914. This barren scene has now been replaced with a beautifully-landscaped area with paved roads. (City of Green River photo)

The day was sunny and warm, with no wind, so peaceful. The area looked cozy and inviting as we passed by wooden benches which had been constructed by the City and placed in cement at appropriate places for the convenience of those visiting the cemetery. This was one of the many projects visualized and brought to completion by Caretaker Allan Wilson, who was recognized for his dedication as the City's Outstanding Employee in 1992.

Wildlife abounds in the area. In the Spring of 1998, Allan reported that there was an average of ten deer, with two does and two spotted fawns visiting the cemetery. The deer many times enjoyed eating the flowers, which wasn't too popular with those bringing flowers for their loved ones, although many probably wouldn't mind sharing.

Allan also advised that there had been a fox with four to six babies observed behind the water tank. Of course, there always were rabbits, with approximately 50 in 1998 -- "a rabbit year," he commented. Also, red-tail tree squirrels had been spotted.

As one entered the front gate, it was very apparent that this cemetery was very well kept and landscaped compared to the plain dirt evidenced in the photo from several years ago. The pine trees and lilac bushes have flourished through the years.

The individual cement copings had been removed and turf had been planted throughout for perpetual care. River rock, plus many new trees and shrubs, lined the roadways.

Straight ahead from the gate was the Ten Commandments monument which formerly stood at 91 West Flaming Gorge Way in front of the Town Hall building occupied by the Town of Green River from 1954 to 1982. The monument had been donated by the Wyoming State Aerie Fraternal Order of Eagles in June of 1968. It was moved to the cemetery and later destroyed by vandals. It was completely replaced by the City of Green River in the Fall of 1996.

From 1868 until 1913, Green River's original cemetery was located at the site of the town's present Sweetwater County Library at 300 North First East, formerly Elizabeth Street. In 1913, the Town Council passed a resolution to purchase 80 acres of land from the U.S. government for a new cemetery, which became Riverview Cemetery. The gate and fencing were purchased in 1914.

In 1926, the town transferred known bodies and grave markers from the old cemetery to Riverview. Throughout the years, additional graves have been uncovered: in 1944 during construction of World War II veterans' temporary housing; in 1978 during construction of the new library; in the spring of 1983 during library landscaping; and, again, during structural work that was necessary to the library in 1985 and 1986.

In 1943, the Town Council designated Section "I" of the Riverview Cemetery as the Veterans' plot for the burial of veterans only. I spoke to James Ringdahl in 1998, who was Quartermaster of Green River's V.F.W. Pilot Butte Post No. 2321. At that time, he reported that there were 76 veterans buried in the Veterans' plot. Other veterans had chosen to be buried in their private lots.

Ringdahl, who had been with the V.F.W. since 1951, further advised that, in the Veterans' plot, there were two from the Civil War, one from the Spanish American War, and the remainder from World War I, World War II, the Korean War, and the Viet Nam War.

Thomas Whitmore, Second Lieutenant with the 153 Illinois Infantry, Civil War, is buried in the Veterans' plot. According to Ringdahl, the Green River Thomas Whitmore Post of the American Legion was named in honor of this person, its founder.

According to Edith Sunada, who has been with the Green River American Legion and the V.F.W. for many years, Whitmore was the grandfather of Thomas Whitmore Siegel, Margaret Kemp and Lillian McCoy.

HISTORIC GREEN RIVER: CROSSWORD PUZZLE NO. 1

By: Bill Thompson

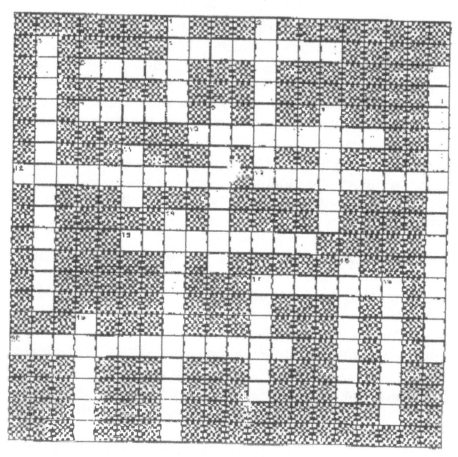

OK you crossword puzzle fans with an interest in history, this should be an easy one for you. The questions (clues) come from past publications of "Echoes" and *The Green River Star.* If one has lived in Green River for a significant amount of time, some of these clues can be answered from general knowledge.

Our members hope you have fun with this historical puzzle. Oh yes, speaking of history, this puzzle was created from a program on a five and a quarter inch floppy that was loaded in an Apple II and run off an a C Itoh printer. So, for you computer buffs, that's history.

Across Clues
4. Historic building designed after Chicago's
    famous water tower.
5. Famous western trail running through the
    City of Green River.
6. Former city clerk and recipient of Green
    River's Distinguished Citizen Award.
7. Explorer who began both trips down the Green
    and Colorado River systems in Green River 1869 and 1871.
9. Shoshone name for the Green River.
10. Owned beauty shop and received Green
    River Distinguished Citizen Award.
13. Rock Formation painted by Moran several-
    times and the name of one Lions Club in
    Green River.
15. Name of house that served as a maternity
    hospital in Green River.
17. Steamboat on the Green River!
18. Destroyed by fire - except the gym.
19. Rock formation that looks east.

Down Clues
1. Who is buried in vaults in Centennial
    Park?
2. Green River is "The -?- Capital of the
    world!"
3. Used to preserve Union Pacific Railroad
    ties.
6. Oldest bar in Green River. The building has
    continuously housed a bar since constructed in 1872.
8. Widely copied anti-peddling ordinance
    passed in 1931.
11. Highest point within the city limits of
    Green River.
12. Former deputy sheriff, county commissioner, and
    historian ... George ?

14. Former Green River citizen, first woman
Jury Foreman in United States ... Louise ?
16. "Sorry we're open", ? Taxidermy.

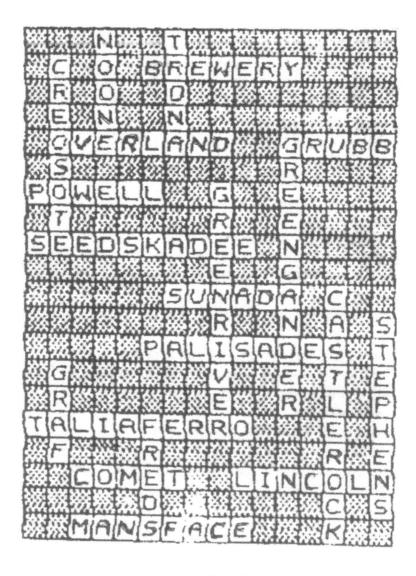

TOUCHING THE PAST

By: Terry A. Del Bene

There is something about the past which touches all of us:
It might surprise one to find out that more Americans visit museums and historical sites each year than attend all the professional
sporting events combined. Why is this? Why do more people get
in the car, drive for miles, and pay admission to see places where
things once happened rather than go to a place where things are
about to happen?

We are most fascinating creatures because we walk through
this world leading multiple lives. We all walk with our feet firmly
in the present but our minds are allowed to wander the halls of
the past. So ... there you are driving to the grocery store in your
van, perhaps one of the children is snoring away in the car seat
and you turn on the radio. You start hearing the sounds of one of
your favorite songs from a few years ago. Suddenly your mind
starts doing some very interesting things. Without a wish from you
it starts recreating aspects of the time when that song first meant
something to you. You can encounter flashes of weather, space,
people, smells, flavors, and events; all purely involuntary and all
too strong to ignore. Some find that the smells of certain foods,
flowers, or perfumes have even stronger powers to bring on an
attack of nostalgia. Perhaps this is some exercise by the mind to
reinforce our memories. Perhaps it is an extension of our natural
defenses. Perhaps it is a divine gift or curse. Whatever the nature
of this phenomenon it is clear that most humans like to time-travel.
Museums and historical sites are very important to us to serve as
the catalyst for the start of our mind wandering down those halls
of time. It seems that for many it's not enough to relive aspects of
our own pasts that we are compelled to travel further down those
dark halls, and find the pasts of others. Therefore, the artifacts and
places associated with persons and events of the past become sin-
gularly critical to our time travel experience.

One can get a far better "feeling" for events which happened in the past by visiting the original ground or place where
things happened than by any other media. For example, we here
in southwestern Wyoming are fortunate to have the majority of

the surviving intact portions of the Oregon, Mormon-Pioneer, California, Cherokee, Pony Express, and Overland Trails. Many of the tourists who come to visit the trails have seen images of our trail ruts and have read about the events. However, something interesting happens when you take them to a place like the Dry Sandy Swales or South Pass. Here, our visitors get to physically and mentally touch the past. They can feel the wind and the temperature of the place. They can smell the plants and the dust. They can experience the whole vista and view a scene which is almost unchanged since the days those trails were in use. Many of our visitors shortly develop a thousand-yard stare and they find that for one of the few times in their lives they are able to mentally go to the past and physically be there. Such powerful places are true national treasures. Would that we recognize the value of these few remaining places.

The feeling of "being there" drives many to take up living history as a hobby or even as a job. Roughly 25,000 to 30,000 Civil War reenactors went to Pennsylvania in 1998 to recreate the Battle of Gettysburg. That doesn't even count the crowds which came to watch. Living history involves shedding the outward present-day person and putting on the clothes, mannerisms, and attitudes of people from the past. It is not easy to do. It takes a lot of research, dedication, money and support from other living historians to make one into an accomplished living historian. It is a powerful teaching tool. Those who visit historic sites find the experience much more rewarding and informative if there are people bringing the location to life. A visitor can see a static display of a store and take away what they can from that experience or they can see the store and the storekeeper (a living historian who looks, talks, acts, and smells like what a shopkeeper should).

I remember seeing a recreation of a Confederate hospital where visitors enter a dark, smoky room filled with sleeping and coughing men on the floor. The visitors hesitate at the door not knowing whether they wish to continue this brush with unpleasant things from the past. Those who go through the door become quiet, as if afraid to disturb the illusion around them. They almost walk on tip-toes seemingly unwilling to acknowledge their own presence in a room filled with the suffering. As a young housewife passes by a teenage boy who has been blinded ... he reaches up and grabs her hand. "Mother, oh Mother I knew you would come ... I can smell the rose water you love to wear." The young woman, with tears in her eyes puts her other hand over his. For a moment she has been pulled into the 1860s and she will carry her memory of the Civil War for the remainder of her life.

The educators who study such things tell us that retention of information of the situation where a living history program is present increases over 30 percent. It is especially helpful with teaching children the importance of the past for them. After all, most children are too busy building up their own stores of personal memories to focus on those of others. However, living history programs allow them to do both at the same time and can foster a powerful appreciation of the past. I encourage each of us to support our museums and historic sites. Sometimes it's easier to send the children to a movie or buy them a computer game than to pick them up and let them walk the parade ground at an historic place like Fort Bridger. Perhaps it's easier to put a video on at night than to read to the family from a book. However, in doing so I wonder if we are not cheating the children out of a gift which our parents gave us... the ability to take our minds on our own journeys through time.

GREEN RIVER'S SWEETHEARTS
RUTH ANN AND ALTON HERMANSEN

By: Bill Duncan

"I first noticed her when I was a senior in high school and she was a sophomore," Alton said. "Next September, we'll celebrate our 60th anniversary."

What has happened in between those times is the story of a well-known couple that found Green River a "good little town" to grow up, raise their family, and mature in. Their record of community service stands as a high mark for succeeding generations to try to reach.

How did we get started? "Like most kids in the 1930's, we made our own fun, watched movies at the Isis, listened to the radio together, and we never missed a high school ball game or play. Like any other small town of the time, everybody knew what we were up to."

The site of Alton's home is now occupied by Green River Cable Television. Alton remembers, "Kids had a lot of home chores like bringing in coal, keeping care of the yards, and shoveling snow to keep them occupied during the day. We played a lot of games in the evening like kick-the-can, run sheepy run, and punch the iceman. Every kid had roller skates and the main track was around the Merc block. Kids socialized on the old Courthouse lawn afternoons and evenings.

Ruth Ann's home (the Mortimer house) still stands east of the Casa de Oracion Church behind the courthouse. She particularly remembers being a member of the high school's Booster Club when Green River hosted the District Basketball Tournament each March. The Boosters had a tea and welcomed teams from all over this part of the state. Teams included Superior, Reliance, and of course Rock Springs and the others we have now. She also baby sat, sometimes with Alton's "help".

Since only two kids in town had their own cars, dates were walking dates on the North side of the river. One social center was the Eklund and Cottle Confectionary, next to the Isis Theater at the corner of Railroad and Center Street. "We could get in for

Ruth Ann and Alton Hermansen visit Catalina Island shortly after their marriage. (Photo courtesy Ruth Ann and Alton Hermansen)

12 cents apiece. So for a quarter we could have a sundae or soda before the movie, get in, and still have enough left for penny candy or popcorn. Of course quarters were pretty hard to come by in those days," Alton says.

Alton started collecting those quarters going to work for the Piggly Wiggly grocery when he was 12. The store delivered three times a day to the customers who called in their orders. One of Alton's jobs was driving the delivery truck. After graduation, Alton went to work for the Green River Mercantile Co. The manager of the Merc's clothing department was Bill Mortimer, Ruth Ann's father.

As they began to date, Alton had a sudden interest in the Carnegie Library and Ruth Ann found lots of topics she had to research there. When he visited her at her home, they would often sit on her family's enclosed porch. A gas heater provided comfort on cold evenings. When Ruth Ann's mother thought it was time for Alton to go home, she would come out and turn the heater off. It didn't take long for things to cool off and Alton would be on his way. On warmer evenings one of Ruth Ann's sisters "liked to keep track of what they were doing" so they had to behave.

Alton was able to buy a car after he graduated, so he and Ruth began to spend evenings up by the City Cemetery. After

Ruth Ann graduated, she worked as a secretary for the County Extension Agent in the basement of the Post Office and then in the Court House.

The Mortimer's decided that Alton had a steady job, went to the same church regularly, and was a likeable chap, so Ruth Ann and Alton were married in the Union Congregational Church on September 10, 1939. Marriage ended her working career for awhile because, "In those days before the War, married women didn't work."

"I made $80 a month then," Alton remembers, "and we thought if I could only make $125, we would be in second heaven." The rent for their first apartment was $20 a month.

Entertainment then? We visited other young families and we played cards. The men would meet to play poker and the gals would meet for bridge or pinochle. The Hermansen's moved into a house on Fifth West and raised their two children, Janet and Jerry, who both graduated from the University of Wyoming.

Alton was serving on the school board when Superintendent John V. Bernard asked him to come to

Ruth Ann and Alton Hermansen after fifty-five years of marriage. (Photo courtesy Ruth Ann and Alton Hermansen)

work for the school district. Alton resigned from the Green River Mercantile, after 25 years of service, and from the school board. He spent another 22 years serving as Superintendent of Buildings, Grounds, and Transportation.

Ruth Ann was already working for the schools as secretary at the high school and district's combined offices. Peanuts, their dog, came with them every day and watched over the students (usually from his place on the mats just inside the front door) for many years. They both retired in November 1980.

Over the years both Hermansens constantly gave back to Green River. Ruth Ann served her church as organist for 46 straight years – don't forget to count the Wednesday night choir practices, marriages, and funerals as well as the Sunday services. Both are active in Eastern Star.

Need an MC? Get Alton if he's not already booked; he's the best around. Who can we get to be pallbearers? Let's see, after Alton....of course Ruth Ann will play... she always does.

Ruth Ann and Alton booked trips for their TNT (travel 'n talk) group to Spain, Alaska, Michigan, Mexico, Massachusetts, and Hawaii (four times). Alton's chairmanships include Red Cross, Flaming Gorge Days, AARP, Senior Citizens Advisory Board, as well as serving for United Way, Boy Scouts, Castle Rock Medical Board, and the GR Centennial Calendar Committee. Ruth Ann and Alton were Grand Marshals of the Flaming Gorge Days in 1994, the same year they won the City's Beautification Award for their yard.

What kept us together? Their eyes meet simultaneously and they smile. "A sense of humor" they say together. "Marriage is a 50/50 proposition," Alton adds. "There's got to be cooperation," Ruth Ann continues. They agree that attending church regularly and their church family have helped keep them together over the years. But it's their give and take unity that has carried them through the good times as well as the bad. People tend to say Ruth Ann and Alton as one word. Green River also knows they are one unit with separate personalities that blend, merge, and strengthen. Congratulations to Ruth Ann and Alton Hermansen, Green River's sweethearts for over 60 years!

The author thanks Mike Realing Hanks for her oral history publication on Alton Hermansen and Ruth Ann and Alton for their interview. Ruth Ann (and probably Alton) was one of my earlier baby sitters. She later helped me when we both worked with the School District. Alton has been my mentor for many years, reminding me that life is too serious to be taken seriously.

THE QUESENBURY SKETCHES: AN EARLY VIEW OF GREEN RIVER

By: Ruth Lauritzen

Photographic views of what is now the Green River area were first taken in the late 1860s. Prior to that time, visual evidence of what the area looked like is found in sketches done by travelers. Two such sketches exist in a larger collection known as the Quesenbury Sketchbook. The *Omaha World-Herald* purchased the sketchbook, and in a public/private partnership, the newspaper allowed the Nebraska State Historical Society full use of the material.

These sketches were created by William Quesenbury (pronounced "cush-in-berry"), an Arkansas journalist who was also a poet, artist and political cartoonist. Quesenbury, who often wrote under the pen name of Bill Cush, was associated with several newspapers during his lifetime, including the *Sacramento Union*, *Southwest Independent* and the *Arkansan*. He served in both the Mexican and Civil Wars and later taught art at Cane Hill College in Arkansas. He died in 1888.

In 1850 Quesenbury went along the Cherokee Trail. In what would later be Sweetwater County, he struck north and picked up the main emigrant trail, the Oregon-California Trail, at teh ford on the Green River about thirty miles north of the current city. He then continued on to California where he worked briefly at the *Sacramento Union*. In 1851 he returned east on the Oregon-California Trail. It was on these western journeys that Quesenbury produced his sketchbook. It includes images of Pike's Peak, Bent's Fort, Devil's Gate, Independence Rock, Fort Laramie, Scott's Bluff and many other sites.

Two images of most interest to students of Green River history were made on the westward journey. These include a depiction of the bluffs east of Green River and one of Tollgate Rock made on or about July 4, 1850. His time in the area was described in his diary entries as quoted in the August 1979 issue of *Flashback*, the quarterly of the Washington County (Arkansas) Historical Society.

July 4 (Thursday)

The Glorious Fourth! Dry times with us. Left early, going over rolling ground as usual. Went down a high, steep slope. After going about a mile and a half, Mr. Mitchell discovered that the mare had shaken off his pistol again.

I turned back with him and found the pistol about two thirds up the steep slop we had passed. Found our men at a spring in the high prairie on the side of a slope. The spring water was exceedingly cold, clear and pure. Rested here a few minutes and then went on. Dreary prospect ahead. Traveled several miles down a hot dry valley which was tolerably in our course. Struck once a ridge and came to another valley running west with water running in it (probably the Bitter Creek Valley)

Followed on several miles and came in sight of a stream running apparently east. It seemed from the highlands where we were to be small–not more than twenty steps across.

Descended the highlands to the stream and camped. Before we had been here long several began to suppose we were at Green River.

We were delayed a while this evening by Crum's mule stampeding.

July 5 (Friday)

All agreed this morning we were on Green River. Crum went back and found his coat which he lost yesterday.

Walked a while for Strickler who tried to wade. Found it impracticable. Packed and started up the river. Went about two miles before I overtook the most of the company.

Thought I saw a canoe with willows on the other side. Some of the men were of the same opinion. Mr. Mitchell came up and we determined to go back and examine with spyglass. One look satisfied us that it was a canoe. Strickler and myself made a paddle and started over by swimming. We got us chunks to swim on in case we should be beaten below by the current which drawed to the north bank. I got over safe, but Strickler turned back. Found the canoe, a small one. Paddled it over and the others got a couple of logs to put to the sides We made seven trips before we got everything over. Our horses were disinclined to enter the water, but after a couple of hours hard work we made them all swim. Camped just below our landing place in the cottonwoods. Good grass. Left some of our things above.

July 6 (Saturday)

Got a late start. Went up the river, but had to leave it as it was impossible to follow on account of the bluffs. Turned out and struck our old course veering a little north. At twelve came to a stream so large as N. Platte which from the map must be Black Ford. [Black's

Fork] Nooned. I cooked bread. Whilst engaged at it there blew up a very hard gale of wind.

Passed a pond near the river in which there were a good many ducks. They were as wild as if they had been hunted a gerat deal. In the evening about four o'clock we came to a trail evidently made by Californians. Followed it to the river. Looked ahead and saw clouds of dust rising from the main road about six or seven miles off. Camped about a mile an half below the road. We could see the wagons from our camp. We are at the Independence road [Oregon-California Trail] at last.

The presence of a person as artistic and literate as Mr. Quesenbury in the west at this early time is remarkable. The legacy he left in his journal writings and in his sketchbook gives the modern world an early view of some of the marvels of the virgin West.

Tollgate Rock. (Photo courtesy *Omaha World-Herald* Quesenbury Sketchbook)

UNDERPASS AND PEDESTRIAN VIADUCT

By: Marna Grubb

Today, traveling from one side of Green River to the other is accomplished with great ease in a short period of time, but this was not always the case.

For many years, Green River was a town of three-to-four thousand people located north and south of the railroad tracks and north of the river. Getting across the railroad tracks often presented long delays, while citizens would wait for the passing of long freight trains, or the heavy passenger and freight switching accomplished in the railroad yards.

In October of 1935, Green River's town council approved a proposal to the Union Pacific Railroad for the elimination of the railroad crossing at Elizabeth Street (North First East) with the construction of an underpass at West Second South and a pedestrian overhead crossing of the railroad tracks at the Elizabeth Street crossing.

This proposal was reported to have been brought about by the "persistence of Green River's popular mayor and his loyal supporting town council" according to *The Green River Star* of August 1937. Samuel S. Hoover was mayor from 1935 to 1939.

The underpass was opened to public use in August of 1937, and *The Green River Star* reported that "This improvement has been at the cost of approximately $160,000 and one must see this structure to realize its beauty and fine construction, with a pedestrian walk on one side with steel railings for protection. The entire length is lighted by artistic iron lamp posts at the top of which are attractive large globes of the latest design."

The underpass was constructed by the Inland Construction Company of Omaha, Nebraska.

In September of 1937, *The Green River Star* reported that "Police Chief Chris Jessen is making an appeal to children, and particularly to parents, to avoid possible serious accidents by discontinuing the use of the underpass as a playground. Several children were reported to have been using the runways for roller skating and wagon coasting lanes."

In the Agreement of September 7, 1936, the railroad agreed to grant a right-of-way for a pedestrian viaduct over the railroad tracks, the State Highway Department agreed to construct the viaduct, and the town agreed to take and maintain the viaduct. If any major repairs were needed, the town would need to notify the railroad.

In 1937, the Wyoming State Highway Department awarded the low bid of $66,931 to Inland Construction Company of Omaha, who also were the contractors on the underpass project.

The Green River Star, in December of 1936, reported that "The pedestrian overpass will be a decided contribution to the safety of Green River residents, particularly the children who must traverse the dangerous railroad tracks four times daily in their progress to and from school. The cost of the project would be out of Federal funds appropriated for railroad crossing elimi-nation, but would be under the supervision of the Wyoming Highway Department."

Green River's pedestrian overpass spans the Union Pacific's main line and switching tracks. It was opened to the public in June of 1938. (City of Green River photo)

The pedestrian overpass was opened to the public in June of 1938, and Mayor Hoover reported that it eliminated the crossing of 21 double rails, main line and switching lines.

HISTORIC GREEN RIVER: CROSSWORD PUZZLE NO. 2

By: Bill Thompson

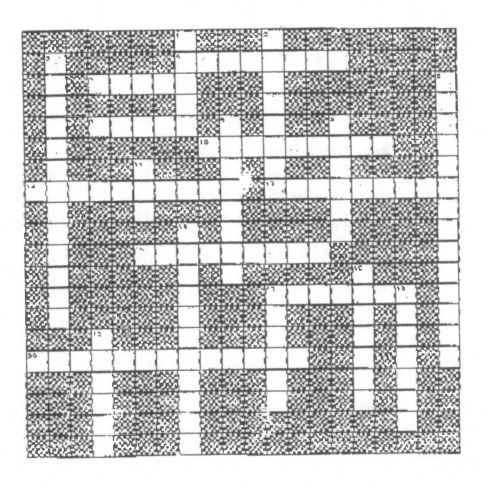

For some people crossword puzzles are fun ways not only to decipher riddles but also to learn new words, ideas, people and so on. With that in mind then we ran the first one a few months back (Historic Green River #1) and got some pleasant responses from you puzzle buffs.

Thank you for the calls. So this one is a little different in that all of the answers you don't know (if any) are found in *Echoes From The Bluffs Volume 1*. This is a collection of articles that the Historic Commission published in *The Green River Star* from 1991 to 1998.

The page number for the answer is given in the clues. No fair peeking at the answers first! Have a great time.

ACROSS CLUES
4. FIRST POSTMASTER. P. 92
5. PETER APPLE'S CROSSING THE GREEN RIVER 1886. P. 139
7. 1896 BRIDGE. P. 58
10. GREEN RIVER'S 1ST RECREATIONAL AREA OR PARK. P. 24
12. BUILDING DESTROYED BY FIRE IN 1940. P. 62
13. 1ST SENIOR CITIZENS ACTIVITIES TOOK PLACE IN BASEMENT OF CHURCH. p. 224
15. CANYON ONCE USED BY LINCOLN HIGHWAY UNTIL THE 1920S. P.36
17. INHABITANTS OF EGYPT ACCORDING TO SOME STUDENTS. P .144
20. THE ORIGINAL GREENBELT. P. 81

DOWN CLUES

1. FOR AWHILE KNOWN AS CORINNE. P. 93
2. A NIP WOULD TEMPT ONE TO STEAL HIS OWN CLOTHES AND TO BITE OFF YOUR OWN EARS. P. 11
3. THE MOST ROMANTIC HOLIDAYS. P. 66
6. ROAD AUTHORIZED IN 1912. P. 102
8. FORMER SLAVE, MIDWIFE AND DRESS-MAKER. P. 29
9. FORMER DIRECTOR OF SWEETWATER COUNTY LIBRARY SYSTEM. P.49
11. 1938 CAMP IN GREEN RIVER. P. 54
14. SPOOKY LIBRARY SITE. P. 73
16. ENLISTED IN NAVY AT AGE 15-1/2 YEARS. P. 164
17. FIRST MAYOR. P. 141
18. 1908 STERN-WHEELER. P. 255
19. TEACHER AT CHEROKEE AND MOM of MARNA, ESTHER P. 87.

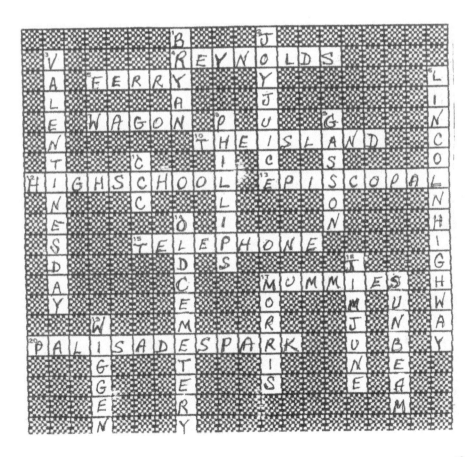

THE TRAP OF HISTORY

By: Terry A. Del Bene

"Those who do not remember history are doomed to repeat it."

History remains a powerful influence on all our lives. Whether we understand it or not history plays a profound role in how current events unfold. At the start of the latest crisis in the Balkans both sides dusted off the history books. One side attempted to explain its actions as defending its most sacred sites which had been alternately won and lost over the past 500 years. The other side drew historical analogies to the Holocaust of World War II, where world powers had been slow to halt the atrocities of Nazi Germany. Both of these are powerful examples of how we can allow ourselves to fall into the trap of history. The trap is that history teaches most of us only those lessons we are willing to learn from it.

When we use history we need to be careful of how and why it is being used. The facts do not and never have spoken for themselves. We all use the "facts" to make points which we think are important. The "facts" rarely are discussed within their entirety and with a complete context. Of course, it would not help one to make an argument by bringing in examples which disprove one's point. Accordingly when we hear anyone attempting to justify a recent action or decision by some historical analogy it would do each of us well to question just what was left out. We should use such instances as a chance to look for the whole story, not just the part of the story someone is trying to sell.

There is a unique chemistry which occurs when history and religion are mixed together. If we look at the world's most enduring conflicts this unique mix of religion and history appear to work together to assure the continuance of conflict. The continuing difficulties in places like Ireland, Central Africa, the Middle East, and the Balkans all show similar patterns of the interplay between history and religion. Religious groups have been extremely adept at "spinning" history to produce specific slants to events. In these regards history becomes a tool for molding opinion and justifying continued conflict rather than a tool for helping us to understand previous conflicts and head them off altogether. In such instances the opening quote perhaps should be modified to read, "Those who remember history are doomed to repeat the past."

The "facts" have proven themselves to be readily moldable. Americans can see this in our present interpretations of the War between the States (Civil War). Debate still rages among us as to what caused the war, roughly 140 years after the event. Contrary to popular belief it's not easy to start a modern war. It takes a lot of shaping of public opinion to get people to dislike each other sufficiently to take such a drastic measure. The American Civil War was no different. The combatants were extremely similar in culture, history, political institutions, and religion. This is not the easiest of situations to start a war in. The flashpoint issue which divided the nation was the role slavery would play in a democratic society. Slavery existed in this nation since it was an English colony. Hence it took years of building tensions between the slave-holding and free states before the war would come.

It is interesting to note that even after 140 years the mere suggestion that the war was about slavery still elicits a knee-jerk reaction from many. These individuals would be quick to point out that the issue was the right of states to regulate their own domestic institutions. There is plenty of documentation to back up the clash between the Federal Government and the states regarding the regulation of slavery. Many free states were quite upset that the Fugitive Slave Act required them to use their own resources to return runaway slaves to slave-holding states. One of the biggest issues in Congress during the first half of the 19th century was how to maintain a delicate balance of power (especially in the Senate) between slave-holding and free states. This was not a clash over state regulation of domestic institutions (the only domestic institution discussed was slavery). Similarly Presidents of the time chose their Cabinets, appointed judges, and appointed Territorial Governors in such a fashion that they would avoid showing favoritism to free states or slave holding states, as well as playing partisan politics. Our ancestors recognized that the war was somehow about slavery. The newspapers, both North and South, recognized this simple "fact." The Vice President of the Confederacy, Alexander Stephens, states in his 1868 history of the war,

"Slavery, so called, was but the question on which these antagonistic principles, which had been in conflict, from the beginning, on divers other questions, were finally brought into actual and active collision with each other on the field of battle."

So... why are we left with such a basic issue still in doubt? Much of it has to do with the remaking of the history to suit current times. It pains many to consider that their ancestors may have fought and died to keep other people enslaved. The "other questions" mentioned by Alexander Stephens above seem much more palatable to 1990's people.

If histories of the war vilified the South they also glorified the North. Northern armies have traditionally been portrayed as carrying freedom in their knapsacks into a despotic and decadent South. A powerful image but an incorrect one. Though the war was about slavery it was only marginally about the condition of the slaves. Though there undoubtedly were thousands of Northern soldiers (especially the 200,000 Black soldiers) who fought for the lofty principle of freeing those less fortunate than themselves, the average soldier held the slaves in contempt. Abraham Lincoln actively supported efforts to remove freed slaves to Africa rather than championing their residence in the country they had labored so hard to build. The image of the pure motivations of the North are just as misleading as those images of happy slaves and of a "genteel" Southern culture which still persist. It is up to us to look deeper into the misty images of the past and find more truth and balance.

The ultimate consumers of historical products are we people in the present. Our perceptions and expectations are different than people in the past. For example, George Washington, Thomas Jefferson, and numerous other architects of this land of the free were slave owners. In the 1990s the 18th century luster of these luminaries of freedom seems somewhat tarnished. George Armstrong Custer goes through interpretive flip-flops from a great general fighting overwhelming odds to a complete fool. Additionally he goes from patriot to egotistical bigot. Events such as the Sand Creek Massacre of 1864 have changed from a grand and glorious blow struck against an evil foe to a crime against society so heinous that we rarely find mention of it in our children's textbooks.

It is up to us as consumers to expect and get the best history available. The spin-doctoring of historical information and the building of cults of personality have made us forget that in each of us there is the potential for a hero or heroine should the right circumstances occur. History has really been made by the ordinary people not merely by celebrities. Our children need to learn that this most wonderful of countries has had its dark corners. Things which seemed natural 100 years ago are quite baffling now. The burden for our children and their children is to learn from these mistakes and to avoid the trap of history. Sometimes the hardest lessons are the best.

CELEBRATING FOURTH OF JULY IN GREEN RIVER

By: Bill Duncan

The glorious Fourth dawned bright and clear, ushered in by batteries of light artillery and cannon crackers. As usual, the first glance of the early riser was toward old Castle Rock on whose pinnacle Old Glory was proudly waving to the winds. *The Green River Star*, July 5, 1907.

What are some local traditions surrounding July 4th? What did people do 90 years ago without 3 on 3 basketball, Green Garboon races, or rock concerts? I checked *Green River Stars*, looking for changes and activities that lasted. Ball games, band music, parades and athletic contests were part of each decade's celebration. Volunteer participation and leadership is the strongest factor in maintaining the fun during the 20th century. Firemen most always had a key role. Early in this century, decorated hose carts from the town's various firefighting units followed the community band. More often than not, it was reassuring to have them in on the celebration.

We were blessed by delightful weather on the Fourth and it was taken advantage of in a manner that was appreciated by the sport loving gathering of people who had joined us in celebrating, as Green River has never celebrated before.

The first spirit of patriotism upon arising was brought about by seeing old glory proudly floating to the breeze on Castle Rock, and the same spirit existed throughout the day.

The day's programme was a large one, and every event a good one. Perhaps, if any, the Leap Year Club ball game may have proved more interesting than the rest, it being a novelty in its line, and the young ladies who so ably played the National game are deserving of much praise along with the prize that they deservedly won, from a bunch of has-beens who thought that they could play ball, but are now convinced otherwise. (The final score was 12-2) *The Green River Star*, July 10, 1908.

Not all games were that interesting. In 1907 "The ball game was a long winded and uninteresting affair and was finally brought to a close in favor of the U.P. Bridgemen with a score of a hundred and something to something."

Prizes were awarded for horse, pony and donkey races. Men raced 100 yards, 220 yards, and in a 3-legged race. Women raced for 50 yards and in an egg race. Boys and girls had separate races for under 8, 8 to 14, and 14 to 18. Other contests included ladies nail driving, greased pole climbing, men's high jump and broad jump, and rope climbing. Events concluded with a Fireman's Ball at the Opera House.

> The only marring feature of the celebration was the fact that high water prevented the use of the Island, as was heretofore the custom.
> An added feature however, and one which should live long in the minds of our citizens, and especially the younger generation was the Opening Reception at the Carnagie Public Library, and everyone who attended that function had nothing but the highest words of praise for mine host Robt. C. Morris and his corps of able assistants. *The Green River Star*, July 5, 1907

The 1917 Celebration was held on North Railroad Ave. and in the U.P. Railroad Park, due to the flooded condition of Island Park. The Red Cross sold hot lunch, ice cream and other refreshments from their booth at the east end of U.P. park. Again the band led the "Patriotic Parade" followed by the "Goddess of Liberty" float and "Other decorated Floats and Automobiles."

> The line of march ended at the band stand of the Union Pacific park, where Rev. Schillinger opened the morning exercises with prayer. Following a splendid overture by the band, the oration of the day was given by Rev. S.A. Webber, who in a most forceful and able manner pointed out the object of the demonstration. Rev. Schillinger done (SIC) full justice to his subject, and his address proved, a word picture of the world's struggle for liberty that will long remain in the minds of all who heard him. The address was followed by the band playing "America." The entire audience joining with the band in this soul stirring National hymn. *The Green River Star*, July 6, 1917.

Buried deep in the social column was the sad commentary for 1918. "Green River did not celebrate this year, and a number of our citizens took in the program at Rock Springs on the Fourth." Long lists named men leaving for Army duty at Ft. Logan, Colorado. A side note added that, "The dance at the Rex

Theatre the night of the Fourth was well attended and thoroughly enjoyed."

"Safe and sane" seemed to be the theme for the roaring '20's. Ball games with Parco (Sinclair), Lyman, and Rock Springs were the total 1926 celebration. The July 1, 1927, *Star* said that, "...most people are arranging to spend the day in enjoying whipping the streams and picnicing, while many will take in celebrations in neighboring towns." A ballgame between the Rock Springs all-stars and Green River's Union Pacific teams plus a dance at Island Park "rounded out the days' doings" in 1928.

The July 2, 1937, headlines crowed "Huge Fireworks Display, Races, Baseball, and Midnight Performance G.R. Program." Green River's Drum and Bugle Corps was known as "one of the best...in the intermountain states." A dance on the evening of the 3rd was... "followed Sunday by a full outline of rides, concessions, picnic grounds, Bingo game, swimming and other amusements during the day at Island Park." Those events were climaxed by a "midnight frolic dance at Riverside starting at 11:30 p.m." Monday's events called for "everything to be open at Island Park...interspersed with a race program for children; all cash prizes; another baseball game...." Plans also called for "a mammoth $200 fireworks display." Still not had enough? The Isis Theater "presents a weird performance, featuring a stage show of "Virgil's Spooks," and a film featuring Boris Karloff...in "The Man Who Lived Again."

World War II put a lid on the traditional summer celebration. The June 27, 1947, issue noted that, "This will be the first time in seven years that an observance of any planned degree has been sponsored in Green River." Prizes were awarded ($1 and .50) for foot, horse and bicycle races for five age groups of boys and girls. The biggest hoopla during this celebration went to the grand opening of the Vet's Club (later a Bingo Parlor at 38 North Center St.), "one of the most beautiful in Wyoming."

Softball results claimed the most newspaper space in 1948. S. Kalivas, J. Valencia, and R. Pershin were league leaders (first names weren't provided) with Rudy leading in both homers and batting average. Apparently there were more fireworks than just on the ball diamond because the town council adopted an ordinance banning the "sale, purchase or the firing of Fourth of July fireworks in Green River" after the celebration.

> It was pointed out that several fires were caused in Green River
> this year by pyrotechnics and firecrackers, some of which could
> have been very damaging. It was also pointed out that youths, es-
> pecially in the "smart" late teen-age group of boys, were gaining
> more headway each year in the careless disregard they hold for the
> safety of other persons, throwing lighted firecrackers under people,
> in the midst of crowds, into groups of small children, and at small
> animals such as dogs and cats. Further, many motorists complained
> about the youths throwing lighted firecrackers at or in cars, which
> could cause serious accidents. *The Green River Star*, July 15, 1948.

An exception allowed "...fireworks for community entertainment."

An estimated 1,500 persons attended the 1949 celebration.
The agenda called for baseball and softball games, entertainment
for the children, swimming races at Riverside pool and a gigantic
fireworks display from "Hutton's Heights", earlier called Hutton's Bluffs. The Eagles Auxiliary drill team and a band concert
entertained the crowd before the third ball game of the day.

Community participation helped the third annual Flaming Gorge Days succeed in 1958. Keenie Wilson received "special
hoorays and a string of posies" for "sparking ... shenanigans like
a belle from the Floradora days." Alton Hermansen, Jim Davis,
and Joe Sanchez were on the parade committee. Glenn Hill and
the Jaycees were in charge of the children's events. Tom Kourbelas won a prize for the neatest beard. Several citizens such as Ed
Lewis, Grant Twitchell, Ada Krause, Lee and Doyle Prince raised
money for the celebration by taking a dip in the dunk tank. Lee
was pictured in her "spectacular new yellow bathing suit". The
Star noted that she raised "12 silver biscuits" (dollars) for taking
the plunge. Square dancers, including Ralph and Muriel Widdop, Erma and Ferren Boren, and Sybil and Leon Brady, put on a
"dandy street dance at three downtown locations in the Rock."

Kay Sorbie (Hansen) garnered 97 out of 100 points to win
the 1959 Flaming Gorge Queen contest. "She received 30 out of
a possible 30 points for her playing of the accordion at the talent
show." Jim Shaw and George Reynolds chaired the celebration.
Parade prizes gave $150 for the best decorated float and $40 for
the winning decorated car. Square dancing, drawing for mer-

chants' prizes at the lot between GR Merc and Moedl Drug, a "mammoth parade", and a horsemanship "SHOWDEO" topped the '59 agenda.

Bill Luzmoor III emceed the 1968 Miss Flaming Gorge pageant. Anything familiar about that? Green Garboon races provided humor and excitement. "With an 'anything goes' (providing it is homemade) rule ...has become one of the hilariously entertaining events of the Fourth of July show." Homemade boats(?), maybe floatation devices would be a more accurate description, entered the river at the Palisades. The fastest entry to stay afloat and get to the Highway 530 bridge was declared winner. The Jaycees arranged speakers, games, a carnival, and music keeping with the old-time theme.

A couple of years earlier, organizers had chosen a "Gay Nineties" theme. The pavilion was converted into a "honkytonk" with beer sold by the pitcher and served by Can-Can Girls and a Barbershop quartet. A Mickey Finn stage show was included in the following years.

Star editor Carl Bechtold lamented the loss of Fourth fireworks in 1978. This was the year that the Flaming Gorge Days board decided to move the celebration away from the July 4 holiday. FGD featured a beer drinking contest, a decorated store window contest, and an RS-GR fire department water fight. Doug Kershaw, Barbara Fairchild, and Roy Head entertained a crowd of 1,300. Jack Evers and Ray VandeKroc (canoe), Terry Phillips (bike), and Ann Evers (horse) split $800 first prize money in the relay race. Relay prizes totaled $1500.

> After this Fourth of July celebration it is obvious that many Green River citizens have gone totally bonkers with firecrackers.
> Our city sounded and looked like a war zone as thousands of firecrackers, bottle rockets and other explosives were set off. Francis Scott Key would have been inspired to write another verse watching all the explosions. It seemed that our city was under siege by the sounds of bottle rocket battles waged by "young Rambos". Keith Bray, Editor, *The Green River Star*, July 6, 1988.

Fire Chief Glenn Hill reminded residents to use extreme caution when setting off fireworks. In 1988 the Star reminded readers that "Local firefighters have battled several grass fires during the spring and summer, and although none caused major damage, the potential exists for it...." That was the summer Yellowstone burned.

Road Damage, Los Banditos, and Tempest offered a free concert from 2-8 p.m. that year. The fireworks display budget had been increased to $8,000. Parks Superintendent Roger Moellendorf promised that the automatic lawn sprinklers, which came on during the show in 1987, would not interrupt the display. Spectators looked forward to the second annual Mud Rally. Events that might have entertained during the Fourth like arm wrestling, kids games, horseshoe pitching, and a flea market had all shifted to FGD.

What kind of celebrations will a new century bring? Committees of volunteers have worked during this century to meet changing participant and spectator appetites. You can rest assured that the next century's Fourth of Julys will have fireworks, music, and money raising schemes. You can bet that volunteers will rise to put the pageant together.

Flags will be carried and saluted. Editors will call for tighter fireworks controls. People will shoot off fireworks. Let's hope that none of the celebrants forget that this day commemorates our country's decision to seek independence and maintain freedom.

FORGET-ME-NOT

By: Ruth Lauritzen

Green River, Wyoming
May 4, 1899

Dear Friend Nellie:
There is a little pale blue flower.
That winds around the sheapards (sic)cot.
And in the latest midnight hour.
Lo softly sies (sic) for-get-me-not.

Yours Respectfully,
Alice R. Viox

In an archival document box in the Sweetwater County Historical Museum lie two small autograph albums, each bearing the same embossed gold engraving and pastel-colored drawings of a young girl and an idyllic small-town scene. These albums belonged to Green River resident Nellie Albertina Dankowski Bishopp Elder and her daughter Jean Flora Bishopp. They bear witness to the tender and sweet customs of old-fashioned girlhood and the love between a mother and daughter.

Nellie Dankowski was born in Green River on September 10, 1886 to Stanislaus and Johanah Miller Dankowski. She was raised in Green River and attended school there. For Christmas in 1898 she received her autograph album from her cousins Chet and Jim Chrisman.

Autograph albums were all the rage at the time. During the entire Victorian era (1830-1910) books holding personal collections of writings, photographs and homemade personal mementos were often kept and treasured by middle-and-upper-class women and girls. Many albums were begun by schoolgirls and kept well into adulthood. Some were quite elaborate, containing beautifully executed watercolors, newspaper and magazine clippings, and extensive writings. They were sometimes richly bound leather volumes, but were more often modest commercial publications, or even homemade treasures with covers made of leftover wallpaper. No matter how elaborate or simple the binding or accompanying material, the messages transcribed in these albums frequently took up the refrain of "Remember Me" or "Forget-me-Not" and were, of course, inscribed by hand.

These albums preserve a very special kind of history, as collector and author Starr Okenga, opines in her book about friendship and autograph albums, *On Women and Friendship*.

> Published history is usually about major events and the well-known figures who shaped them. This history is of a quieter sort. The owners of these albums wove the social fabric of an age, but very few of their names are remembered. The montage of words and mementos created by the last century's forgotten women have, for me, become a tender document of connections and feelings, as delicate and fragile as their braided hair wreaths.

Nellie's book consists mostly of writings from her fellow students at school in Green River. The only school in town at that point was housed in what is now the Masonic Lodge, located at 129 E. Flaming Gorge Way. Penned in childish hands are such literary gems as follows.

Green River, WY
Oct. 6th 1899

Friend Nellie
The largest is not the sweetest flower, the longest not the happiest hour, fewer words are best.

I wish you well.
Blanch D. Bingham

Green River, WY
Dec. 5th 1899

Dear friend Nellie.
There is a word in every clime to every heart most dear, in English 'tis; forgetnot in French 'tis Souviner.

Your Friend
Dottie Ethel Bingham

Some are of dubious poetic merit, but heartfelt nonetheless:

Green River, WY
Dec. 11, 1899

Friend Nellie
When your husband is sick and cross just kick him out of the house
and call it square.

Your Friend
Geo. Washington Scott

Feb. 13, 1899

Dear Nellie,
Violets are blue and roses are red.
Sugar is sweet and so are you. And if I had time. And a barrel of
pitch I paint you all over you sweet witch.

Your School-Mate
Norma Riley

    In 1907 Nellie married Edward Thomas Bishopp. She bore three children; Edward, Jean Flora, and John.
    The last entry, save one, in her album was made in 1902, five years before her marriage, however, it is obvious that she kept the book and took it with her when she left home because, the final entry, by date, is as follows:

Green River, WY
May 2, 1917

Dear Mama
For-get-me-not

Your loving child
Jean Flora Bishopp
I love you

Shortly before this entry was made in her mother's album, Jean, at age eight, began her own album. Though a generation had passed, the sentiments in the book remained very much the same as demonstrated by the following entries:

April 24, 1917
Green River, WY
Who comes dancing over the snow? His soft little feet all bare and rosy. Open the door though the wild winds blow. Take him in and hold him ever dear. For he is the wonderful glad new year.

Mareese Gravelle age 10
Green River, WY

April 24, 1917

Dear Jean;
When you see a monkey climbing a tree. Pull his tail and think of me.

Your dear friend
Evelyn Esther Mortimer Age 8-1917

Nellie herself inscribed the following message in Jean's book, echoing the same sentiment placed in her own book by a friend fifteen years before.

April 25, 1917

My dear little girl,
When in the course of human life,
Five things observe with care,
To whom you speak, of whom you speak,
How, when and where.

From your mama

Little Jean Bishopp lived just over a year from the time of her mother's loving inscription. She died August 24, 1918 of a septic infection related to an appendectomy. The Bishopp family, like many families of the time, had its share of early deaths. John died of scarlet fever in 1915, Jean passed in 1918 and later that year, in October, her father Edward T. Bishopp died of pneumonia. Nellie married Arthur Elder in 1920 and lived to the ripe old age of 81. The year following her death in 1968, the albums were donated to the museum where they are kept as an example of an interesting literary tradition and as a testament to the love of friends and family.

ABOVE: Nellie Dankowski as a girl. (Photo courtesy Sweetwater County Historical Museum)

RIGHT: Jean Flora Bishopp. (Photo courtesy Sweetwater County Historical Museum)

NEW ADDITION TO MUSEUM

By: Marna Grubb

In 1999, an electric permanent-wave machine was donated to the Sweetwater County Historical Museum by local resident Edith Sunada. Edith had used this machine in her business in the late 1940s. Edith owned and operated Edith's Beauty Studio on North 1st East Street in Green River for nearly 40 years.

This event brought back many memories to me of being hooked up to such a monstrous machine while I was a child growing up in Green River. I must say that permanents have come a long way since that time! Plus the price for a permanent has jumped from $5 at that time to $35 to $60 now.

When training to become a beautician in 1947, Edith was taught to use a Marcel curling iron which needed to be heated on a stove. I can remember how attractive the ladies were looking with their beautiful, soft waves created by the Marcel curling iron process. This became obsolete with the permanent.

Except for nearly three years while in Salt Lake City, Edith had lived her entire life in Green River. During this time she was busy volunteering her services for the community and those in need.

Edith received the City's Distinguished Citizen Award in 1989. Also in 1989, Edith received a certificate from Governor Sullivan and the Wyoming Volunteer Assistance Corporation in appreciation for exemplary volunteer service in Wyoming.

Edith's list of services is endless, but she had been especially active with the VFW Auxiliary 2321, the Sweetwater County Historical Society, the Golden Hour Senior Citizens, the Food Bank, and as Memorial Chairman for the American Cancer Society for nearly 20 years. Her story needs to be told.

Edith was born April 24, 1921, with Green River's first woman doctor, Charlotte Hawk, attending. When Dr. J. W. Hawk came a few days later, her father asked him what they should name this child. Forgetting that it was a girl, he said, "Call him 'Frank'." Then, after clarification, the name suggested was "Edith" after Edith Peters, the respected principal at the Lincoln

Edith Sunada donated her permanent wave machine to the Sweetwater County Museum. (Photo by Marna Grubb)

High School at that time. While growing up, Edith didn't like her name since, whenever she was in trouble, she was reminded that Edith Peters would not be very proud of her, knowing that Edith Peters was a very proper lady. Although, Edith smiled as she said, "Sometimes when I really got in trouble, he still called

me 'Frank'." Later in life, when she became personally acquainted with this highly-respected lady, Edith Peters, she decided the
name was not so bad.

Edith's father, Morijiro, came from Japan in 1915 to work
in the coal mines at Superior. Since he wanted to be in control of
his destiny, he tried a laundry in Superior. Morijiro married Toku
in 1917, who came as a picture bride. She was 22 and he was
34. Superior wasn't too impressive to Toku when she arrived
(no trees, no flowers, nothing green, plus the Indians scared her),
so they moved to Layton, Utah, where he became a vegetable
farmer, and later to Green River where they opened a laundry on
July 4, 1920.

Marijiro and Toku had nine children: Edith, George, Mary,
Agnes, Janet, Kayo, Mae, Leo and Ray. They lived south of the
railroad tracks on Second South Street. The children needed to
cross the tracks to go to school, which was the old Washington
Grade School located by the road to the cemetery. They often
waited for long freight trains; and, if the trains were stopped, the
children would crawl underneath the cars. Looking back, Edith
remarked about how fortunate they were not to have been injured. The pedestrian viaduct over the railroad tracks was constructed in 1938 correcting this dangerous situation. Edith graduated from Lincoln High School with the class of 1940.

When asked about how Green River is different now from
when she was growing up, Edith didn't hesitate before answer-
ing, "I appreciate the indoor bathrooms most of all. We had an
outdoor toilet and, many times, we would come in and stand
by the flat-bellied coal stove to get our bottoms warm! We took
baths in round, metal wash tubs."

For entertainment in the summer, Edith said they enjoyed
riding on the ties that would be coming down the river. From
1868 until the mid-to-late 1940s, the Union Pacific Railroad had an
annual tie drive from the headwater of the Green River to furnish
ties for railroad construction. Tie booms were located in Green
River to catch the ties, which were then loaded onto railroad cars
for shipment to be treated or to saw mills.

Edith's father died in 1938 leaving her mother to continue
the laundry, but this proved to be too much for her. She sold the
business and began doing hand washing. Edith did housework

and George worked for the railroad.

During World War II, her brothers lost their jobs with the railroad. Edith's older brother George then served in the Japanese American 442nd Regimental Combat Team during World War II and her younger brother Kayo served in the Army after the war as a medical technician. Kayo later received a doctor of medicine degree and became director of the State Home and Training School in Wheatridge, Colorado. The remainder of the family avoided an internment camp in Colorado because of the efforts by Police Chief Chris Jessen and Wiley Shaver.

Since Edith couldn't get a job in Green River because of the War, she went to Salt Lake City where she did housework, worked for the LDS Hospital, and then went to the Quish Beauty School. Edith then returned to Green River and worked at Thora Monahan's Beauty Shop. A couple years later she bought the shop and managed her own beauty shop for nearly 40 years.

Edith assisted her mother in raising the six younger children and helped in providing higher education for all of them. She was the one who took care of their mother until Toku died in 1982. Edith retired from the beauty shop in 1986 and has been a "busy volunteer" helping many in the community.

The world needs more "Ediths"!

JAMESTOWN

By: Bill Thompson/Gay Collar, guest author

This month we have a, guest contributor. She is a second-generation native Sheddon from here and a former: student of mine (who was always a chapter ahead of me). She is one of the pleasant and knowledgeable voices you might hear when calling the Green River Chamber of Commerce for information.

From time to time we hope to have contributions from people in our community who have some little known or hard get informative historical highlights about this region. We feel that this guest spot might stimulate more residents out there to add to our written knowledge of this area. Please feel welcome to submit them to our President Ruth at the Sweetwater County Museum.

JAMESTOWN, WYOMING
ALSO KNOWN AS JAMESTOWN - RIO VISTA SUBDIVISIONS

By: Gay Shedden Collar
granddaughter of Charles Johnson

This area was originally homesteaded by two friends; J.T. Moriarity from Kansas, and Charles W. Johnson from Missouri and Colorado. According to Sweewater County records, Mr. Moriarty filed homestead in November 1917, and Mr. Johnson filed for his in March 1918 for 160 acres or a quarter section. Each homesteader had to work the land by building a house and raising crops and/or livestock .

Mr. Moriarty lived on his homestead only part of the year, as he had previously built a house in town where they continued to live in the winters.

Mr. Johnson and his wife, Nellie May, built a two room house, and lived on their homestead year-round, raising crops to sell such as potatoes and strawberries, as well as having a small herd of dairy cows and goats. Johnson also worked for the water works in Green River some summers while his wife and two daughters, Bernice and Audrey, worked the farm. He also drove the school bus and did odd jobs around town for extra income as well as making headstones depicting local scenery. Some of. those headstones can still be found in Riverview Cemetery.

During the early years on the homesteads, there was no electricity; the families used coal oil lanterns and cooked on wood stoves and used wood and coal for heat. Water for irrigation was pumped from the river with gasoline powered pumps. Household water was hauled from town or pumped from the, river. When the Johnson family added a room made of railroad-ties for a kitchen, a large tank was installed above it to store their household water.

Perishable food was stored in an icebox cooled with ice cut from the river; vegetables were canned or stored in a root cellar which was built partially underground. One corner of the root cellar contained a raised bed of soil where they grew mushrooms. Electric service arrived at the homesteads in the spring of 1930, shortly before Mrs. Johnson's death.

During the Great Depression hobos were riding the rails which were visible from the homestead. They came and asked if there was any work they could do in exchange for a meal. They never asked for a handout but always wanted to work for what they got. A one-armed fellow insisted on chopping some wood.

Mark and Lottie Moriarity sold their family's property to James D. Maher in January of 1924. Maher filed a subdivision plat at the courthouse in March 1930. He named it Jamestown. The first lots recorded sold were in 1936 and 1941. Buyers pumped their water from the Green.

Johnson filed his subdivision plat, Rio Vista Townsites (Spanish for River View) in the early 1950s and started Rio Vista Water Service for the new residents. After his death in 1956 his daughters platted and filed two more subdivisions and expanded the water service.

Bernice ran the water service until 1982, when the Jamestown-Rio Vista Water and Sewer District was formed and bought the water rights and installed a new water treatment plant and storage tank.

The Rio Vista Subdivision starts about two miles west of Green River at the east edge of Section 7, Township 18 North, Range 107 West. A street called Sweetwater Lane runs along that section line.

The subdivision extends westerly a little over a half mile to Washington Street where the fireworks store and campground are. The Jamestown subdivision extends from there almost to the Highway 374 bridge over the Green River.

A NEW MILLENNIUM

By: Terry A. Del Bene

In the year 2000 the world was getting ready for a new millennium. There were tourist extravaganzas planned all the way from the Pyramids to Times Square. The media was filled with stories about the changing from the 20th Century to the 21st. One heard stories on ABC, NBC, CBS, Fox, PBS, and even the famed BBC about the last days of the 21st Century. How about all those end of the millennium sales and deals which business offered? We were reminded to get that 21st century car, boat, or home now. The 20th Century stuff was all obsolete.

Well, there was one thing wrong with all this hub-bub. The new Millennium really did not begin until January 1, 2001. That's right, the media convinced the public that the millennium had changed when they really had more than a year to get ready for the BIG ONE.

It seems this same confusion occurs every hundred years. There were similar difficulties at the end of the 18th and 19th centuries. As happened for the 20th century there will be two years of celebrations to mark its end. No duels were fought over which is the correct date but there was lively discussion. It's amazing that our news media, who will take sublime pleasure in ripping every detail out of a murder or sex scandal added to the misinformation regarding the Millennium. It's probably more interesting to be "investigative" on the court cases than it is to expose all the big-business hype which showered the public. After all, to expose the latter all you have to do is be able to count to 1,000. In a world of calculators and computers perhaps this task is beyond the capabilities or sensibilities of too many of us. Maybe this should be part of the standards of education which seem to take up a lot of discussion in Congress. Have any of you wondered how many of our representatives in Congress fell into the same trap of allowing advertisers and reporters to do our counting for us? Where was the scientific community and historical communities during all of this? This was one of those great times to provoke, interpret, and educate. Even the History

Channel seemed to drop the ball.

The problem started when in the year 526 A.D. the now-recognized-universally, Roman calendar was adopted. This calendar did not include a year zero. Hence the date presumed to mark the birth of Jesus of Nazareth was 1 A. D. The year prior to that was 1 B.C. Now it doesn't take a degree in mathematics to count and realize that first Millennium ended on December 31, 1000. Accordingly this is the 999th year of the current Millennium. Despite all the media and business hype the Millennium is still a period of 1,000 years in length. We have a year and a month (plus) to go.

Whew! That means we had more time to prepare for this momentous, if completely arbitrary, recognition of the passing of time. Those model year 2,000 cars which people are buying were really 20th century cars. The Y2K bug was really a 20th century glitch. The New York Yankees had chance to add one more world series to their list of 20th Century accomplishments.

So, if you wanted to see the Pyramids on the actual night the Millennium turns, you should have saved your money for 2001. There were smaller crowds and the prices were much more reasonable. Remember we're actually embarked on the traditional two years of celebration... one for those who can count and one for those who like to have an excuse to celebrate. All in all, both are wonderful reasons for marking the accomplishments of an era... recognizing the contributions of those who came before us... and to allow M&M candies to actually have some intellectual content to their commercials. I'm saving my big time for December 31, 2000, but was happy to watch all the wonderful fireworks displays and take advantage of any real bargains in those end of the Millennium sales. Just remember it was all done with a wink and a smile and perhaps those ghosts of the individuals, who thought up this system 14 centuries ago, had a chuckle with us.

PEARL LANE, 20TH CENTURY PIONEER

By: Bill Duncan

As the buzzer sounded, the 14-year old girl rolled sleepily from her cot and walked to the telephone switchboard. "Number please?"

" Pearl, can you get Dr. Hawk for me? Eunice has a terrible case of the croup."

"Yes, ma'am."

Pearl made the connection, glanced at the clock and waited to pull the plug when the call finished. Maybe she could grab a couple more hours of sleep before she got up to go to school.

"It wasn't so bad," Pearl Lane said recalling her switchboard operator days, "I only got three or four calls a night."

Pearl Lane celebrated her 99th birthday on November 29, 1999. She was born in the Burntfork country south of Green River. Her family moved to the Bridger Valley when she was five. When she was six, her mother took Pearl and her two sisters and moved into Green River. She says she's "always worked, even in high school" and graduated when she was 18.

Pearl is very proud that her father rode for the Pony Express. "He was a small man and loved fast horses," she remembers. "That's why they hired him." "He rode between Cheyenne and Salt Lake City." "He used to tell stories about how he lay down on the horse or on the side of the horse when the Indians shot at him." "It must have been exciting," she says with a twinkle in her eye.

What was the 4th of July like? " We used to put a lunch together and go picnic on the island," she said. "I remember some parades with firemen and lots of horses," she said. "They always had a speaker, I remember Taliaferro from Rock Springs, he was a good speaker."

"Of course it was different," she snorted when I asked her about Christmas. "Christmas was a lot more practical." "When we lived out on the ranch, we didn't get to Evanston more than once or twice a year." "Our kids were glad to get an orange with their rock candy." "That was a real treat." Pearl's kids did most of the tree trimming with homemade decorations. "We had popcorn, dried fruit, and paper chains," she said, "the oldest would take charge." She said most of the presents were practical—like clothing. "We always tried to make dolls for Christmas," she said.

"We used to have dances on the Island, take in a picture show, and picnic up the river." "I never took a vacation, though," she said, "my life was mostly about raising kids and taking care of my family."

Pearl married right out of high school. "The (first) war changed everything," she said. "The flu was terrible and lots of people died." "I lost two brothers. " Cars got more affordable and they began to fix up the roads. "I had three kids."

Her first husband was a mechanic for the Union Pacific. She lost him when her kids were teenagers. Pearl was left to raise and support her kids alone. Pearl's second husband was a dispatcher for the railroad. "He was an office man," she said of her second husband," he didn't know how to use a screw driver."

Pearl established a reputation (which she brought with her) at the Castle Rock Convalescent Center for her card skills. She likes Pinochle, Bridge, and is always up for a game of Cribbage. "Mother wouldn't allow us to play cards," Pearl said, "Playing all these (card) games just came to me." If she can't find a game, you are likely to see her nimble fingers busy knitting or crocheting.

Pearl worked as a dental assistant to Dr. Stapleton, who practiced in Green River from the 30s to the 60s. "The depression didn't affect us much," she said, "I had no money to invest, so it didn't bother me much."

She was looking forward to celebrating her 100th birthday. What do you think helped you live this long? "Well, I don't really know, but I never smoked or drank," she said. Pearl would be having relatives visiting from California. Having her family around her was important, as it always had been for her. She had seven grandchildren and "several" great-grandchildren.

"We take what God gives us" guided Pearl through the entire 20th century. Through it all, Pearl Lane gave Green River an example that we may all take into the next millenium.

1999 GREEN RIVER GEMS

By: Ruth Lauritzen

Morris house presents a Victorian facade to passersby. (Photo courtesy Sweetwater County Historical Museum)

Sponsored by the Green River Historic Preservation Commission, the *Green River Gems* program serves to recognize significant historic structures and sites in the City of Green River. The designation is honorary only and there are no financial advantages or regulatory obligations attached to membership on the roster. Each year two additions are made to the roster. Additions for 1999 include the Morris/Dickinson House at 6 West Second

North Street and the Carnegie Library/Circuit Court Building at 177 North Center Street.

The Morris/Dickinson House

This historic residence was built in 1888 as the home of Edward J. Morris. Morris was the son of famous Wyoming citizen, Esther Hobart Morris, known as the "Mother of Women's Suffrage" in Wyoming. He was a prominent local businessman with interests in Hunter and Morris General Merchandise, Hunter and Morris Bank, Morris Mercantile and Morris State Bank. He served as Sweetwater County Clerk, a Sweetwater County Democratic delegate to the Wyoming Constitutional Convention and a signer of the Wyoming Constitution on September 30, 1889. Morris was elected as Green River's first mayor following the town's incorporation after Wyoming statehood in 1891. He served as mayor from 1891 to 1893 and again from 1896 to 1898.

The structure is of wooden-frame construction and built in the Gothic Revival style. This style is characterized by a steeply-pitched roof, use of gables and the presence of ornate bargeboard (gingerbread) trim. The house is a two-story building which incorporates these elements. The gable roof has decorative barge-

Carnegie building was typical of small-town llibraries funded by the Carnegie Foundation across the United States. (Photo courtesy Sweetwater County Historical Museum)

board and there are several bay windows incorporated into the design. These windows sport decorative stained-glass inserts. Although some modernization has taken place, the structure retains much of its original appearance and is made distinctive by its cheery "painted lady" color scheme of purple, pink, white and green.

Carnegie Library/Circuit Court Building

One of Green River's most beautiful buildings is the historic county library building located at 177 North Center Street. This building was built in 1906 at a cost of $20,000. Funding was received through a grant from industrialist and philanthropist Andrew Carnegie. Carnegie came to the United States as a child from Scotland and amassed a fortune in the manufacture of iron and steel. One of his favorite charities was the building of libraries and during his lifetime he provided funds for the construction of 1,689 libraries in the United States. In order to qualify for the construction funds, the municipality had to provide the site for a building and pass an ordinance for the purchase of books and future maintenance of the library. The Sweetwater County Commissioners levied this tax in 1907.

The building was dedicated on July 4, 1907 with a program that included a patriotic speech by library board member T.S. Taliaferro, also well-known as the author of the Green River Ordinance. Over 500 people were in attendance. The first libarian was Elizabeth Moriarty who made the princely sum of $10 per month.

The substantial building was constructed of brick and stone in Greek Revival style. This style includes classical elements such as the symmetrical window placement and a triangular pediment supported by columns. The building was renovated for use as a Circuit Court in 1980 and has undergone some minor remodels in the years following. However, it still looks very much the same in spite of the passing years and changing styles.

In 1999 the *Green River Gems* roster increased to seven sites. These included: (1) Sweetwater Brewing Company/The Brewery; (2) Expedition Island Pavilion; (3) Old Post Office/Sweetwater County Museum; (4) St. John's Episcopal/Casa de Oracion Church; (5) Union Pacific Depot; (6) Morris/Dickinson House; and (7) Carnegie Library/Circuit Court of Sweetwater County. Two more sites may be added each year and the Green River Historic Preservation Commission welcomes citizen input in the nomination process.

THE MAKING OF A GEM

By: Ruth Lauritzen

The Green River Historic Preservation Commission established *Green River Gems*–A Local Register of Historic Places in 1998 as a means of designating structures, landscapes and locations of local historic interest. While at the time there were three properties in Green River recognized by the honor of being on the National Register for Historic Places, the commission felt that there are many more which, though they could not meet the stringent criteria for National Register status, were quite important to local history. For that reason the commission decided to develop a local register.

The City Council was notified by letter of the intent of the commission to institute this program, and on November 2, 1998 approved the creation of the *Green River Gems* program through a Council action item. Five properties were submitted to the *Gems* list the first year with the intent that two more properties may be added each calendar year. Two properties were added in 1999 bringing the total number to seven.

In order for a property to be considered for the *Gems* register it must meet the following criteria for inclusion.

1. Location–the property must be within the actual or visual boundaries of the City of Green River. Visual boundaries include that area which is normally visible from within the actual boundaries of the City.

2. Significance–The site is of historical importance. The subject property must embody or represent an important aspect in the history of Green River, or have a significant association with a person or persons of importance in Green River history. The site is of architectural significance. The property must be a noteworthy, rare, or unique example of an architectural style or method of construction in Green River, or represent the work of a known professional architect.

3. Integrity–Significant properties, which have been cosmetically changed but otherwise are substantially intact in terms of location and form, will generally qualify.

Nominations for inclusion on the register should be made by submission of a nomination form. For forms and further information on nominations please contact a member of the Green River Historic Preservation Commission. The commission also accepts suggestions for properties to be nominated and will make the nomination themselves if the property warrants it.

The nomination forms are reviewed by the commission, which then makes recommendations to the City Council for approval by the end of each calendar year.

Though not binding, the commission requests that the City Council provide an opportunity for commission comment on any actions affecting sites on the *Gems* roster.

In 2000 the commission undertook a project to mark the properties. Permission was sought from all of the *Gems* property owners to mount plaques on the sites designating them as *Green River Gems*. The commission appreciated the support of these property owners, both public and private. The plaques feature the *Gems* logo and a date of designation.

Green River Gems logo appears on signs marking additions to the local roster of historic places.

Green River Historic Preservation Commission

BRIDGES OVER THE GREEN

By: Marna Grubb

The Green River has been an oasis in the desert through-out the years providing much-needed water for the Indians, the mountain men, the pioneers, the Union Pacific, the settlers of our community, and the abundant wild life.

Today, it winds its way through the center of the city of Green River, Wyoming. It continues to be an ever-faithful source of water for Green River and Rock Springs. It is a tremendous asset to our community.

Our citizens can relax with a leisure walk along the river enjoying the many benefits derived from the addition of Green-belt pathways and parks. Expedition Island is a constant attrac-tion.

The Green River wagon bridge was consructed across the Green in 1896. It was considered to be unsafe in 1954 and demolished. (Jim June photo)

High-country springs, streams and lakes in the Bridger Wilderness and Bridger Forest create the headwaters of the Green River. The waters then begin their long journey, emptying into the Colorado River which eventually flows into the Gulf of California.

The first bridge to span the Green River was the Union Pacific Railroad bridge in 1868. When the railroad reached Green River City in October of 1868, the Union Pacific proceeded to bypass Green River City by laying tracks to a new town, later to be known as Bryan. Therefore, a temporary railroad bridge was built across the river.

It was replaced by the present railroad bridge in 1910 using some of the original quarried stone abutments.

The Green River wagon bridge was built across the Green in 1896 by the Town of Green River and Sweetwater County. It was a single-lane, iron structure with a wooden deck.

In 1913, with the coming of the automobile and transcontinental travel, the wagon bridge was used by the Lincoln Highway, later called US 30. Prior to the building of this bridge, travelers either had to ford the river or use a ferry located further east down the river.

In 1910, a bridge to the Island Park area was constructed, replacing a wooden bridge, to give safe and easy access to the popular recreation area. It was a steel bridge with a wooden deck.

In 1922, the Wyoming State Highway Department built a new highway bridge across the river approximately five miles west of Green River. The route of the Lincoln Highway (US 30) was then changed from going south across the wagon bridge and up telephone canyon to going west through town and past Tollgate Rock to the new bridge.

In 1951, the Wyoming Highway Department built the Wyoming Highway 530 bridge across the river just east of the 1896 wagon bridge to handle increasing traffic with town expansion south of the river.

In 1954, the 1896 wagon bridge was considered unsafe and was demolished. During low water periods, the remains of the bridge abutments and pier can be seen in the river, and have actually become a gauge for determining how much the river has risen until they are completely covered at high-water stage.

In 1966, the bridge across the Green in the FMC Recreation Area was constructed by volunteer FMC employees. According to one of the volunteers, Jim Bucho, the Blacks Fork bridge near FMC had been dismantled into two sections and then put back together at the FMC recreation site.

It is a 12-foot-wide bridge, roughly 30 feet long, with two steel beams and wood cross planks covered with wood length planks. On October 9, 1986, the Green Acres Recreation Club (a FMC employee group) conveyed the FMC Recreation Area to the City of Green River for public recreational purposes only.

In 1982, the Wyoming Highway Department built a second bridge next to their 1951 Wyoming Highway 530 bridge to accommodate two lanes of traffic with the ever-increasing growth south of the river.

Green River's trona bridge was set into place on September 17, 1994. It is a pedestrian bridge linking Expedition Island with Riverside Park and the Greenbelt, thus connecting the north and south sides of the city. It is a single, 250-foot-span bridge, 10 feet wide, with a metal superstructure and wood decking.

Funding for the attractive bridge was made possible by FMC Corporation, General Chemical, Rhone-Poulenc, Solvay Minerals and Tg Soda Ash, each donating $50,000 for the project – such a wonderful gift to the community.

SOME OBSERVATIONS ABOUT
PRESIDENT'S DAY-FEBRUARY 21, 2000

By: Bill Thompson

We are aware that some time ago Congress decreed that February 21 would be a national holiday to honor our first president, George Washington. Later they expanded the day to include all of the former presidents of the United States. But there is a point of interest to some of us, for George was born on February 11 not 21. Is this another goof by Congress? Nope.

George Washington was born on February 11, 1731 and celebrated his first nineteen birthdays on February 11. But an act of the British Parliament in 1750 discarded the Julian calendar and adopted the Gregorian calendar in its stead for Great Britain and the Colonies. In the Julian calendar the first day of the year had been March 25, but the year 1751 ended on Dec. 31. The days between January and March 24 were omitted from the calendar. This legal year then, contained only 282 days. The period from January 1 to March 24 was dated 1752 (a little over 2-1/2 months). Thus George was nineteen years old on February 11, 1750, but his twentieth birthday was on Feb. 11, 1752 not 1751.

Now since the vernal equinox had been displaced by 11 days in the Julian calendar, it was ordered that the difference be removed by taking out 11 days from September 1752. So there were no days dated September 3 to 13 inclusive in the year 1752. The day after September 2 was September 14! This required the addition of 11 days to compensate. Thus in 1753 George Washington celebrated his birthday February 22 instead of on February 11...... and you thought Y2K was a big deal.

HOW DO THEY DO THAT?
THE STORY OF THE GREEN RIVER
HIGH SCHOOL WRESTLING PROGRAM

By: Bill Duncan

Traditionally, people gather on the mat after a match to congratulate coaches, wrestlers, and each other. Little kids roll around underfoot shooting takedowns or trying to pin each other. Was 72-0 the largest victory margin ever? How are things looking for State? Is anyone hurt or ineligible? The crowd includes a 96-year-old great, great-grandmother and babes-in arms. Folks come from Pocatello to Cheyenne watching brothers, sons, nephews, grandsons, or just enjoying the "Green Machine's" dominance.

Wrestling came to Green River in 1964 when Mel Baldwin began practices in the basement of Monroe School. Baldwin, then a teacher at Washington Elementary, remembers,"the first year we practiced on tumbling mats. When we bought our first wrestling mat, it had to be cut into eight pieces so it would fit through the basement doors." Monroe's basement was a designated bomb shelter with a sharp "S" entryway. Baldwin says, "I had no assistant and I drove the bus to practice across town every day and to all the away matches. My wife washed towels and uniforms." Baldwin initiated the Green River Invitational Tournament in his second year. Dr. Baldwin was the Evanston schools Superintendent, retiring in 2004.

Larry Heslep's initial season was 1968 when the Wolves tied for 8th at the 3A tournament. Heslep wasted no time in urging his high school participants and younger grapplers to get involved in the AAU program. "I know we practiced some on the Monroe stage," Heslep says, " because that was where Mike Mehuron dislocated my elbow." Having to share the basement with a target shooting range and solid support pillars (Baldwin recalls at least one kid knocking himself out), practice eventually moved to a portion of the bus garage at Lincoln. "We could really heat it up in there," Heslep reminisces, "the moisture would condense on the ceiling and drip into puddles on the mats." Heslep is currently Assistant Superintendent at Gillette.

The first state championship trophy arrived in 1970. Both Dave Gomez (elected Mayor of Green River in 2002) and Gary Gomez were undefeated that season. Rick and Rusty Owens were 22-2 and 22-3. Rusty is the father of the current varsity 152 pounder Jake Owens. That was the same year that the Green River Wrestling Club (AAU) was named outstanding club in the state against wrestlers from schools of all sizes. Wolves placed in 7 of the 11 weight classes.

It was also the first of Green River's 13 state championships. Coach Bill Hodges noted that if any grappler stayed in the program for all four years, he would have been part of at least one state championship team. The championships have come that often and that consistently.

Consistency is one of the keys to the Wolves success. Hodges was only the fifth head wrestling coach in 36 years. That even counts Ted Adams's half year when Heslep left to become a school Superintendent in the middle of the season. Heslep guided the Wolves to 7 state crowns his 17 years.

Tom Seamans's teams grabbed 5 state titles in 13 years. Like his predecessors, Seamans was a product of the UW program. His 1989 team set a high-water mark when six individuals grabbed state championships. Seamans, later an elementary principal in North Carolina, still kept up on the Wolves' results through weekly phone calls with Hodges, his assistant all 13 years. Seamons is now Gillette's head wrestlng coach.

Although the year 2000 was Hodges first year as a head coach, he had been associated with the program since 1979. That doesn't count his freshman year when he was named all-tourney at the Evanston Freshman Basketball Tournament. Nor does it count his time at UW, where he was a WAC champion.

When growing enrollment pushed Green River's teams into 4A, the program didn't miss a step. Green River took the 3A crown in 1977 and brought home the 4A trophy in 78 and 79. That was the only three-year run in the program's history.

The "Wall of Fame" in the wrestling practice room notes that David Gomez and Kasey Thomas are three-time state champs. Gary Arguello, David Hansen, Dale Hansen, Arthur Maestas, Fernando Flores, Troy Gunter, Rick Yoak, Ryan Hintz, Jason Pacheco, Bryant Birch, Trenton McDowell, Greg Bybee, Dallas Balzly, Justin Salas, and West Busha won two state crowns. Winners of one state title are: Gary Gomez, Dell Brady, Marvin Brady, Eva Castillion, Monte Kester, Bob Thoman, David Drinkle, Scot Duncan, Ron Stassinos, Dan Arguello, Bill Hodges, Gary Dallmann, Mike Beck, Mike Hamel, Steve Ortega, Joe Hamel, Chad Brakke, Brad Hill, Bryce Johnson, Scott Waters, Paul Hardy, Matt Kraft, Anthony Gibson, Jamie Lewis, Leon Castillo, Seth March, Blake Gunter, Eric Wright, and Steve Harmon.

Winners alone do not measure a successful program. At a recent double dual, GRHS wrestling graduates coached for Cheyenne Central (Rob Hodges), Cheyenne East (TJ Castillion), Rock Springs (head coach Joe Hamel and assistant Scot Duncan) and Green River (Bill Hodges and Darren Heslep). Mike Beck was an assistant at Gillette. Monroe Principal Mike Hamel returned after head coaching stints in Rawlins, Gillette, and Alaska. Chad Brakke lead a wrestling program at a Wisconsin college and now heads a high school program there. Johnny Webb assisted at BYU. Monte Kester, member of the three state winners in the late 70s has officiated at state tournaments for 23 years. Jack Hamel, an early 80s competitor, also officiates at state tournaments. Nando Flores works many home meets and enjoyed his first state tournament this year.

The Gary Dallmann Memorial Scholarship gives $500 to GRHS grads currently competing in college. The scholarships in 2000 were awarded to Blake Gunter, a junior college All-American at NWCC in Powell and Eric Wright, wrestling for WWCC in Rock Springs. John Anastos, another program graduate and local official, founded the scholarship and raises the money each year. Dallmann was a wrestler who first made famous Green River's hallmark, the cobra hold.

Rudy Gunter began driving the team bus in 1986. It was a great way to watch his son, Troy, wrestle. He still drives, sponsors the cheerleaders, films some of the matches and is one of the Wolves most avid supporters. Pretty good for a guy who spent nearly 20 years coaching basketball at GRHS, some as a successful head coach.

No program is successful without cooperation. Parents travel long distances over icy roads to provide support. They raise money, conduct shirt sales and raffles and form the core of Green River's knowledgeable fans. Green River's fan support is legendary from Reno to Grand Junction. Senior moms continue a 15-year tradition of making illustrated history quilts for their sons. Most of all they provide guidance, perseverance, and counseling. No other sport demands that a participant humiliate an opponent by keeping part of his body motionless on the mat, then shaking his hand and his coach's hand. Yet parents seem to be able to help keep fragile teen egos together.

The Green River Grapplers feeder program starts kids as early as 4 or 5 years old. Ex-coaches, ex-wrestlers, parents, and high school wrestlers help coach. Mac McCulley, a retired elementary art teacher, provided leadership for many years. Former grappler Raul Gardea, father of varsity 135 pounder Ricky, coached in the feeder program for years. Local businessman Charlie Stickney currently leads the state's USA effort. Hodges has participated in this program most of his life.

Each wrestling team reflects the work of several people. The year 2000 varsity had one freshman, six sophomores, two juniors, and five seniors. Most of these kids didn't wait until high school to start wrestling. They came out of the USA program, were groomed in middle school by coaches like Don Borchardt, polished by long-time high school assistants Greg McClure and Byron Stahla. Their final honing came every afternoon in the room with Hodges, Darren Heslep and Marshall Rhodes.

Three rows of young fellows shouted themselves hoarse in the middle of the GR section at the Casper Events Center. They were the excited members of the junior varsity and freshman GRHS wrestling teams. Think they're not excited about the next few years?

In an era when educators struggle to measure student success, in a time when taxpayers demand accountability, they need to look no further than Green River High School's wrestling program. Are all the men who come out of this program model citizens? No. But considering college success, graduation rates, job stability, community service and personal growth – look at the products of the GRHS wrestling program. They know the value of hard work, the need for discipline, the thrill of competition and the rewards of success.

RANGE WARS, A CONTINUING SAGA

By: Terry A. Del Bene

> Well, they have just got through shelling the house like hail. I heard them splitting wood. I guess they are going to fire the house to-night. I think I will make a break when night comes, if alive. Shooting again. I think they will fire the house this time. It's not night yet. The house is all fired. Goodbye, boys, if I never see you again. (Nathan D. Champion April 8, 1892).

Shortly after putting these words to paper, Nate Champion fled the burning ranch house within which he had withstood a siege of several hours. He managed to run almost fifty yards before he was struck by a succession of four bullets. The Johnson County War had started in earnest.

The words quoted above came from a diary which Champion kept during the siege. The pocket memorandum book was soaked with his blood and was taken off Nate's corpse by one of his murderers.

It is remarkable that Champion's account of the fight was ever written. Imagine, taking the time to write about being besieged by somewhere around fifty gunmen. Imagine, tending your wounded friend for over two hours and watching him die. Imagine, withstanding hours of gunfire and knowing that the next move would be to burn you out of your only cover. Champion's cool observations during the siege mark him as an inordinately brave human being.

After his friend Nick died, Nate wrote, *"I feel pretty lonesome now. I wish there was someone here so we could watch all sides at once."*

It is even more remarkable that his last writings survived the fight and made it to publication. Champion's killers easily could have disposed of the document. However, the world learned of Nate's courage through the publication of a book called *The Banditti of the Plains* or the *Cattlemen's Invasion of Wyoming in 1892* (The Crowning Infamy of the Ages), penned by Asa Shinn Mercer. The story also was told in scattered newspaper coverage.

Asa Mercer was a reporter in Wyoming while many of the events of the famed Johnson County War were unfolding. He quickly became the arch-foe of the Wyoming Live Stock Association. Mercer, who is perhaps best known for arranging for eastern brides to be shipped to the Pacific Northwest, published *Banditti* on his own. The publication of the book unleashed a series of bad events in his life, all done at the behest of the Wyoming Live Stock Association.

Mercer was arrested and thrown in jail. Many copies of the book were confiscated and burned. He was charged with publishing and distributing pornographic materials (that being *Banditti*) through the mails. His paper was closed and he found himself hounded for years to come. Apparently copies of the book which found their way into public libraries, including the Library of Congress, were stolen or destroyed.

Some believe that history has a way of repeating itself. There may be a grain of truth in that. The year 2000 legislative session generated substantial controversy over *The Western Range Revisited, Removing Livestock from Public Lands to Conserve Native Biodiversity* by Debra L. Donahue.

Professor Donahue of the University of Wyoming Law School found herself under attack for things such as misuse of university stationary. The Legislature rumbled about eliminating the University of Wyoming law school, and with it Donahue's job.

The two books have something in common, besides having excessively long titles. Both paint the agricultural elite and political machines of Wyoming in a poor light. In both cases, the reactions of the stock-growing industry's supporters make Wyoming seem more like a third-world country than part of a vibrant democracy which cherishes free speech. In both instances, the public would better be served by an open debate of the issues and facts. Both books are very issue-oriented and whatever interpretive biases exist could easily be answered by a candid debate.

However, the message to many will be that if you try to discuss certain controversies, there are people who will try to get you and silence your voice. Ask Professor Donahue. For the record, I take no stance for or against the slant in either book. I recommend that persons interested in the topics at hand read the books and examine the facts for themselves.

Several years ago, Hollywood took on the Johnson County War in a movie called *Heaven's Gate*. You may wonder what this movie was like. The reason for that is that the movie was not released in many domestic theaters. At the time of the decision not to release the film it was indicated that the movie was just plain bad. Some thought it was just too hot a topic to handle. One might wish to pick up the recently released DVD and make one's own decision. Was it unpalatable or unimaginable?

Perhaps the ghosts of those politicians and other influential people who were responsible for killing Nate Champion and hounding Asa Mercer are still with us. Or maybe they just thought Kris Kristopherson is not much of an actor. Maybe they thought the events of 1892 were unbelievable, even in Hollywood.

BRIEF HISTORICAL INTERWEAVINGS

By: Bill Thompson

My maternal German grandparents, Albert and Tilli Schultz, immigrated to this country on the good ship BREMAN in the last part of the 19th Century, arriving in Boston (not Ellis Island). Grandpa could have had a lucrative job as an interpreter for the U.S. Government, but Grandma wanted land.

So they homesteaded in South Dakota where later Grandpa and his brother Fred worked in the Homestake Gold Mine at Lead. By the 1920s various circumstances led the family to the famous Tea Pot Dome oil field in Wyoming, 35 miles North of Casper.

Now divorced, they went their separate ways. Grandpa was the powder man for the Alcova Dam project on the Platte River. Grandma worked in the Salt Creek Oil Field near the Tea Pot Dome.

By now the rest of their scattered family had arrived and found employment in the oil field too. This included my mom, Edith. Here is where she met my dad, Bill, who had grown up on the Bannock Reservation in Idaho. In the Salt Creek Field, using a "Rig Ax", which ironically resembled a tomahawk, he built wooden oil derricks for the then-fabulous wage of $5.00 a

Pioneer burial unearthed near Green River/Rock Springs in the 1940s by the author's uncle Al Carlson. (Photo courtesy Bill Thompson)

day. He also ran a dance band. It was not unusual to find 40-50 musicians playing each night in the various "clubs" at the height of that boom period.

Grandpa's brothers had immigrated also. One brother, Fred Schultz, had been blinded in an explosion at the Homestake gold mine. The company paid for his schooling to become a chiropractor. Widowed he had, married again. Later, opening his office in Rock Springs he was able to keep Great Aunt Louise and their sons (Ace, Virgil and John) in comfort. His first son, Ray, also had moved to Rock Springs and found work in the coal mines.

Great-Uncle Fred and Great-Aunt Louise would come to visit us in Midwest, Wyoming in the Salt Creek Oil Field from time to time.

As a very young kid I was amazed that he could get around so well and even lace and tie his own shoes...which patiently he would do over and over for me.

Sometime after Uncle Fred's death in 1947, Aunt Louise married contractor Al Carlson. Among his various assignments included the dismantling of water towers and other such structures for the Union Pacific Railroad. Driving from one job location to another in several states, he too would stop by our house in Midwest for a visit.

On one of his trips in the late 1940s, he fascinated me with a story about the rails being moved and some pioneer graves being unearthed near the Green River-Rock Springs area. Due to the arid conditions of this region they were perfectly preserved. Also, all of the several bodies had red hair! It was assumed that chemicals in the soil caused this effect. The air began to cause rapid decomposition so pictures were taken as quickly as a camera could be found. "Uncle" Al said he thought he had the pictures. He wrote the following letter to me in March 1950 from the Calmez Hotel in Clinton, Oklahoma:

Dear Billy,

Enclosed are snapshots requested. When I can locate negatives I will have others reprinted and sent to you. Here we have dust storms most impossible to see any distance and very unpleasant dust goes right through your clothes(sic). May see you soon. I wish to get up to Wyoming and home.

Sincerely Yours,   A.L. Carlsen

And there you have it in a nutshell folks; German immigrants, gold and coal mining, the world's largest light-oil producing field (at that time), Indians, a reclamation dam, a major railroad and pioneers, all historically woven together through time and geography.

GREEN RIVER'S HISTORIC JEWELS

By: Ruth Lauritzen

The additions for the year 1999 to the *Green River Gems* register of local historic places, the Morris/Dickinson home and the Carnegie Library/Circuit Court of Sweetwater County building were previously profiled. This article describes the other five properties on the register as of that year.

Sweetwater Brewing Company/The Brewery

This building is the most architecturally distinct historic building in Green River. Built by Hugo Gaensslen in 1899, it replaced a much smaller frame structure on the same site. The original brewery was established by Adam Braun in 1872 and was the first brewery in the Territory of Wyoming.

The new structure was built of stone quarried in First Spring or Mormon Canyon and was designed after castles along the Rhine River in Gaensslen's German homeland and the famous Water Tower in Chicago, the first place he settled when he arrived in the United States. The cornice on the building is unusual because it is fabricated not from stone like the rest of the building, but rather from cast metal.

The current building was part of a larger complex, which included an attached engine house and brew house as well as a nearby icehouse and bottling shed. Most of these buildings have been torn down, although the bottling shed, located across the alley, is still standing.

The Sweetwater Brewing Company operated as a successful venture for nearly fifty years, employing between thirty and forty men and producing a beer of sufficient quality to win silver and bronze medals at the 1904 and '05 World's Fairs

The beginning of Prohibition in 1919 brought hard times to the company. "Near beer" and soda pop were bottled during the ten years the Volstead Act was in force. In 1934 two con men leased the building and reopened the brewery for a brief time, only to flee the area, taking stockholder's money with them.

In the years following the building housed several businesses including a laundry and a plumbing shop. In 1976 the building underwent a renovation and has since been home to a bar, appropriately named the Brewery.

Expedition Island Pavilion

Expedition Island has long been a pleasure spot for citizens of Green River. Early in the town's history it was used as a picnic ground and later an open-air dance pavilion was installed for summer entertainments.

In 1930 the Town of Green River floated a bond issued to finance the building of the present pavilion. It was used in the following years for a dance hall, public gathering place, roller skating rink, National Guard Armory, "Teen Town" and for Flaming Gorge Days activities.

The building was renovated as a Bicentennial project and dedicated in June 1979. The Pavilion is owned by the City of Green River and continues to be one of the most heavily-used recreational buildings in the town. It and the surrounding Island Park were placed on the National Register of Historic places in 1968.

Old Green River Post Office/
Future Sweetwater County Museum

This building was the first federally-constructed property in Green River and was completed in 1931. Green River's post office had been located in various buisness houses until that time and many citizens worked for years to bring the building into being.

Constructed of brick and stone, the building represents the Classical Revival architectural style so popular with federal buildings of the time. The exterior has changed very little since its dedication on April 29, 1931.

The building served as the town's post office until 1981 when the current post office was opened. At that time the building was sold to the City of Green River who leased the property to be renovated and run as Trudel's Restaurante. The building came into the hands of Sweetwater County in August 1995. Over the next few years the building underwent an extensive internal renovation and opened as the new home of the Sweetwater County Historical Museum in November of 2001.

St. John's Episcopal/Casa de Oracion Church

The St. John's Episcopal Church was the third church building built in Green River and is the oldest one still standing.

The Episcopal Church of Green River held its first services in the courtroom of the Sweetwater County Courthouse in December 1883. The St. John's Episcopal Church opened its doors in 1892.

The church is a wooden-frame building with a gable roof with bargeboards having exposed overhead eaves. There are elaborate wooden shingle designs on the steeple, with brackets on the upper ledge or cornice of the bell tower and pedestal for the steeple. The gothic windows have curved, triangular stained-glass window circles. There is a cross-shaped finial on the spire and a circular finial on the gable. The study is an attached wooden frame structure with a gable roof and exposed overhead eaves.

The Episcopalians left the building in 1970 when they built a new facility. Beginning in 1976 the building was used as a senior citizen's center until 1979 when the Casa de Oracion congregation purchased it.

Union Pacific Depot

The Union Pacific Railroad Depot was constructed at a total cost of $75,000 and opened to the public October 24, 1910. This construction followed a petition by the Commercial Club and the citizens of Green River for an improved railroad facility to replace a small and outmoded frame structure.

Construction began in October of 1909. The structure is made of pressed brick with Bedford stone trimmings and a red tile roof. It is the second largest Union Pacific depot in the state, surpassed only by the one in Cheyenne.

The main building is two stories with a colonnaded main entrance from the tracks. It is flanked on the east and west sides by single-story wings connected to the main structure by brick archways. Historically, the west wing housed a restaurant while the express office was located in the east wing. There was also a lunch counter located in the main building. The second floor of the main building was dedicated to offices.

The building is not currently being used as a depot since there is no passenger service on this line. It contains offices, staff rooms and technical services for running the Green River terminal.

The Sweetwater Brewing Company building was built in 1898 and quickly became a Green River landmark. (Photo courtesy Sweetwater County Historical Museum)

Expedition Island has been a playground for Sweetwater County residents since the settlement of the area. The old open-air Pavilion was used seasonally for dances. (Photo courtesy Sweetwater County Historical Museum)

St. John's Episcopal Church as it appeared around 1900. (Photo courtesy Sweetwater County Historical Museum)

Green River's large depot shows the importance of the town to the Union Pacific passenger service. (Photo courtesy Sweetwater County Historical Museum)

BACK IN TIME: GREEN RIVER 1940-1950

By: Marna Grubb

In the year 2000, Green River was visited by several class members and spouses of the Green River High School Class of 1950 who were celebrating their 50th class reunion. After two Star Transit buses toured the group around Green River for two hours, many were awed with the positive changes to Green River since their graduation 50 years prior.

One commented about how beautiful Green River had become, remembering the dirty little town with cinders from the train engines blowing in their eyes.

All were impressed with Expedition Island, the Trona Bridge and the Greenbelt, such assets to the community!

The cemetery was another pleasant surprise to everyone, since it was plush green since the coming of perpetual care, the beautiful landscaping, and paved roads. Many of the large pine and lilac

The popular Isis Theatre provided a place for residents to gather to view the latest in cinema attractions. The sing-alongs were popular also – follow the bouncing ball! (Sweetwater County Historical Museum/Proctor photo)

bushes had been planted while these people were growing up back in the 40s, although the remainder of the cemetery had been quite desolate.

The Reunion Committee compiled six pages of "Green River As We Remember It" and I would like to share a summarized version with you.

Back in the 1940s and 1950s, Green River, Wyoming, was a sleepy, slow-paced, little town of approximately 3000-4000 people located entirely north of the river. It was a great place to grow up! The railroad was a busy place and provided employment for many of their parents.

Before the underpass was built in 1937 and the walking viaduct was put over the tracks in 1938 because of safety concerns, there was a small gatehouse for directing cars and people across the tracks and a park nearby with a bandstand for concerts.

There was a "rough" landing strip on the flat below Man's

RIVERSIDE SWIMMING POOL: The Green River, outdoor, swimming pool was located near the river and northwest of the Island bridge. It was opened to the public in July of 1931. This municipal pool furnished enjoyment each summer for people throughout the county until the Monroe indoor pool was built in 1962. (Sweetwater County Historical Museum/Proctor photo)

Face Rock (later the location of the Hutton Heights Subdivision) and the old town landfill was in the same area.

Tie drives came down the river from 1868 and continued until the mid-to-late 1940s causing "jams" in the river which had to be dynamited. Ties were collected in "booms" and gathered and loaded onto cars for shipment for treatment and use in railroad-track construction. The ties provided fun for some as they caught a ride down the river.

In their early years, the boys were playing marbles, rubber guns and mumble peg, while the girls were playing with their Shirley Temple dolls, paper dolls, jacks, hop scotch, jump rope and roller skating. They also traded comic books. Through the years, outdoor games were popular, such as hide-and-seek, kick-the-can, red-rover, run-sheepy-run, and anti-i-over. In the winter, they ice skated on the pond west of town by the Palisades. In the summer,

Digging out a Union Pacific train engine buried in snow during the blizzard of 1949. (Ed Bratke family photo)

they swam in the outdoor Riverside Swimming Pool in "ice" water, or so it seemed!

They spent many hours at the Isis Theatre watching such movie stars as Gary Cooper, Claudette Colbert, Humphrey Bogart and Lassie. Bing Crosby and Bob Hope were doing their "Road to..." shows. Saturday matinees were Hop-a-long Cassidy, Roy Rogers, Zorro, Superman and Batman, usually with a cartoon, the serial and the 20th Century Fox news. They didn't have cars, so they would walk or ride their bikes.

Evers Field (later Evers Park) provided a place for softball games or rodeos with spectators under covered wooden bleachers.

Soda fountains could be found at the Moedl Drug and the Tomahawk Pharmacy, also at the Sugar Bowl. Some served as "soda jerks" at these places. They remembered the old post office, the old court house, the Carnegie Library, the old Red Feather, the Star Café and the Covered Wagon west of town – and Bill Hutton taking care of the court house and Adrian Reynolds as editor of *The Green River Star* – and later the McGowans.

Their "hangout" was the Sugar Bowl with Dave and Eva Zumbrennen providing hamburgers and other light snacks, but most importantly providing a place to socialize. The juke box played many songs popular at the time (six songs for a quarter): Stardust, String Of Pearls, In The Mood, Candy Kisses, Harbor Lights, Slow Boat To China, Now Is The Hour, Memories Are Made Of This, Chattanooga Choo Choo, The Old Lamp Lighter, Sincerely, etc., etc., etc.

The theme of their Junior Prom was Stairway To The Stars. Their class colors were blue and silver. Their class flower was the white rose and their class motto was "Success lies in ambition." Their Prom Queen was Marilyn Mills with attendants Mettie Anderson, Carol Hill, Anita Horton and Barbara Weimer. Junior class president was Marna Grubb, Gordon Hoover was vice president, and J. Pewtress was secretary-treasurer.

The school paper, the Wolves Howl, was strictly amateur, but they had fun publishing it. The Wolves Howl of May, 1950, listed the Top Ten Tunes for dancing as the Johnson Rag, Blue Moon, Twelfth Street Rag, I Can Dream Can't I, There's No Tomorrow, Again, Stardust, Chattanooga Shoe Shine Boy, Sugar Foot Rag and My Dream Is Yours. Although the Juniors at that time stuck with their Prom theme song, How Deep Is The Ocean. They listened to the radio and played 78 and 45 rpm records.

They were saddened with the loss of their typing and gym teacher, Julia Malonek, and they dedicated their School Annual in memory of her.

At school, they answered correctly that there were 48 states in the United States. The territory of Alaska didn't become the 49th state until January 3, 1959, and the territory of Hawaii, the 50th state, not until August 21, 1959.

The only United States president they knew for many years while growing up was Franklin Delano Roosevelt, who became president in 1932 when many of them were born. In April of 1945, Roosevelt died while in office of a massive cerebral hemorrhage. His vice president, Harry Truman, took command and was president when they graduated in 1950.

In October of 1940, Green River High School burned down, all except the gymnasium. After the fire, students were having classes in various buildings throughout the community while a new high school was being built. The Lincoln School was built at the same location and encompassed the old gymnasium.

World War II was the world-changing event of the 40s while they were in the lower grades. It began for our nation on December 7, 1941, with the bombing of Pearl Harbor. They used ration stamps when they shopped for sugar, coffee, butter, shoes, gasoline, etc. The town's people enjoyed driving down to the railroad depot parking lot to watch the numerous trains coming through. Many were troop trains of soldiers, while others carried war supplies such as tanks and trucks. They helped to collect paper, magazines, rubber and metal for the war effort. They would buy savings stamps at school and savings bonds. House windows displayed small banners with blue stars for each person from the household in the service – or a gold star to designate you had lost someone in the war. On August 15, 1945, they heard on the radio that Japan had surrendered and the war was finally over. Train whistles and the fire whistle were blowing for a long time.

On Sunday, June 25, 1950, shortly after they graduated, the Korean War was precipitated when North Korean Communist forces invaded the Republic of South Korea, crossing the 38th parallel at several points. On June 29, President Truman announced he would pledge American armed strength for the defense of South Korea. This resulted in many of our boys serving in the armed forces. Following a storm of controversy, Truman announced he would not run again for the presidency.

With World War II in the early 40s followed by the Korean

Conflict, they became very patriotic, showing great respect for our flag. This respect seems to still linger in their hearts today, even though later generations are at times very disrespectful. They sang the Star Spangled Banner with great gusto, along with America, The Beautiful. Kate Smith stirred their hearts with God Bless America.

Ed Taliaferro was mayor from 1943 to 1947. During his term, the City began purchasing some land south of the river, which later was developed into the first subdivisions south of the river. Dr. Stapleton (dentist) followed as mayor from 1947 to 1949. During his term, an ordinance prohibiting gambling in the town was adopted. When the Class of "50" graduated, Frank Wilkes was mayor (1949-1955). He served again from 1959 to 1963. Wilkes Drive in Green River was named in his honor.

The trona industry had its beginnings in 1946-47 with the arrival of the Westvaco Chlorine Products Company west of Green River, now known as FMC Corporation. Since that time, several more companies have mines and processing plants west of town, which provided jobs when the coal mines in Rock Springs and the railroad in Green River began downsizing.

When they picked up the phone, they would get a friendly voice asking "Number please." These operators usually knew everyone in town and where to find them, especially the doctors, firemen and law enforcement officers.

Many townspeople still speak of the "Winter of 49." The most severe storms in the Rocky Mountain area over the past four decades were recorded. In January, snow and high east winds piled snow up to 10-to-14-feet deep, halting road and train travel. Travel on the U.P. had been slow and erratic. Stockmen were having a very difficult time feeding their sheep and cattle. Antelope were being killed by the trains and were coming into town. Temperatures were staying from 1-to-30-degrees below zero. On January 24, 1949, President Harry Truman put into effect "Operation Snowbound" with planes dropping food to snowbound livestock, wild animals and snowbound ranchers.

In February, drifts of snow on the U.P. right-of-way between Wamsutter and Rawlins were 20 feet deep. Highways were closed between Wamsutter and Rawlins and west from Green River to Salt Lake City. On February 6, 1949, 2000 travelers were stranded in Green River. Food demands taxed the local business houses to supply the passengers. An Emergency Red Cross Office was set up in the old VFW building on Railroad Avenue to aid those stranded and to meet the needs of the community. After a 15-day tie-up, train and highway traffic began to move again. A heavy blizzard hit again on March 15 causing heavy losses to calving and lambing livestock. On April 1, 1949, Chinook winds caused snow to melt as if under a blow torch, with flooding in many areas near Green River.

All this time, the Class of 1950 was struggling through its senior year and not paying much attention to all this, since Green River was not as hard hit as surrounding areas.

The Reunion Committee for the Class of 1950, composed of Marna Jessen Grubb, Carl Williams, Sharon Rhodes, Dick Hodges and Eva Merrell Cauthorn, had great fun reminiscing and gathering these memories.

THE VOTE

By: Terry A. Del Bene

Before we begin this month's installment, we would be remiss if we were to allow the passing of a good friend to go unmentioned. Ray Lovato, of Rock Springs, was one of the true pillars of our community. He was a man engaged in living life to the fullest and one could not be but swept along in his enthusiasm for making the life of all our citizens better. Ray also was very interested in the history of this area. Without his assistance the popular Trail Tales series probably would not have happened in Rock Springs. There are fond memories of a steam-engine trip where all were caught up in an animated game of Three-Card Monty. It was great living history and great fun. Ray, you are missed!

Vox Populi, vox dei?

"I'm your top prime cut of meat... I'm your choice... I wanna be elected! I'm Yankee Doodle Dandy in a gold Rolls Royce...I wanna be elected!" Alice Cooper.

November brings that time again... the trees are turning fall colors (well after that early snow they're turning white), the hunters wear orange, and there are electioneering signs in the front yards. Americans have always had a love/hate relationship with politics. We love the horse-race but hate the stable-yard droppings and flies. Every year we're bombarded with messages about getting out to vote and every year the numbers of eligible voters who do exercise their right to vote declines. Voter turnout for Presidential elections has been hovering around 50%. Was it always like this?

Records for the earliest elections are not clear. The vote was much more restricted in the early days of the nation. Voting was often tied to land ownership, gender, and race. The first women voters in this nation were late 18th century widows in Virginia who had inherited property (and the right to vote until the voting law was changed). In the Presidential election of

1828 upstart Andrew Jackson unseated incumbent John Quincy Adams. The voter turn-out was a modest 57.5% of the electorate. Today that would be a massive turnout.

Elections later in the 19th Century would eclipse these numbers. As the country became more polarized over sectional issues (like slavery) there seemed to be more of a moral imperative to vote. The 1856 election (won by James Buchanan over John. Fremont and Millard Fillmore) saw a turn-out of 78.9% of the voters. Even this astounding number was surpassed by the pivotal election of 1860, the result of which was a civil war. The 1860 election had a turn-out of 81.2%! Winner Abraham Lincoln only received 39.9% of the popular votes, while opponents Stephen Douglas, John Breckenridge, and John Bell carried the rest. The trend was for voter turnout to be extremely good through the end of the 19th Century. In the last election of the century (which was a repeat of the 1896 election) President McKinley won re-election over William Bryan with a voter turnout of 73.2%.

How is it we've become a nation obsessed with ducking our responsibilities? Have politics suddenly become more dirty? What is causing voters to turn-away? Why is it with all the high-powered marketing tools at our disposal and millions of dollars asking people to vote that the American public is "just saying-no" to voting?

Politics is, and was a dirty business. After all, politics is about power. Candidates have fought each other tooth, nail, verbally and occasionally with fists/knives. It is a rarity for anything so dramatic to happen in this century but one can imagine that if the current Presidential candidates were going to roll up their sleeves and have at it the debate would be one of the most watched pay-per-view events rather than one carried by a few major networks. The hope for the unexpected made 19th Century politics more exciting. Imagine Davy Crockett running for his re-election to Congress when he sees his opponent has brought several witnesses to certain events which would brand him as a liar. He has been caught! Crockett, in 19th Century fashion declares, "Fellow citizens, I did lie. They told stories on me, and I wanted to show them if it came to that, I could tell a bigger lie than they could. Yes, fellow citizens, I can run faster, walk longer, leap higher, speak better, and tell more and bigger lies than my competitor, and all his friends, any day of his life."

Imagine a time where the Presidential candidate only makes a few speeches the entire campaign and spends much of the election year sitting on his own porch. A loser you think? Not at all... that's what Abraham Lincoln did for the 1860 Presidential campaign. Some politicians of the period actually thought it undignified to go around "speechifying" the public and begging for votes. Mr. Lincoln's supporters clearly went around spreading the word about "Honest Abe." There were no debates... which we have come to expect. What about those Lincoln/Douglas debates? Most Americans forget that these were for an 1858 Illinois Senatorial election. However, unlike our present incredibly dull, "info-mercial" debates... the candidates had a series of several hour debates where issues (real issues) were discussed back and forth. The audience (who for the most part stood through the entire thing) heckled both participants while the debate was in progress and the responses reveal much of the character of the two candidates. The result was that Mr. Lincoln lost the election but was catapulted to national recognition through his homespun eloquence.

Some say it's the endless problems with campaign financing. For years America has had the best national government which money can buy. Whether it's the issue of awarding a defense contract in the year 2000 or building the transcontinental railroad in the 1860s our elected officials often have worked at the behest of donors and supporters. The founding fathers probably intended for the public to only be able to influence their representatives with one form of bribery... the vote. However, that's not how it worked and the state which contains the teapot dome need not look far for examples of how this flaw in the system has been exploited.

In the 18th and 19th century special interests had ways of influencing representatives and their elections but one gets the impression that those interests usually took a side. Hence, there is a little bit more of the aspect that they were supporting those who supported the special interests' position on issues, be they grazing, mining, slavery, immigration, railroad construction, tariffs ...etc. Today we've taken a strange path. Now corporations/individuals routinely throw their financial support at all sides.

This means either the various parties are so much alike that there is no effective difference on issues or the corporations/individuals are overtly purchasing influence.

We've certainly come a long way in homogenizing and dulling down the nature of public debate. It is common to hear complaints about negative campaigning. A curious thing because public opinion has for generations been molded largely by negative advertising. All sides throw slick, Madison-Avenue campaigns at the voters and bombard them with a host of sound-bites. Even in campaigns where there seemed clearer choices, such as the Nixon/Kennedy campaign of 1960, voter turn-out was much lower (64%).

Perhaps the decline in voter turn-out is a plea to get back to real issues with clear choices of visions for our future. More time seems spent on debating how we'll manage entitlement programs than on how we'll manage the next generation of scientific discoveries. More time seems to be spent on looking for flaws in the characters of the candidates than fixing the flaws in our legal system.

Perhaps the public just finds the whole thing predictable and boring. The more hum-drum the candidates make the election, the less likely folks will be to participate. The Bush/Clinton campaign of 1988 was about as hum-drum as they come and the turnout (50.1%) reflected that. The pollsters are so accurate and immediate that many may feel it's all decided before they even cast their vote. Each election seems to be a re-run of the previous elections. The signs look the same... the commercials look the same... there are few policy differences... the rhetoric sounds the same... the candidates look the same... even their buses look the same.

Who would have thought just 30 years ago that by the end of the 20th century the totalitarian system of the Soviet Union would give way to a republic which would outshine the leader of the free world? Yes, while we have been waiting for more entertainment value in our political system, the Russian people have embraced the responsibilities which democracies entail. While we pray for a turnout of over 50% the Russians managed a 69.8% voter turn-out for their last Presidential election. Maybe they understand some things which we forgot along the way. Please vote!

LAND OF THE FREE

By: Ruth Lauritzen

"Wyoming is the first place in God's green earth which could consistently claim to be the land of the Free!"
-Susan B. Anthony
Laramie, Wyoming Territory, 1871

Esther Hobart Morris is known as the "Mother of Women's Suffrage" in Wyoming. Her twin sons, Robert and Edward, were prominent Green River businessmen and civic leaders. (Photo courtesy Wyoming State Archives)

The cause of women's suffrage reached a major milestone in 1890 when Wyoming became the first state granting universal suffrage to be admitted to the Union. The story of women's rights in Wyoming was one marred with amazingly little bitterness and controversy when compared to the protracted battle fought in many states, particularly in the east. A combination of astute leadership and the existence of a social and political climate right for the revolutionary new idea fortuitously came together in Wyoming during the spring of 1869.

Wyoming Territory was organized in May of 1869. Elections for the first territorial legislature were held the following September. One of those elected was William H. Bright from South Pass City, then county seat of Sweetwater County. Bright introduced the bill for women's suffrage to the first Wyoming Territorial Legislature.

Bright, it has been said, was heavily influenced by women in his efforts for universal suffrage. There is a persistent story about a tea party held in South Pass City hosted by Esther Hobart Morris at which Morris persuaded both Bright and his opponent for the territorial legislature seat to introduce a bill if elected. In more recent times this story has largely been discredited. Mrs. Morris was a believer in the cause and did serve as the first female Justice of the Peace in the nation, but she was not extremely active in the cause, never campaigning for public office nor expressing her views publicly in voice or print.

However, many believe that Bright's opinion was most influenced by his young and much-beloved wife who was a believer in the suffrage cause. Of course, there are also those who maintain his inspiration was Edward M. Lee, Secretary of the Territory. Lee was a supporter of universal suffrage and possibly helped Bright draft the bill. Regardless of his influences, Bright introduced the bill at the first territorial legislature which met on October 12, 1869. It read as follows:

> That every women of the age of twenty-one years, residing in the territory, may, at every election to be holden and under the laws thereof, cast her vote; and her rights to the elective franchise, and to hold office, shall be the same, under the election laws of the territory, as those of the electors.

This territorial legislature also enacted acts which provided for the property rights of married woman. Under the system of English Common Law, which was the basis of most state law in the United States at that time, married women could not control their own property and they were not guardians of their children upon their husband's death. The school law also provided that, "in the employment of teacher no discrimination shall be made, in the question of pay, on account of sex when the persons are equally qualified."

The methods employed by Bright and his supporters to get these measures passed were recalled by John W. Hoyt, Territorial Governor from 1879-83. Quoted in *History of Woman Suffrage*, he says;

> So he (Bright) went over and talked with the other members of the legislature. They smiled. But he got one of the lawyers to help him draw up a short bill, which he introduced. It was considered and discussed. People smiled generally. There was not much expectation that anything of that sort would be done; but this was a shrewd fellow, who managed the party card in such a way as to get, as he believed, enough votes to carry the measure before it was brought to the test. I will show you a little behind the curtain, so far as I

can draw it. Thus he said to the Democrats: "We have a Republican governor and a Democratic Assembly. Now then, if we can carry this bill through the Assembly and the governor vetoes it, we shall have made a point, you know; we shall have shown our liberality and lost nothing. But keep still; don't say anything about it." They promised. He then went to the Republicans and told them that the Democrats were going to support his measure, and that if they did not want to lose capital they had better vote for it too. He didn't think there would be enough of them to carry it, but the vote would be on record and thus defeat the game of the other party. And they likewise agreed to vote for it. So when the bill came to vote it went right through! The members looked at each other in astonishment, for they hadn't intended to do it, quite. Then they laughed and said it was a good joke, but they had "got the governor in a fix." So the bill went, in the course of time, to John A. Campbell, who was then governor the first governor of the territory of Wyoming–and he promptly signed it!

However, it took more than astute political maneuvering to ensure passage of the bill. Conditions in Wyoming were right for the idea of universal suffrage for several reasons. First, the idea was hardly a new one. Much had been said and written about the idea of enfranchising women since the begining of the movement in the 1840s. Indeed, there was limited suffrage in many states where women were allowed to vote on school issues. Second, the lack of women in the frontier territory made the idea of female suffrage less threatening. With only one woman of voting age for every six men listed in the 1870 census it was unlikely there would be any great revolution at the polls. And finally, the leaders of the new territory were eager for the publicity being the first to grant suffrage would bring and the population it would hopefully attract.

Miss Anthony's stirring procalamations aside, universal suffrage was still an experiment. While women voted freely in elections, females rarely held office or served on juries except during the first few years after getting the franchise. There were also major challenges to the law. These included an 1871 attempt to repeal the act by the territorial legislature, an attempt seek another vote on the issue at the 1889 Wyoming Constitutional Convention and a heated debate in the United States House of Representatives and Senate during statehood proceedings in 1890. Through it all Wyoming proved to have a commitment to universal suffrage that earned its moniker, the "Equality State".

COMIN' TO THE DANCE?

By: Bill Duncan

"Get the kids ready while I hitch up the wagon and finish the chores, Ma. We're not going to miss the big dance tonight. You know they always have the Grand Promenade right at 9 p.m."

"Put those quilts and blankets in the back seat with the kids, Ma. I'll gas up the T and get it ready to go to town. We have to be back in time for chores tomorrow morning."

The first part of the 20th century Wyoming people were hitching up wagons and buggies or climbing in the Model T and driving over rutted tracks to go to a dance.

Folks could forget drought, bad prices, long winters and isolation by getting together at a community dance hall. People from Lonetree to Linwood shook up dust at the old yellow and white McKinnon schoolhouse. Farson's community hall hosted "hard times" dances where the farmers and ranchers could wear their hard-worn work clothing. It was the Swanson Place (a deserted homestead) in the upper Wind River country. Around Lander the popular spot was Iiams barn.

In Green River an "open air" dance hall graced the West End of Expedition Island. The wooden structure had "windows" that were lowered to let in the night air. Chicken wire kept the bigger varmints from being too curious. An adjacent concession stand served the dancers' refreshment needs.

My mother was lucky. Sometime in the mid-1920s her parents, John and Josephine Grice, decided to hold dances every couple of weeks. They remodeled a large room over their lumberyard storage in Sundance, Wyoming. When they had finished, they had a large room with benches along the sides, some smaller rooms on one end to serve as rest rooms, and a band stage at the other end. They saved enough room down one side for a long, rather narrow lunchroom. Mom and her sister, Darlene, were thrilled with the idea, even though it meant helping fix and serve lunch and cleaning up the next morning.

Each evening began with a Grand March, which served as

a mixer. After the rather formal processional, the crowd ended up making a big circle around the hall. A few allemandes later, every person had a new partner and got acquainted with the evening's crowd. Young and old all joined in. Aunt Darlene said, "We learned many of the older dances from Dad. We also danced with the older men, as well as the young ones."

Music varied from waltzes and foxtrots to round dances. Both old and new dances were popular. The Charleston, Lindy and Black Bottom made some of the older folks gasp because they were scandalous, not strenuous. The foxtrot, waltz, seven step, two step, Baltimore, and rye waltz were crowd pleasers. A few ladies choice dances added variety. Dancers were treated to one square dance each weekend.

Both jazz and blues tunes were popular. Aunt Darlene remembers singing "Where the Lazy Daisies Grow" with the local orchestra. Some of the other songs included, "Bye Bye Blues", "Five Foot Two", "I'll See You in My Dreams", "Girl of My Dreams", and "Bye Bye Blackbird".

The band took a midnight break for lunch. Fifty cents each bought sandwiches, coffee, and pastry. The lunchroom had places for 64 people. My grandmother hand-ground chicken, ham, or pork roast; mixed the meat with mayonnaise and chopped in sweet pickle. She and her daughters spread white bread with butter before piling on the thick filling. My Aunt Darlene remembers that the "hundreds" of sandwiches were carefully made, making sure the butter and filling went to the edge of the bread. These sandwiches were cut into triangles and served from big platters in the middle of the table.

How was the coffee made? My grandmother sewed a little cotton envelope, filled it with coffee, and tossed it into a huge, open pot. This "wash" boiler was often used to boil shirts and underwear. Of course, my aunt and mother assured me that the boilers they used for coffee hadn't been ever used for laundry. When the coffee was ready, the hosts filled big, blue enamel coffee pots and filled each person's china cup. Refills were free and plentiful. Coffee was the only drink offered. Because this was in the middle of prohibition, other drinks were probably available outside.

Desserts were special. Usually war cake, a spicy concoction with raisins, was cut into squares from huge, flat pans. The recipe had become popular during WWI because it was delicious, but contained no milk, eggs, butter or sugar. Other times my grandmother fried donuts, glazed them and served them instead of cake. On special occasions ice cream was mailed in 30 miles from Spearfish, South Dakota. It came wrapped in insulated canvas containers.

Babysitting was no problem. My grandparents set up a double bed as part of the ladies room. When kids got sleepy, they were stacked on the bed like cordwood. Younger kids, wrapped in blankets, were tucked away under the benches that lined the dance hall or in beds made of coats and blankets in the ladies room. My aunt says that, "Someone who liked music and did not care to dance would take care of the kids."

When the band played "Three O'clock in the Morning," it was a signal to dance with your date because it was the last dance. The last musical sequence was "Home Sweet Home", "Show Me the Way to Go Home", and finally "Good Night Sweetheart." If the weather were bad outside, sometimes the dances would last until 3 a.m.

The next morning my mother and my aunt would take the phonograph up the stairs and clean the dance hall and wash the dirty dishes. Their friends would help. They swept, waxed, and polished the floor. There were always dishes to do and leftovers to eat.

My grandfather really became worried when he discovered burns on the wooden benches of the gentlemen's smoking room. Just a few more moments and a smoldering cigarette or cigar butt could set the wood smoldering. That was too steep a risk for a lumberyard. Cost and risk put insurance out of the question. So John and Josephine went out of the dance business.

Better transportation and smoother roads changed people's dance habits after the depression. Couples hired a babysitter and moved from bar to club to bar throughout town seeking the best music. Home entertainment, like radio, television and video rentals, encouraged people to stay put. Tighter, more enforced laws meant that some stayed home to party rather than drive.

People still dance. Young folks know which bars have

Green River Historic Preservation Commission

live music to suit their taste. Some couples still belong to square dance clubs. But the days of community-wide street dances have been replaced with live concerts or parking lot dances sponsored by adjacent bars. Portable, personal music means that you can listen and do your own thing. Dances just aren't for families any more.

Thanks to my mother, Theresa Duncan, and my aunt, Darlene Hayward, for their information, memories, and the fun we all had sharing. Thanks to Alton Hermansen for the local information.

MAN ABOUT TOWN: DICK PAXTON

By: Marna Grubb

When I'm out and about town, it is always great to visit with Dick Paxton and his wife, Norma Jean. Dick served two terms as a Ward 1 council member for the City of Green River.

Bowlers in the community have enjoyed his, and his wife's, participation for approximately 38 years, as he reported it was about 1961 when they first began bowling.

When I think of Dick, I think "Mr. Baseball" since, a few years ago, the east field of Veterans' Park was named Paxton Field in recognition of more than 50 years of Dick's dedication to the baseball and softball programs in Green River.

He said he began playing baseball when he was about eight or nine years old and continued his involvement as a player, a coach, a sponsor, a co-sponsor and a spectator.

Dick played on Green River's first American Legion baseball team in 1947, organized by Bill and Lucy Bramwell.

He was recognized as the Most Valuable Player by the state American Legion. He later played in the Independent Baseball League on weekends.

He was a catcher in fast pitch softball and a pitcher in slow pitch softball. He was elected to the Wyoming State Softball Hall of Fame and also to the National Softball Hall of Fame. We often forgot that we had a "celebrity" in our midst.

Through the years, Dick helped others in the community by sponsoring Little League boys baseball, men and girls softball, ladies basketball, childrens basketball and bowling.

Richard A. (Dick) Paxton was born in Marysville, Kansas, on June 11, 1930. He was the son of Gerald and Leota Paxton. The family moved to Green River in 1940 and Dick began attending the 5th grade in the old Washington Grade School.

For the first three months, the family lived in a boxcar-type home. There was no pedestrian viaduct at the time, so everyone had to cross the tracks to get from one side of town to the other.

They remembered often getting cinders blown into their eyes from the many train engines in the railroad yards.

Later, they moved into a home in the area under Castle Rock. Dick has brothers and sisters: Geraldine Stephens of Green River, Peggy Carillo of Rock Springs, Carol Sue Stover (deceased), Fred Paxton (deceased) and Jackie Sanchez of Green River.

I first remember Dick Paxton and Norma Jean Krause when they were attending the old Lincoln High School in Green River. They began dating in their junior year, graduating in 1948. We enjoyed sharing our memories of two high school teachers, Edith Peters and Helen Haynes.

Dick was playing football, basketball and baseball, receiving All State and District awards while he was a junior and senior. Dick was a member of Green River's first district basketball championship team in 1948.

Norma Jean reminisced about the school dances, saying that none of the boys would dance with her except Dick. She said, "I began to think I was a wall flower!" In later years, Dick informed her that he had advised the boys that he would "kick butt" if they didn't leave her alone.

They also shared their memories of circus trains stopping in Green River to water their animals at the stockyards. Parents would take their children down to see the animals.

Dick Paxton and Norma Jean Krause, daughter of Frank and Jean Krause, were married on June 6, 1950.

Dick was employed as a pipe fitter on the Union Pacific Railroad from 1948 to 1958. During that time, in 1950, he served in the Korean War with the 141st Tank Battalion, Company C, and was discharged in 1952.

He was commissioned as a 1st Lieutenant Service Battery Commander in the 351st Field Artillery in 1957. From 1958 to 1968, Dick was an Express Handler for the Union Pacific Railroad.

Later Dick was a partner in B&P Plumbing with Cliff Brandner. Then he managed the Paxton Digging business for approximately 35 years.

They listed the births of their children as the main highlights in their lives. Their four children were Pamela Finch, Larry Dean Paxton, Jerry Paxton and Ricky Paxton (deceased). They have seven grandchildren and seven great grandchildren.

Dick listed the other highlights in his life as being the pre-

viously-mentioned naming of Paxton Field in honor of his service to the town, and being chosen as Grand Marshal of a Flaming Gorge Days parade in Green River.

Dick Paxton graduated from Green River's Lincoln High School in
1948. (Dick Paxton family photo)

THE CRIME(S) OF THE CENTURY

By: Terry A. Del Bene

Do things ever really change? Americans have a love-hate relationship with murder trials. The stakes are rarely higher in our court system than when handing down justice regarding the ultimate crime, murder.

The criminal trial of former football star O. J. Simpson held the world's attention for roughly an entire year. The press hailed it the "trial of the century." Coverage was unprecedented. A major news network took all the other news off the air to cover it live in its entirety. The trial even had a theme song! We can blame television for shaping the case and dragging it out far longer than it should have taken. With the handing out of the criminal verdict, the public seemed to lose interest in the case. The subsequent civil suit and its appeal have hardly received any coverage. The third decision on the so-called "trial of the century" was handed down. But was it really the "trial of the century?"

It seems that there usually are several "trials of the century" in every century. Clearly the 20th Century left us with no shortage of high profile murder trials, though the war crime trials at Nuremburg and similar trials in Asia should get consideration as the trials dealing with the most heinous crimes. How can a football star compare with the architects of the Holocaust? Having a celebrity involved makes for public interest and increases the chances that the trial will catch the public eye.

The trial of millionaire Harry Thaw, accused of murdering Stanford White in 1906, had all the elements of sex and violence; but occurred in the days before television. Stanford White, one of the most famous architects in the nation, was murdered in full view of hundreds of people in one of the buildings he designed, Madison Square Garden. White was murdered by one of the richest men in the country in a fit of jealous rage over his past relationship with Evelyn Nesbitt, who we all recognize as the original Gibson Girl.

Evelyn and Harry were married, but it was a stormy marriage, full of jealously and abuse. Thaw was extremely jealous and could not abide that White had been intimate with Evelyn at the tender age of sixteen. It was a chance meeting the night that Thaw pulled a pistol and shot White. Thaw managed to beat the rap by pleading temporary insanity in the first trial and complete insanity in the second. This was one of the first times that plea of insanity was used successfully to beat a murder charge. The case had many similarities to the 1850's plea of temporary insanity won by Daniel Sickles.

In the Thaw case, the evidence was not circumstantial. There was no shortage of witnesses to Thaw shooting White. There was a silent movie of the whole affair completed well before the trial was done. Thaw's family owned newspapers and were quick to get out his side of the story. A book about Thaw's tribulations appeared in almost no time at all. Thaw was found innocent by reason of insanity and served seven years in a prison for the criminally insane. His family assured that his stay was one of luxury. Harry and Evelyn divorced and she went on to a career in vaudeville and remained one of the most famous women in America.

The 19th Century was not without its "trials of the century" candidates. Clearly the Lincoln assassination, the Mankato Massacre Trials, and the John D. Lee trials rate up there as major contenders. Other more local inquests, such as that over the murder of Ellen Watson (a.k.a. Cattle Kate, according to her enemies) took on wide-spread interest. The Lincoln assassination trial resulted in the multiple hanging of several of the conspirators, including a woman. The Mankato, Minnesota trials resulted in the mass hangings of 38 Santee Sioux charged with murder and rape during the Dakota uprising of 1862. The John D. Lee trials eventually resulted in the execution by firing squad of Lee for his role in the Mountain Meadow Massacre of 1857. The inquest for Ellen Watson came to naught, with a crucial witness to the murders disappearing on his way to testify at the trial in Rock Springs.

The century closed with perhaps one of the most famous murder cases of all time, the Fall River murders. In this case, Andrew and Abbey Borden were brutally slain with an ax. A daughter of the deceased was in the general vicinity but did not hear the grisly murders in progress. The accused murderess, Lizzie Borden, would inspire songs, poetry, plays, movies, and a host of books. Her trials were the talk of the day and continue to inspire significant interest.

The press had a field day, even inventing a story about Lizzie being pregnant and naming the likely father. When the poor fellow tried to escape the crush of the press following out the fabricated story by fleeing to Canada, he was run over and killed by a train. The inquest trial had all the makings of great theater. There was a long period where the cause of death for the two bloodied and hacked up bodies was thought to be poison. (Police science seems to have improved enough to accept the obvious these days.) Lizzie's confused recollections and the fact that she had no representation at the inquest led to the actual murder trial in 1893.

Lizzie had competent representation for her real trial and he managed to have the damaging testimony from 1892 kept out of court. Still it is difficult to argue how she could have been in the house while two brutal and bloody murders were in progress without having any inkling that something was wrong. Lizzie fainted away listening to the gory details of her father's and stepmother's deaths. The prosecutor "accidentally" allowed valuable evidence (being the hacked-up skulls of the victims) to tumble from a valise onto the floor. The all-male jury (women did not serve on juries at that time) deliberated on the events and returned a verdict of not guilty. The verdict in light of the overwhelming circumstantial case creates controversy to this day. Some consider this an early example of jury nullification.

Earlier in the century there were other candidates for a "trial of the century" which the Fall River murders eclipsed. Our memories of the Bond Street murders of 1857 are not very strong. This was a circumstantial case involving complex and confusing love relationships between the participants.

On January 31, 1857 Dr. Harvey Burdell was found strangled with fifteen stab wounds. Though the house was full of boarders the night of the murder, no one heard what must have been a very vicious struggle.

A new periodical, *Harper's Weekly*, caught upon the trial and generated interest. The beautiful Mrs. Emma Augusta Cunningham and two other men were indicted for the murder. One of these men, John J. Eckel, was thought to be her lover as was Dr.

Burdell. It was quite the scandal. Mrs. Cunningham claimed to have been Burdell's wife but, while alive, Burdell denied the marriage. The clergyman who performed the marriage was not sure who he married to Mrs. Cunningham; Dr. Burdell or Mr. Eckel. It was thought that Cunningham, Eckel, and an accomplice named George Snodgrass plotted the murder to take over the reclusive Burdell's substantial property. A phony marriage was thought to be part of the plot, followed by disposing of Dr. Burdell. Once again, the press had a field day. Mrs. Cunningham was tried and convicted in many newspapers. She was even accused of having murdered her first husband with poison.

Hundreds would stand outside the court waiting to hear the latest word from the trial and hoping to catch a glimpse of the beautiful widow. Mrs. Cunningham became a celebrity. After deliberating for one-half hour, the jury acquitted her of the charges. Eckel and Snodgrass never came to trial and the murder remains unsolved to this day.

How could we have forgotten the Flickenger Farm murders of 1872? A disturbed Civil War veteran named Ervin Porter, on a cold December morning, had breakfast with his family. He seemed in a most melancholy mood and after breakfast he took a hatchet and within hearing of the rest of the family, murdered his two daughters: Minda, three, and Adeliade, one. He escaped but was captured in a short while and denied having committed the crime. His defense was based upon the family history of mental disorders, depression, temper, and instability. It was pointed out that he was the child of the marriage of cousins. Over 85 witnesses testified, but his insanity plea came for naught. There was no shortage of witnesses attesting to Ervin's "insanity". His cold demeanor during the trial and the nature of the crime worked against him. He was sentenced to life in prison. He lived roughly two years in prison before giving up his own ghost. During the trial, the press raised what might have stayed a local story to national significance.

So, the next time you hear the press talking about the "trial of the century," remember every century has several such trials. All murder cases are the "trial of the century" for those affected by the crime. Think of what they (and we) all have lost.

A CITIZEN'S DUTY

By: Ruth Lauritzen

Jury from *State of Wyoming vs. Long*. This was the first jury to empanel women since Wyoming statehood in 1890. Louise Spinner Graf, first woman selected as jury foreman, stands on the far right of the front row. (Photo courtesy Sweetwater County Historical Museum)

A significant case tried in the Sweetwater County Court-house began as a rather routine murder. Otto Long was charged with the shooting death of Joe Pearce during an argument on the road between Rock Springs and Green River in 1949. However, the case came to trial shortly after a law enacted by the Wyoming State Legislature allowed women to serve on juries. Women had served on juries in Wyoming during territorial times, but no female had been empanelled to serve since statehood in 1890. The law was appealed to the Wyoming Supreme Court, but was upheld as constitutional.

Thus, on May 8, 1950 court convened in the Sweetwater

County Courthouse in Green River and a jury was was empanelled to decide Criminal Case Number 2362, the *State of Wyoming vs. Long.* Six women were selected for jury service including Louise Spinner Graf of Green River who was named as foreman. Other jurors included Donna Schultz, Kathryn Auld, Mrs. Dave Rauzi, Mrs. D. G. Marshall, Mrs. John Wilde, George Palko, Bill Wonnacott, Alva Qualls, Floyd Henry, Merton L. Schultz and Hugh Sweeney. Elmer F. Parton served as alternate.

Graf described the receipt of her summons for this historic event in a paper on file at the Sweetwater County Historical Museum in Green River.

> Mike Maher, who was the sheriff at the time, personally served my summons. We were good friends and he told me afterwards he wanted to see my reaction. This was it "Oh, I can't go! Monday is wash day!" I can still hear him laugh and dance around when I said that.

The biggest problem encountered by the jury was not a legal one, but rather one of a more personal nature. When a jury was sequestered, as it was in this case, the requirement that the members stay overnight presented some logistical problems. The old courthouse lacked segregated facilities for a jury of both sexes. Mrs. Graf recalled the solution to the problem:

> They had accommodations for the men–but now the women presented a problem. All six of us were put into one large room. It had a wash basin and toilet in one corner. Mr. Wm. Hutton Jr., who was the custodian at the time, got us a mirror and made everything pleasant as possibel (sic) under the circumstances. At mealtime we were marched to a cafe and then marched back.

In her memoirs, another female juror commented on the newness of the situation. Gisela Bertagnolli Wilde mentioned the historic event in her handwritten memoirs, a copy of which is held at the Sweetwater County Historical Museum.

> In May of 1950, women were allowed to serve on the jury so I was one of the 6 women to serve. Our case was a murder trial. It was very educational and very informative. It was all very new to me. Now we see many trials on T.V. and I can understand them a lot better than I did 31 years ago.

After deliberating for one hour and thirty-five minutes the jury return a verdict of guilty. The attorney for the defense, Walter Muir, was very upset with the verdict and was said to blame the loss of this case on... "those damn women on the jury!"

THE ROCKY MOUNTAIN POLKA FESTIVAL

By: Bill Thompson/
Richard Kaumo, and Jim Frost, guest authors

Polka fans across the United States and parts of Canada fondly recall the great music and fellowship provided by the Rocky Mountain Polka Fest. There were 12-14 big name polka bands performing continuous music in two buildings from start to finish every day of the event. Sixty volunteers a day came from Rock Springs and Green River to take tickets, to run the various

Myron Floran, Richard Kaumo, and Bill Thompson (left to right) play at an early Rocky Mountain Polka Festival. (Photo courtesy Bill Thompson)

booths and to help out in general. "How do you get all these people to donate their time?" one Minnesota band leader marveled. The answer was that imbedded in this area was the pride, respect and love for the historic polka tradition. Without those volunteers the "Fest" could never have

made it. Even though some of the nationwide bands had lowered their prices to help out the Fest, the cost for the bands alone ran around 32 thousand dollars. The total cost

Dancers fill the floor at a Rocky Mountain Polka Festival in the 1980s (Photo courtesy Bill Thompson)

Governor Mike Sullivan dances with his wife Jane at the Rocky Mountain Polka Festival in the 1980s. (Photo courtesy Bill Thompson)

was around 40-45 thousand in the 1980s. The "Fest" made a small amount of profit which was used for the next year's nation-wide advertising.

For the official background history of this event I have a guest author. He is this year's nominee for the World USA Polka Hall of fame in Chisholm, Minnesota. From the bandstand for many years I have introduced my friend to polka lovers around the country in this way: "Ladies and Gentlemen, the leader of our band and the father of the RockyMountain Festival, Richard Kaumo!"

The Rocky Mountain Polka Fest "Polka's High" - 1984-1992

By: Richard Kaumo

What became known as the Rocky Mountain Polka Fest began as an idea in 1979 when my cousin Karl and I went to Duluth, Minnesota, to do some TV shows with State Senator Florian Chmielenski. He was the creator and producer of the Chmielemski Funtime TV Show.

We became life-long friends. He told me about the International Polka Festival being held at the Pine City Fairgrounds which he had also created. I thought, "This guy has really got something going!" and I asked a lot of questions. Then Florian invited me not only to come play at his Third Annual Festival in 1980 but to come and learn the "ins and outs" of such an event.

Along with wife Kathy and the accordion, I took an address book. I became acquainted with some great musicians and band leaders and made sure that I had their phone numbers and addresses. These people became great friends of ours and remain in touch.

On our return to Rock Springs, my goal focused on organizing an Oktoberfest. With the variety of nationalities in the area, polkas and Grape Festivals held at the Slovenski Dom were always popular. In 1980, I organized a committee that started the Rock Springs Oktoberfest.

It was a one-night affair at the Civic Center and was an instant success. Since the seating capacity was only 550, the event was sold out days in advance. With modifications throughout the years, it remains successful to this day.

"Always listen to the people; they will let you know what they want" was an important piece of advice from several great band leaders. So when people asked me during the second Oktoberfest and told me to, "do these dances more than once a year ... or make it longer," I listened.

Using contacts from the address book, I sought advice on how best to put together a three-day event. Some of the questions were: Is Rock Springs ready for such an event?... Could it succeed? ... Don't you need more time to make sure that it is what people want?

Richard Kaumo, Myron Floran and Bill Thompson (left to right) at a polka festival. Floran was well known for his performance on the Lawrence Welk Show. (Photo courtesy Bill Thompson)

In 1982, the third successful Oktoberfest convinced me that the time was right for a three-day polka celebration. I formed a Polka Fest Committee consisting of Bill and Rita Thompson, Kathy and myself. The planning stages were immediately implemented with our major goal being to stage this event in the summer of 1984.

Some of the concerns were what to call the event? We registered the name with the Wyoming Secretary of State for protection. If we so desired, the event could be moved to other geographical areas. We incorporated, too.

What bands to hire? (The ones that had the biggest following) How much to charge? How many people would we need in order to break even? I did not want to file for bankruptcy, and how do we promote and advertise?

We spent much time formulating a realistic budget. We had about two years to put it all together. The last week in August was selected and the Sweetwater County Fairground was reserved. I contacted the bands and put them under contract.

In that first year I worked hard studying event promotion. I knew that the local population alone could not carry this event financially.

Radio stations and newspapers in the intermountain area that promoted polka music nationwide were contacted. I also got in touch with newspapers and radio stations in cities and towns in the intermountain region where I felt polka music was popular. I knew it would take a year of intense promotion to make this event successful.

And then the big day arrived! It was unbelievable the success this event had. It went beyond my wildest dreams. Over the years, it became the favorite polkafest for thousands of people and many nationwide bands and performers.

Bill Thompson speaking here - In closing, here is a reprint from The Green River Star Tues. Aug. 25, 1987. It was written by then news editor, Jim Frost. Viewed from today's perspective (2004) in regard to interest in economic development in this area, the authors find his editorial message somewhat ironic. The last two paragraphs in this article were written by the authors.

Well-known accordionist Frankie Yankovick is interviewed by KSL-TV during a polka festival. (Photo courtesy Bill Thompson)

Polka Music Offers Sound Economics

By: Jim Frost

Polka may not be the savior of our economic plight here in Sweetwater County, but if you listen closely, you can hear money falling out of the dancers' pockets into local businesses.

Three years ago, Richard Kaumo sat out on his front porch telling me his plans for a polka festival that would give the county a much-needed shot in the arm. The festival would not only bring in money for our ailing economy, but it would also give Sweetwater County and Wyoming a good reputation around the country, especially among polka-loving folks.

The polka tunes coming out of Kaumo's tape player sounded okay, but Kaumo's words were kind of hard to swallow. A polka festival did not seem to be my idea of what this county needed to turn things around. I always believed polka was invented to just make North Dakota interesting, and that other than Lawrence Welk, not a lot of guys advocated the music. That's the problem, or possibly a blessing, with growing up in a non-ethnic, non-Midwestern neighborhood - you're not exposed to much polka.

Kaumo, the leader of a local band, the Polka Knights, apparently not only knows his music, but knows how deep the popularity of polka runs in this country, not just among ethnic groups. His idea paid off in big dividends. Since the first Rocky Mountain Polka Festival in 1984, the annual event has attracted as many as 8,000 people over a weekend, and many of them come from Ohio, Wisconsin and beyond. They come for the music, beer and good times, but also bring a lot of cash with them, which makes sweeter music to local retailers and innkeepers than an accordian.

The reason the festival paid off is because it was dreamed up by someone who believed it would work. Co-organizers Kaumo and banjo player Bill Thompson of Green River tapped into an attraction they knew existed and made it into something more successful than any economic committee or expensive study has thus far turned up.

The best part about the polka festival is that it was not created as a self-serving event on Kaumo's or Thompson's part. They wanted people to have fun, and for the county to reap the benefits it has had under its nose for a long time. Besides, if the festival failed, it would have been their problem, not ours. They took the risk, not the taxpayers.

The moral of the polka festival, or maybe crescendo is a better word, is that this county needs more people like Kaumo and Thompson to take the initiative rather than waiting around for some major company or business to come down the road to bring economic salvation.

Unfortunately short-sighted economic actions such as continuous unrealistic rising costs and charges from locals who should have known better overcame the cooperation from the Big

Bands and local volunteer efforts. Those actions were instrumental for the demise of the Rocky Mountain Polka Festival in 1992. They killed polka's Golden Goose. The event that had helped to overcome past negative publicity about this area and which had put Rock Springs, Sweetwater County and Wyoming on the positive nationwide and Canadian polka map for years, was gone.

Subsequent attempts (under another polka title) by the Sweetwater County Fair Board and others to continue the high standards set by the Rocky Mountain Polka Fest cost the taxpayers thousands of dollars. Crowds dwindled. Some national polka bands avoided the event. After several years the county-sponsored polka attempt was canceled. Nationwide participants and band leaders said that it was due to lack of Polka Fest know-how, leadership, and promotion.

GREEN RIVER'S STREET NAMES

By: Bill Duncan

Green River's street names mix western culture, geograph-ically inspired names, slightly warped botanical names, a direc-tional grid system and commemorative names. Nobody won-ders about Boulder Drive, Riverbend Drive or Mansface Street. But some street names are just downright mundane.

The original 1877 plat numbered streets running east and west (North 1st through 4th and South 1st through 4th). Those streets running north and south had names like Elizabeth Street, Sage Street, River Street, Highway Street and Great Northern Street according to Green River historian Jim June.

June says the 1928 town council passed an ordinance re-quiring house and business numbering and hired Utah consul-tants to number the houses, business places and rename Green River streets. Sage Street became Center Street and North Rail-road Avenue became Railroad Avenue

A 1930 map shows "Salt Lake Style" street names with compass directions and numbers. That leaves us with streets like North 3rd West (or is it West 3rd North?).

The Southeast part of town has names of states, with no alphabetical or geographical order. Alaska runs by Maine and intersects with Tennessee.

The tree streets branch off of Riverview. The original idea was to name streets after locally growing trees which is OK if you accept Driftwood (it was originally Dogwood), Knotty Pine and Pecan.

Pioneer Park names streets after pioneer heroes Kit Car-son, Daniel Boone and Davy Crockett. Bridger Drive separates two stages of town development.

But there are pockets of streets named after local people. Who are they? Why did these particular people have a street named after them?

A left turn at the first stoplight going south after crossing the river is the part of town settled just after WWII. The Veterans Addition has streets named after local servicemen killed in that war. Ruth Lauritzen notes in "Peace At Last: The End of World War II" in *Echoes from the Bluffs Volume 1* that Sgt. Floyd C. Hoover, Lt. Donovan Astle, T/Sgt. Ernest Pelser, Cpl. Howard Schultz, Lt. H. Bert Jensen, Pvt. Darrell Barnhart, Pvt. John Logan, and Pfc. Robert James Bramwell are immortalized. Streets east of Wilson School, now Expedition Academy, honor past presidents. Evers Street is named after former mayor Bill Evers. The origination of some street names in the Paxton Webb addition is lost in time. Guesses are that Evans Street may be for Day Evans, city maintenance foreman during this time. He was one of those guys who knew where and how all city utilities underground were connected. Wilkes may have been for Frank Wilkes, a visionary Green River mayor. Wilkes was instrumental in procuring land south of the river from the Federal Government insuring room for the town to grow. Powell might have been for General John Wesley Powell, leader of scientific expeditions after the civil war.

Green River's population quadrupled from the mid-1960s to the mid-1980s. Modular housing was eventually replaced with more permanent structures. Eldon Collier developed several areas west of Uinta Drive called Hutton Heights. Collier Circle branches southwest from the west end of Riverview and marks his legacy.

In those days the developer submitted street plats and names to be approved by the city council. Although most Hutton Heights streets were named for locally growing trees, the southwestern part had an Easy Street and Easy Circle. Branching off of Knotty Pine Street were a handful of streets named after local people. Collier submitted the names and the council approved them, according to Dave Brandner who was on the council then.

Hutton Street, Hutton Circle and Hutton Heights were named for Bill Hutton. For a short time at the beginning of the 20th century, he grew potatoes and alfalfa on the bluffs south of the river. Originally, this area was known as Hutton's Bluffs. Hutton was a custodian at the county courthouse for over half a century. Hutton established an athletic reputation early in the 20th century by racing against the clock to carry a flag from the local brewery to the top of Castle Rock as part of the July 4th festivities. Hutton is known for his wry wit and artifact collection.

Stephens Street was named for George Stephens who worked in the Union Pacific's car shop. Probably due to his early career as an undersherriff, he amassed an extensive collection of guns, badges and historical memorabilia. Old timers remember him as a long-time county commissioner and "a real Green River booster."

Yates Street was named for Bill Yates, another avid Green River supporter. Yates was a Boy Scout leader and held an elected county office for some time. He was a friend of both Collier and Hutton.

Brandner Circle was named for David Brandner, who served on the city council during the boom times of the late 70s and 80s. According to Brandner, the smaller city staff size meant that the council members had to work more closely with developers and townspeople. Collier appreciated Brandner's knowledge of plumbing, electrical, and paving/curbing needs in a housing development.

Dick Waggener was mayor during Green River's boom period on the late 70s and early 80s. An engineer who worked at FMC, Waggener was dedicated to structured growth according to some who worked with him during this time. If no city laws or charters covered the situation, Waggener favored council edicts. The local zoning plan is one of the most influential products of his administration.

Adrian Reynolds was the editor and publisher of the Green River Star for many years. A keen student of politics, Reynolds served in the state senate for several terms. His column "Chewin' the Fat" entertained his readers each week. He was best known for his stance on water conservation and keeping western Wyoming's water on the western side of the Continental Divide. Brandner says that Reynolds taught him many things about politics. Reynolds thought that Brandner might make a good state legislator, but Brandner says that he didn't want to go that far.

Sometimes changing street names really helps. Flaming Gorge Way sounds much more descriptive than East (or West) First North. Heather Moody Lane honors Green River's Olympian. But other streets, like the "view" streets, lack imagination.

Given the traditions of naming streets for men killed in war and streets for local dignitaries, wouldn't it be appropriate if five streets were named for Green River men killed in Vietnam? Lt. Dennis King, Lt. Colonel Bruce Jensen, Sgt. Bennett Evans, Pfc. Douglas Rogers and Pvt. Robert Maurer deserve such recognition.

PUTTING THE GREEN IN GREEN RIVER

By: Marna Grubb

Robert Morris was the inspiration for the planting of Green River's first trees. (Wyoming Division of Cultural Resources photo)

The Spring of 2001 produced a spectacular burst of blooms around Green River with the crab apples and lilacs leading the way. Green River's Flaming Gorge Way had blossomed with the installation and planting of 20 large flower pots. This was the result of a Boy Scout project for an Eagle Scout award envisioned by Aaron Hayes. As the result of Aaron's contact, the Garden Club purchased 10 cement pots and the other 10 were purchased through the Mayor's special projects account. The Garden Club, assisted by Trudel Lopez, planted the pots, bringing great beauty to the area. After contact by Aaron, some businesses, along with the City, had agreed to water the planters. This was a great accomplishment of people working together.

The City's Centennial Park, also on Flaming Gorge Way, has become quite the show place for Green River with the dazzling array of colors provided by the well-kept flower beds. The "green thumb" provided by Trudel Lopez was very instrumental in this accomplishment.

The Green River Garden Club deserves recognition for providing several places of beauty throughout the community; most notable was the area in front of the Forest Service office. I noticed a tourist as he photographed the colorful array of hollyhocks in bloom. They were spectacular!

Throughout the years, Green River has often been referred to as the "Garden Spot of Wyoming." Our bluffs are natural beauties which have been carved through millions of years of geologic change. But, it was the waters of the Green River that created the natural greenery along its banks in the middle of an otherwise desert area. High country springs, streams and lakes in the Bridger Wilderness create the headwaters of the Green River.

It took the inspiration of many devoted people, working together, to bring Green River to its reputation of a beautiful community. Many comments have been heard from attendees at conventions, tournaments and class reunions of "What a beautiful community Green River has become." That they had "driven by on the highway many times, but never knew how beautiful it was down here!" This did not happen by itself, but came through the inspiration, dreams and hard work of many who have donated their time and talents.

Researching the June 12, 1936 issue of *The Green River Star*, we find that Robert C. Morris "was the inspiration of the planting of the first trees in Green River, which today (in 1936) is designated by many tourists as the garden spot of Wyoming."

We learn more of Robert Morris as it further reports that he was "a man who had in his heart the best interests of Green River, and through his efforts, with the assistance of such men as T. S. Taliaferro, Jr. and Hugo F. Gaensslen, Green River secured the beautiful Carnegie Library, which adorns the northeast corner of the court house square." Currently, in 2003, the building houses the Sweetwater County Court.

The Green River Star of January 15, 1909 stated that "Some years ago Mr. Morris took the active management of the Morris Mercantile company and the Morris State Bank at Green River, business enterprises in which he had been associated for many years with his brother, the late Edward J. Morris." Edward J. Morris was Green River's first mayor after Green River was incorporated under the laws of the State of Wyoming in May of 1891 following Wyoming becoming a state in 1890. Edward Morris died in 1902 and Robert Morris died in 1921.

Robert and Edward Morris were the twin sons of Esther Morris, a pioneer woman of the state, credited as being the author of women's suffrage in Wyoming. She also had the honor of being the first woman justice of the peace while living in South Pass.

The Green River Star of June 12, 1936, reported that "In memory of a man who was the inspiration of the planting of the first trees in Green River. William Hutton, for many years custodian for the county court house in Green River, had placed at the southeast corner of the court house square, directly facing the Lincoln Highway" (now Flaming Gorge Way) "through the town, a beautiful specimen of a petrified tree stump, which he had secured from the petrified forest near this city.

"The stump is set in solid concrete, in which is embedded a brass plate bearing the inscription, 'In Memory of Robert C. Morris'." This petrified tree stump and brass plate survived the demolition of the old court house building and the construction of a new one, and today can be found in the southwest corner of the court house square.

While growing up in Green River, I remember the huge cottonwood trees lining the highway street and other areas in town. Many of these have since died and have been cut down – or maybe been blown down as in recent storms. These trees would be 80 to 100 years old. As Green River was expanding, the fast-growing elm trees were planted along with a few apple trees.

In more recent years, Bonnie Pendleton, Green River's first woman mayor (1981-1986), was a strong advocate of beautification projects and was instrumental in initiating the Flaming Gorge Way and Uinta Drive landscaping projects. These were expertly completed by the City's Parks Supervisor and later Director of Parks and Recreation, Roger Moellendorf, with many new varieties of trees being introduced to Green River; such as Littleleaf Lindens, Green Ash, Autumn Purple Ash, Bur Oak, Honey Locusts, varieties of Flowering Crab Apples, Scotch Pine, Austrian Pine, Pinon Pine, Hawthorns, Black Hills Spruce, White Fir, Ohio Buckeye, Northern Red Oak, Canada Red Cherry, Norway Maple, Western River Birch, Willow, and Hackberry. Also shrubs have been planted such as Potentillas, Barberry, Mugo Pine, Russian Sage, Cotoneaster, Dogwoods, Currants, Viburnum, Junipers, Willows, Spirea and Flowering Almond.

Green River Historic Preservation Commission

Mr. Moellendorf also was instrumental in establishing an annual National Arbor Day Foundation celebration in Green River in 1983, with Green River being designated as a Tree City USA every year since that time.

Green River was the second city in Wyoming to be so designated; Cheyenne was the first.

In recent years through the City's Tree Program, people in the community have been able to have trees planted in honor of or in memory of someone. The first tree planted was in appreciation of Richard W. Waggener, Green River's boom-town mayor (1971-1982), and was planted in front of the current City Hall building constructed during his administration.

In 1991, the Greenbelt Task Force was formed and incorporated with John Freeman as chairman, followed by Richard Watson, and again John Freeman.

Through the efforts of this group composed of volunteer citizens of the community, the Task Force obtained funding for development of pathways and for the Kill Deer Wetland Area along the river through grants and land donations.

They solicited donations from the five industries west of Green River to build the Trona Bridge. One of Green River's greatest assets is our river; and, through this group, it has become more accessible for everyone to enjoy. Hats off!

Bonnie Pendleton, Green River Mayor from 1981-1986 was instrumental in initiating landscaping projects along Green River's main streets and thoroughfares. (City of Green River photo.)

MOB VIOLENCE AMERICAN STYLE

By: Terry A. Del Bene

Once again the headlines are carrying the all-too-familiar story of violence in our streets. Recently we've seen numerous examples of people taking to the streets for a variety of reasons from perceptions of abuses of power by the police, a Cuban child rescued and turned into a geopolitical pawn, a home team losing a championship, a home team winning a championship, the operation of clinics which perform abortions, a concern over the globalization of our economy. Today we even have social events which are little more than entertaining oneself with mob violence. What could any of these have in common with one another? They're all examples of a continuing pattern of American mob violence as an expression of the degree of passion which people have for some subject.

In listening to the pundits talking about the current spate of mob violence which is sweeping the nation one must ask... is this really a growing problem? Did those Vietnam-War-protesting-baby-boomers create a generation of mobocrats which is spawning a generation of even more violent protestors? Perhaps we should look at America's roots in our search for the answer.

The age of enlightenment was replete with notable acts of mob violence. One can still find, even in our sanitized, politically correct textbooks, examples of 18th century mob rule. In fact, the mobocrats in some of these events are now made out to be the noblest of American heroes. That is especially true in events such as the Boston Tea Party and the Boston Massacre. The former involved a political and drinking society vandalizing personal property. The latter involves an assault by a mob on British soldiers where the British overreacted to being assaulted with chunks of flying ice and shot into the crowd.

Perhaps it was the canonization of the mobocrats of the 18th Century which made the 19th century the century of mob violence in this country. That may surprise those of us who remember the 1960s, or those who remember the mine wars in West Virginia, and the numerous instances of labor unrest. All of these pale in scale to the frequency and lethality of mob violence in the 19th century.

In 1835 alone there were 147 riots in the United States. Most of these (109) occurred between July and October. This was in a time of relative economic prosperity (none of these were bread riots). Though slavery and overall race relations loomed large, these factors were not the cause for all the riots. The "bank-war" of 1834-1835 clearly was an important story, but only accounted for a single riot. Many of the riots were anti slavery, many were pro-slavery, many were anti-gambling! In this year alone, roughly 91 Americans would be killed (83 in Southern riots). The latter figure appears more a reflection that Northern riots in general were handled by the authorities with a sterner, swifter hand. That year would see lynchings, beatings, shootings, stabbings, a beheading, tar-and-feathering, castration, and rape all as part of the American experience. How this fits in a nation which guarantee free speech and freedom is not clear... but then free speech and freedom were ideals not always met in a country where people were allowed to own other people and debate about the very issue was forbidden even in Congress.

One of the stranger incidents of American mob violence occurred in New York City on May 10, 1849. Roughly 10,000-15,000 rioters would take to the streets that night forcing the authorities to call out the cavalry and infantry of the New York militia to quell the violence. The issue? The mobs had taken to the streets over who was the best Shakespearian actor, William Charles Macready or Edwin Forrest. The two actors had a long history of interfering with each other's performances and their fans took up the fight for them. Macready was an Englishman and was preferred by the higher classes of society. Forrest appealed more to the common man and was what one might call a darling of the tabloids. When Macready was playing MacBeth at the Astor Opera house a mob surrounded the building. The militia arrived some time later and charged the crowd, being repulsed by a hail of bricks. Then the shooting started, with the military and police killing somewhere between 17 and 20 rioters. Another 60 were subdued and arrested. Poor Macready was forced to disguise himself and managed to sneak out of the theatre, eventually to leave the country for good.

There were a host of other reasons for mob violence during the century. Local election results were often good for a turnout of mobocrats. In 1857 there was violence in the streets of New York which involved both the police and allied gangs as to which police department (that of the City or that of the State) would control the streets. In that same year the U.S. military was called out to the streets of Washington D.C. to keep gangs from preventing naturalized immigrants from voting in local elections. Mobs took the the street immediately following the election of President Lincoln and shortly thereafter America's most costly war was started. New York City was in flames in 1863 as draft riots forced the government to bring troops fresh from the Gettysburg battlefield to fight in the streets.

We were very fortunate the events of past Presidential election did not occur in the 19th century. The Democratic protests in Florida and the verbal assaults by G.O.P. thugs upon the election officials seem tame to what our ancestors likely would have done. Taking a look deep into our past I, for one, am relieved that the American penchant for mobbing seems to be on the wane. Modern mobocrats rarely show the stuff our ancestors were made of. The mobocrats no longer storm the Bastille and topple heads of state. They seem to prefer storming the local appliance store so they can watch themselves on T.V. Charles Macready was born just a century too soon.

ELECTRONIC NEWSLETTER BRINGS BACK MEMORIES: GREEN RIVER'S SWIMMING POOL REMEMBERED

By: Ruth Lauritzen

Green River's outdoor pool provided a haven from summer heat for both young and old from its completion in 1931 until 1960s when it was closed. (Photo courtesy Sweetwater County Historical Museum)

A big part of the fun of class reunions is the chance to get together and talk about old times. Some alumni of Lincoln High School in Green River have taken this one step further and carry on a weekly, ever-expanding electronic get-together via the Internet. *Lincoln High Mirth and Missives* (LHM&M) was begun by Mark Hoffmann who graduated in 1958. In September of 2000 Hoffmann contacted several classmates including Gary Cain, Ronda (Trumble) Burnham and Bobbi (Lee) Kofoed to gauge interest in an on-line newsletter for graduates of Lincoln High School. The group decided that the focus of the project would be 1958 plus or minus five years, although they are flexible. Thus LHM&M was born and continues to grow.

Hoffmann acts as the central control and all messages are sent to him. He then sends them out to the people on the e-mail list. Hoffman will add anyone who is interested to the list. Participants are included at their own convenience and a person's name can be removed simply by contacting Hoffman. Regular participation is the most important thing, according to Hoffmann. "Anyone can start the thread of a conversation. Everyone else is cordially invited to chime in with whatever you want to say about a current subject or a new subject. We always like to have new joiners tell us what they have been doing for the many years we have been out of school."

The Sweetwater County Historical Museum also receives the newsletter and keeps back copies.

What follows is a sample of the material in LHM&M as supplied by Al "Egghead" Stevens who graduated in 1955. His summertime memories center around the old swimming pool, which was located in Evers Park near the picnic shelter.

It was summer and the White boys (Joe and Gary) wanted to go to the swimming pool to go swimming. I had never heard of such a thing but my mother bought me a pair of trunks and the three of us set out to go to the swimming pool.

Just the trip to the pool was an adventure. We, of course, had to cross over the railroad tracks by using the viaduct. The time was during WWII and the Union Pacific Railroad used coal fired, steam driven locomotives. These were huge engines that belched large plumes of smoke that was full of cinders and gases that contained all of the carcinogens known to man. It was great sport to run and position oneself over the engine as it crossed under the viaduct.

After arriving at the pool even more wonderful experiences were in store. For, as I recall, about 20 cents admission you could spend the entire day frolicking at the pool (a season ticket was sold for $2.50 as I recall). The pool had a concession stand where, if you had money, (none of us did), you could buy hamburgers, hot dogs, ice cream, candy and what we called them, bottles of pop.

I spent the day with my buddies having just a marvelous time. After a time the skin on my back seemed to start feeling tight, but I thought little of it. I was having too much fun.

I showed up at my grandmothers' house glowing bright red and in great pain. I had never heard of sunburn let alone think to provide for any protection.

My mother went to the Moedl Drug Store for some medicine for my sunburn. Karl Moedl sold her a concoction that had the smell and consistency of coal tar. This foul smelling substance was applied liberally all over my body and I was put to bed. During the night the coal tar congealed. In the morning, I awoke to find the bed sheets had fused to my body by this epoxy-like substance. Removing the sheet from my body was like being skinned alive.

After all the sun blisters broke and the dead skin peeled away I was anxious to return to the swimming pool. This time, educated by experience, I limited my time in the sun and used liberal amounts of sunscreen. Except for the time recovering from sunburn, I became a fixture at the pool. I don't remember missing a day of going to the pool when it was open until I graduated from high school.

Initially, the pool was not heated or filtered and going in the water was an experience not for the faint of heart. It was frigid! There was a ritual of just putting part of your body such as your legs into the water first and wait for that part to become numb. Then, progressively inch further into the pool until your entire body was submerged. This process could take a long time. Only the brave or foolish would simply dive or jump into the pool without performing the numbing ritual.

As the water sat in the pool, because of the warming effect of the sun and copious amounts of urine, it gradually warmed. Each week, however, the pool was closed for a day and it was drained, scrubbed and refilled with fresh water. As a result, after cleaning, the water was crystal clear but again frigid. As the week progressed the water became warmer, but murkier. Near the end of the week, due to cinders from the railroad and wind-borne dirt, the pool resembled a mud pond that was just a little too thin to plow.

The pool was the summer Mecca. It seemed as if every kid in Green River spent at least part of the summer at the pool. I made friendships at the pool that will last for a lifetime.

HISTORY OF THE GREEN RIVER POLICE DEPARTMENT

By: Bill Thompson/Sgt. Mike Kinniburgh, guest author

One of Green River's own – Mike Kinniburgh – is my guest author. Mike is a former student of mine. His ready smile and personality have made him a favorite officer among Green River residents. Welcome Mike!

The town of Green River had its first election August 11, 1868 with Thomas J. Smith being elected marshal. At that time, Green River was in Carter County, Dakota Territory, which is now known as Sweetwater County, State of Wyoming. Some of the first ordinances prohibited the carrying or discharging of fire-arms or other deadly weapons, public intoxication, any disturbance of the peace or fighting, and indecent public exposure. The first census of Wyoming Territory in 1869 indicates that Green River had a population of 101 people.

The town of Green River was incorporated under laws of the newly-formed State of Wyoming on May 5, 1891. The town marshal was John D. Payne. Since that time, there have been 23 changes in the marshal and later, the chief's position. From 1891 to 1925, the longest any marshal held the position was eight years. That was when Mike Maher served from 1925 to 1933. The other marshals served shorter times. There were some marshals who served a year or two, then came back several years later to serve a year or two again.

It was during these times that the mayor was elected every couple years, and the marshal's position was appointed by the mayor.

On November 16, 1931, the town council adopted the original "Green River Ordinance."

This ordinance prohibited people from going door to door selling items. At that time, as now, a large. population of the town worked shift work and did not want to be disturbed by a door bell. This law has been taken all the way to the Supreme Court and upheld. It is enforced in many towns throughout the United States, and they also call it the "Green River Ordinance."

From 1925, the average time a person served as a chief for Green River was five years. There have been two exceptions.

The first was Chief Chris Jessen who served for 30 years from 1933 until 1963. The second is our current Chief Greg Gillen who, to date, has served 14 years since 1987. Chief Gillen began his career as a patrol officer and worked his way through the ranks to become chief. When Chris Jessen started as the chief, there were only two officers. The chief worked from 7 a.m. to 7 p.m., seven days a week. The chief at that time was paid $143 per month.

During his time as chief, Chris Jessen did not routinely carry a gun. He had one in his desk drawer at his office if it was needed. The only weapon he carried was a pocket sap. This was two pieces of leather sewn together with a piece of lead in the end. This could be used as a club if needed. In the early 1950s and 1960s, before the town began to grow, some of the officers worked two jobs. They would work for the railroad during the day and work as an officer at night. They slept at the jail and went out to take any calls that might come up. They worked by themselves.

From 1968 to 1974, Cal Ringdahl was the chief of police. It was during this time that the first dog catcher was hired. He was John Ogden, who later became a police officer. John's replacement for dog catcher was Neldon Brady. Neldon was paid 75 cents for each dog and 50 cents for each cat that he caught. He used his own vehicle for work and kept the animals in his father's barn, located in the area where the present city corrals are.

In the early 1970s, the Police Department had six full-time officers. There were also part-time officers working for the City. The part-time officers covered the swing shift from 7 p.m. until 5 a.m. on Mondays. At that time, there were 13 part-time officers. They had the same uniform as the full-time officers. It was also at this time that the town experienced a boom. This was caused by the startup and expansion of several trona mines. In 1973, the City budget went from $1.38 million to $3.8 milion. This was a 175 percent increase. The department now had 15 sworn officers and six auxiliary officers. The auxiliary officers rode with the full-time officers when they were out.

Ed Kiernan was chief. There were two sergeants. One worked from 6 a.m. to 4 p.m. The night sergeant worked from 4 p.m. to 2 a.m. The night sergeant would then be on call until 6 a.m. They worked four 10-hour shifts per week.

Uniform allowance was $160 a year. Officers were allowed

450 rounds of ammunition a year to train. Salary was based on years of service.

As for the City Court, in the 1970s Jere Ryckman was the judge. The officers prosecuted their own cases. There was no formal training. The judge would meet with the officer over a cup of coffee after court, or the officer could go to the judge's office to ask questions.

The training for the officers at this time was done at the Wyoming Law Enforcement Academy in Douglas. The buildings used were at the fairgrounds. The basic class was four weeks long. The teachers were all volunteers. The main idea of the training was to get to know other officers around the state. If you had a problem or needed help you could call around and get help from someone you met in basic.

In 1976, the town's population had grown to 9,500 people. A this time, the full-time employees were entered into the state retirement system. The police budget went from $160,800 to $292,780. The department now had its first investigator. The patrol cars went to blue with white tops. The department also went to a new light bar. To the officers at that time, this was looked upon with a great deal of pride.

In 1978, Green River had slowed down to a 10 percent growth in population. The department put on its third sergeant. He covered the days that the other sergeants were off.

In 1979, the population of Green River was 13,000 people. The department now had 23 sworn people. At this time another investigator was hired, making two investigators. There were eight auxiliary officers. The department began paying for the cleaning of uniforms. It was one uniform a week per officer.

At this time a step pay system was started by the City. There were 5 percent increases to each step. If you received good evaluations every year, it would take 10 years to reach the top. The reason for this was that the chance to advance in rank took a long time. People who did not want to become a supervisor would be rewarded for doing their jobs well.

1980 became a time when a second full-time animal control officer was added. It was at this time that the auxiliary officers were no longer used. This came about because all officers were now required to attend basic in Douglas. The department changed its uniform from brown to dark blue. The brown uniform had gone through some changes during its use. The brown pants had a stripe down the outside of each leg. Then the Department went to a brown Levi-type western pant.

The Police Department got its first polygraph operator in 1983, Lt. Mont Mecham. He is still the polygraph operator. In 2000, the department added another operator and a new machine. The polygraph operator is Sergeant Burke Morin.

As the department moved into 1984, Green River accepted into the City Code of Ordinances all of the new State laws. The Green River Police Department was the first department in the state to incorporate the DARE Program. The program is still being taught in the schools. The two officers who started the program in Green River were Sergeant Dave Hyer and Officer Bill Young.

In the 1990s, the department kept moving ahead. The badge was changed to a custom badge,

This was the third badge design change for the department. A juvenile officer position was added. To work the drug problem, two narcotics officers have been added. Computers are being used both for reports and information. The department has its own dispatch center, started in 1997. There are four full-time dispatch officers and three part-time dispatchers. The population is now 12,800 people,

The department now has 29 sworn officers, a bomb technician, and a SRT Team with negotiators. The department has had a mounted horse patrol and bike patrol. To serve the people of Green River, the department still performs lock outs and vacation house checks. While patrolling at night, it is still common to see deer and, once in a while, a fox or moose in town. If you counted just the time that the current officers have worked for Green River, it would be 298 years.

That comes to an average of 10 years' experience with the department per officer.

THE PASSING OF AN ERA: THE OXFORD CLUB

By: Marna Grubb

Green River's Red Light District

In September of 2001, the demolition of a building on Second South Street stirred many memories for people in Green River. I'd hear, "Oh, they tore down the old laundry." With a twinkle in my eye, I'd think, as did many others, that it was not only the old laundry, but it was the old Oxford Club. It signaled the end of an era, as the "South Side" of Green River has a very lively and colorful history.

The railroad arrived in Green River in October of 1868 and found that a town already had been established. The town had recently been incorporated and a town council, marshal, clerk, treasurer and assessor had been elected in August of that same year.

As reported in Maury Klein's history of the Union Pacific, "As the track laying proceeded, the supply bases at end of track sprang magically into bustling, brawling boomtowns that presented many problems. Traders, gamblers, saloon keepers, and prostitutes poured in to feed on the railroad men, teamsters, miners, soldiers, stagecoach travelers, and adventurers who gathered in these stop points."

Red light districts sprang up in towns along the railroad, and Green River was not exempt. Webster's World Encyclopedia 1999 explains the name origin of the "red light district" with a story of the early American railroad men who spent some of their spare time, either when off duty or between trains, with the "ladies of easy virtue." They took their red signal lamps with them, which they left - still lit - outside the brothel. Should, unexpectedly, their immediate help on the rails be required, they could easily be located by their red lamps. Soon the lit lamp became identified with the section of the town in which the brothels were situated.

Isaiah "Cat Eye" Willis

Green River's prostitution was controlled by a person

There was no doubt that Isaiah "Cat" or "Cat Eye" Willis was the man in charge of Green River's South Side. (Sweetwater County Historical Museum/Proctor Photo)

known as "Cat" or "Cat Eye" Willis and various madams such as Dorothy Weddington, Ruby LaRue, Rose, Dolly and "Little Bit." Prohibition forced most of the girls to brothels, such as the Green House, Pandora Rooms, Oxford Rooms, Teton Rooms and the Y-Bing Rooms. The girls were required to have a monthly check-up from the local doctors.

According to City records in the mid 1940s, the City purchased land south of the river for the Rancho, Liberty, Valley View, Hutton Heights and Paxton Webb subdivisions with funds collected from gambling and prostitution. Gamblers were charged $75 a table and $15 for slots. Green River Mayor E. L Taliaferro was quoted in *The Green River Star* as saying, "The girls had to pay $25 a month. I guess some would call it a 'fine' every month. I made sure the money went to the town, not into somebody's pocket. The land south of the river was paid for by community vice."

Throughout the years in Green River, the Greek game of Barboot was very popular, and it was reported that large sums could be won or lost in one sitting.

For many years, the South Side referred to the area of town located south of the railroad tracks to the river, as Green River did not expand housing south of the river until the late 1940s. Discrimination was prevalent in early-day Green River with whites living north of the tracks and mainly others south of the tracks.

In visiting with many who grew up on Green River's South Side through the years, they added that they found it an enjoyable place to live. According to Glenn Hill, a 1951 GRHS graduate, it was the playground for many who were children at that time, and many reported not feeling threatened. Glenn explained that, "We kids would go down to the river and catch suckers, which 'Cat Eye' would buy from us for 25 cents each."

Nighttime seemed to present a different atmosphere, especially in the business district. In Mark Nelson's interview with Angelie Scarpos in 1997, Angelie reported that "at night you didn't dare walk up the alley behind the business establishments. You didn't know if you'd get your throat cut or not." Angelie was a 1932 GRHS graduate.

Property records indicate that a property transfer to I. Willis in 1918 resulted in the building of the Oxford Club in 1919 at 13 West 2nd South Street. The lot had been purchased from Peter Scarpatheotis. The Oxford Club was a bar to service those living south of the tracks, but soon became an attraction for others also.

Isaiah Willis was a black man known as "Cat" or "Cat Eye." There was no doubt that he was in charge of the area which could provide women, liquor and gambling for the man "out on the town." He usually could be found at the Owls Club, which was located a few doors west of the Oxford Club.

In visiting with Doyle Young, a 1946 GRHS graduate, he commented that "Cat Willis was always a mystery. No one seemed to know much about him or where he had been before arriving in Green River."

"Cat" Willis had two children; Isaiah (Ike) and Dora, and he also raised another child named Millard (Snooks). After being informed by Ethel Hill Morris, a 1936 GRHS graduate, that "Cat" Willis was buried in Rock Springs, I checked burial records at Rock Springs City Hall and then visited the burial site in the Rock Springs cemetery. Three graves were reported to be on the lot, but only one was marked, and that was the son's, Isaiah's, grave.

In checking the obituary in *The Green River Star* of July 2, 1959, I found the following: "Isaiah Willis, 91, of 110 South Center street, Green River, passed away Saturday, June 27, at the Sweetwater County Memorial Hospital at 11: 10 a.m., after more than 40 years residence in Green River. Mr. Willis, generally known as 'Cat', was born in Chattanooga, Tenn., Dec. 20,1867. He is survived by a daughter, Mrs. Dora Smith of Los Angeles, and three grandchildren. Funeral services will be held at 2:30 Thursday afternoon at the Rogan Chapel, Rock Springs, with the Rev. R.

Interior of Green River's Oxford Club located at the corner of 2nd South and South Center in 1937. Bartender was Jimmy Passerelli; Manager behind the bartender was Henry Rizzi; Barmaid standing on the right was Mae Kizer. (New Studio photo)

T. Hawes of the Methodist church officiating. Burial will be in Mountain View cemetery in Rock Springs. Mr. Willis originally came to Green River to establish a restaurant for railroad waiters and porters who ran into here. He became one of the town's widely-known figures. Twice his establishments were burned in fires, but he rebuilt each time. His establishments included the Owls Club and a restaurant until a disastrous fire that destroyed his buildings and a store adjoining. Only the Owls Club was rebuilt. He had been a colorful figure in the town's history."

Doyle Young had advised me that "The Union Pacific Railroad had moved in and donated the South Side Rooms to 'Cat' for use as a place for the Union Pacific Pullman porters and waiters to stay, since they were not allowed to stay on the North Side." Doyle further advised that blacks had to sit in the back, right two rows at the Isis Theatre, and they were not allowed in the swimming pool, nor in any of the bars except the Owls Club. He said this didn't seem to change until the late 1950s. I was born and raised in Green River and didn't realize this was happening. In school we enjoyed all of our classmates, regardless of nationality, and many were, and still are, our best friends.

Hiney Krause offered his memories of "Cat" Willis, one of which was, "I was standing on top of a box car on the U.P.R.R. repair track, which was just across the street from the South Side business district. On the east corner was a brick building called the Oxford Club. There was a black man sitting in the V-shaped entranceway. His name was 'Cat Eye' Willis who lived there with his family. A two-story hotel was built on the back of the lot. This was a summer day in 1926. I was 17 years old. 'Cat Eye' was known from coast to coast. If someone knew you were going through Green River, they would say to stop and see 'Cat Eye.' Of course, a lot of that was after prohibition."

John Bacila was a bartender at the Owls Club. He informed that, in 1950, he had hitched a ride on a freight train. When he got off in Green River, he stopped at the old Stanley Hotel and indicated what he was looking for. He said that Irene Bowers and Mrs. Moerke directed him across the tracks. He later married and has been a resident of Green River since that time.

Prohibition

According to *The Story of Wyoming, Frontier Spirit* by Craig Sodaro and Randy Adams, "The Roaring Twenties was a decade of recklessness and rebellion in young people, and with it came prohibition. Under prohibition, people were not to buy, sell, or make any liquor in the country. The 18th Amendment, ratified in 1920, closed bars, distilleries, and breweries across the country. It also opened an age of lawlessness and crime."

It further states that "By 1915 the wild-west, hard-drinking and gambling saloon image of Wyoming was largely a thing of the past. Like the rest of the country, conservative Wyoming now favored prohibition. But problems were quick to develop. If anyone in Wyoming wanted a drink, prohibition or not, he or she could get it. There was plenty of moonshine being made in the stills dotting the countryside. Speakeasies - hidden bars usually located behind or beneath legal businesses - sprang up in many Wyoming cities. By the late 1920s, embarrassed prohibitionists had turned against the 18th Amendment because of the lawlessness it had created. Wyoming had had enough. In 1932, nearly 72 percent of the state voted for repeal, which finally took effect in Wyoming on April 1, 1935."

Hiney Krause commented on prohibition. "My brothers

and I and our friends used to go to the dances that were held in the Oxford dance hall. They had tables around the edges of the hall. Even though it was prohibition, Kemmerer Moonshine, Dago Red and soft drinks were available with most being carried in. There was not much of a bar at that time, and I don't remember 'Cat Eye' around very much. He either leased or rented the place out. I can remember the first two people who operated the Club. One of them was named Tracy. They had some Hollywood

Oxford Club was owned and managed by Jack Evers (right) from 1947 to 1967. (Jack Evers family photo)

entertainers there, and people from all over Green River and Rock Springs would come to see them. You could hardly find a parking place. This was before Jack Evers took over."

Twenty Years with Jack Evers

From 1947 to 1967, John (Jack) Evers managed the Oxford Club. As Hiney Krause said, "Everybody loved Jack and Mary. They lived on the North Side in the big brick house next to the Brewery on Railroad Avenue, but spent most of their time at the Oxford. If one got too much to drink and couldn't make it home, Jack or the help would take them and put them to bed in the back apartment. There was a two-story hotel at the back of the Oxford that sat at the edge of the alley. It was dismantled later."

Hiney further reported that, "Jack Evers was well known, and the ranchers and sheep men from all over would stop by to see Jack. He also had some well-known bartenders. Charlie Viox was an old-time bartender and he looked it. He always wore a long white apron. He was on first shift and Fred Stoll, ex-rancher from out south, but lived in Green River, was the night-shift bartender. Fred had many friends and could tell the best jokes you ever heard, but never told a dirty one.

"Fredie Welsh also bartended. He was a young rancher and cowboy, the son of Tom Welsh. Tom Welsh, along with Dr. Hawk, built the Tomahawk Hotel. Lena Oney and Ada Krause kept books for Jack." Hiney said that he was a relief bartender on his days off from the railroad.

He said, "Jack Evers took good care of anyone that wanted to celebrate a little. The sheep herders and ranch hands, who came in at times with their paychecks or money, would let Jack take their money and give it to them when they sobered up and left. They never lost a cent, except a few dollars he let them celebrate with. He also let people have money from payday to payday, mostly the Mexican people and single guys who were customers."

Hiney reports that "There were a couple of shootings that took place after they had started in the Oxford, but the actual shootings were not in the Club. One was across the street by the Independent Store, and the other on the street by the Eagles Club. The police were called at times to stop a few disturbances outside and in the alleys. One fight was termed a Mexican war."

He continued with "The Oxford Club had very little trouble with the law. In general, the Oxford Club was a respectable place. Married couples, single people, railroaders, business people, single women, and all could come there and be treated with respect. There were no prostitutes hanging around, although they were just a few doors away."

"One time," Hiney reports, "there was a Greek fellow named Mike who was a grocery clerk for the Up To Date store next to the Oxford Club. He was celebrating Greek Easter and had a phonograph playing music out in the middle of the street. He came into the club, pulled a gun out and shot two holes in the ceiling, then turned around and bought everyone a drink. Jack and everyone just laughed and clapped their hands."

Hiney reminisced that "All in all we had some real good times at the Oxford. I learned to do the polka there. I used to get mad at Scritch, the barber, and young Percy Valencia because my wife said they could dance better than me."

NOTE: I thank Hiney for giving us a better insight into life at the Oxford Club with his many enjoyable comments!

Jack Evers was the popular manager and owner of the Oxford Club from 1947 to 1967, which was often referred to as "Jack's place" or "Evers place." On April 10, 1967, City records indicated that Liquor License No. 6 was transferred by sale and change of premises from John Evers for the Oxford Club at 13 West 2nd South Street to James Stahl and Earl Bartlett for the Mustang Bar and Lounge at 530 East Flaming Gorge Way, effective May 1, 1967. Jack Evers had celebrated his 80th birthday at the Oxford Club before selling his business.

At about this same time, the liquor license from the Owls Club was being transferred to Lake Way Liquor Store on Uinta Drive.

Comments By Jack's Son

Jack Evers' son, Jack, a 1956 GRHS graduate who was residing in Laramie in 2001, has shared his childhood recollections of the Oxford Club.

"Some things to keep in mind are that gambling was legal in Wyoming when my Dad first owned the bar. He often described the bar as a 'place for serious drinkers, not social drinkers.' A newcomer once ordered a screwdriver and the bartender got one out of the toolbox. There was an apartment in the back, so we often stayed there. My recollections are of a bar with true frontier spirit. This was the kind of bar that I could, and often did, ride my horse into, starting with my Shetland pony. And mine weren't the only horses ridden into it."

He continued, "Perhaps my earliest recollections were the dances. When there was a big dance that was going to run into the early morning hours, the folks would often take me to the apartment rather than try to get an all-night babysitter. The bedroom that I used shared a wall with the band stand, so I learned to sleep with a dance band blaring a few feet away." It was interesting to learn that Edith Sunada, a 1940 GRHS graduate, had been one of young Jack's babysitters. He praised her saying, "She is truly a remarkable woman. She would be a role model for anyone."

Jack Jr. further informed, "Since most of Green River was north of the railroad tracks, there were few businesses on the South Side. The Oxford Club and 'Cat' Willis's Owls Club to the west of the Oxford were the only bars. This meant that for hunters and fishermen returning from the south country, or ranchers, lumbermen, pipeliners and others who worked out south, the Oxford was the first 'watering hole' they encountered on their way into town. An interesting mix of people could often be found there. There were probably more deer killed, fish caught and tall tales told at that bar than anywhere else in the county."

He remarked that "Characters were abundant. I remember one regular who was limber enough in the hips to rotate his legs until his feet pointed backwards and still be able to walk. He'd often put his clothes on backwards, turn his feet backwards and walk up to some poor drunk to complain that he couldn't seem to get his head on straight."

"On another occasion," he said, "the district game warden came in with his rifle after an unsuccessful day of hunting, but apparently a very successful day of drinking. He spied the Calvert Reserve clock on the wall with a small owl figure in the center. So he remarked that, if he couldn't get anything else, he could get that owl, and he began shooting. He didn't hit anything vital in either the owl or the clock, so the clock continued to run and was left on the wall with the bullet holes to remind Sheff that he shouldn't drink and carry a rifle. The bullets went through the wall and lodged in the ceiling of the dance hall. The holes were never repaired."

Jack Jr. reported that "One of the ranchers who frequented the place before there was electricity or refrigeration on the ranch (REA came about 1952) always came to town with a craving for ice cream products. He would pay the neighborhood kids to bicycle up town and bring him milkshakes, which he would then flavor with whiskey."

Green River Historic Preservation Commission

"Another fellow," he said, "was able to stand at the bar unconscious. The first time I saw it, I looked and then said to Dad, 'Is he conscious?' Dad said, 'No, but he'll fall down in a little bit, the fall will wake him up and he'll go home. He does it about once a month.' Sure enough, that's what happened."

Another character described by Jack Jr. was "a plump, jolly lady named Dolly. There was a boarding house that she ran right behind the Oxford. It had originally been a brothel and she had been the Madam. Dolly was talking to my wife one day and in looking at Ann's figure said, 'I used to have a figure like that. It was necessary for my line of work, but then I moved into management and it didn't matter anymore, so I started eating.'"

Coin Laundry

After Jack Evers retired, the Oxford building was renovated by John and Florence Dallmann and operated as the Coin Laundry from 1968 to 1980. John plumbed the building and installed the washing machines. It was immaculate and their service superb.

In 1980, the Coin Laundry was purchased by Anthony Sawick and later a commercial laundry business was added in the back. In 1999, Brady Bros. Inc. purchased the property. Brady Bros. operate the Brady's Body Shop across the street from the property. In September, 2001, Brady Bros. had the building demolished in contract with Steve Luczak.

NOTE: Many thanks to all who gave comments and assistance as I researched this property. It generated much conversation, and I enjoyed every minute!

CHRISTMAS MEMORIES

By: Bill Duncan

Maybe it's the special evergreen smell or a traditional ornament that prompts nostalgic memory. It might be your unique mix of outside decorations or favorite Christmas tune. The memories that Christmas evokes are private and personal. Perhaps this writing will help you remember the things that make your holiday season special.

My dad told me about his early Christmases on an isolated ranch on the East Fork of the Wind River in Western Wyoming. His Scottish parents decorated the tree during the afternoon of Christmas Eve. While most decorations were homemade paper chains and popcorn strings, they clipped real candles to the end of many branches. The children weren't allowed in the sitting room while the tree was decorated and presents were prepared. After supper, when everything was ready, the candles were lit and the children were allowed in to gather around the tree, sing carols and receive their presents.

One of Dad's favorite stories involves a man in "Santa" costume who was handing out presents. Santa was seated next to the tree so he could reach the packages underneath. When he reached way under the tree, the candles lit his rope beard. Santa made a quick exit out the back door. When the little kids asked where Santa had gone, my dad's Uncle John noted that he had "seen Santa diving into a snow drift at the back fence and was probably headed back to the North Pole."

Trees have changed quite a bit since the early 20th century. Although Louise S. Graf said in a 1972 article in *The Green River Star* that Christmas trees weren't popular in Green River until after WWI, Dad said that he always remembered a tree at Christmas. Even 60 years later I remember candles on my grandparent's tree with homemade popcorn and dried cranberry strings, paper chains and baked ornaments to reflect candle light and to catch the gleam in young children's eyes.

Electricity made a great difference in tree decorations. Strings of brightly colored lights replaced candles. No matter if a whole string went out when one bulb failed. Even the light bulbs were decorated. Heat-driven shades twirled on top of the lights. Today, candle-shaped lights bubble madly from branches. Most families have a traditional tree topper. Ours is a rather bedraggled angel that has lasted for three generations.

Candy makes Christmas special. To me, Christmas candy meant homemade candied orange peel. We would accumulate orange peelings, cut them into strips, cook them in sugar syrup, and let them harden into sugar-crusted orange candy. My Mom also whipped up divinity, cookie-shaped morsels that would melt in my mouth, and Million-Dollar fudge. We always seemed to end up with a box or two of chocolate covered cherries during the holidays.

Toys reflected the times, just as they do now. During WWII we received helmets and wooden Tommy guns, toy ships and planes. One of my favorite gifts was a wind-up toy train that would go down the sidewalk or around the living room without tracks. The full-blown electric train came much later.

Sleds were a big deal in our family. Sixty years ago Green River had an abundance of sledding hills. Although metal saucers and plastic sliding strips hadn't shown up yet, the whole community rode sleds down the steep street just east of old Lincoln School. Police stopped traffic so sledders could cross Highway 30, the transcontinental highway that ran through town.

Technology has made the biggest difference in Christmas. Radios used to mean the big one in the front room where the whole family gathered to listen. Phonographs were cumbersome and needed frequent needle changes. It's hard for people now to remember times before play stations, television, and DVD.

My grandchildren can't believe my stories. "One Christmas we were really thrilled when we got a 45 record player and a few green, red, and yellow records. I thought all records were big and black with a few songs on each side," says one of the older ones.

"No," I said, my eyes glowing with the memory. "We had these neat 45 rpm colored records. Each record was color-coded according to the type of music. I remember country-western was green and popular was red."

"What color was rock and roll?"

"Well, we didn't have rock and roll then, my favorite song was a green record called "Does the Spearmint lose its flavor on the bedpost overnight?" I wanted to tell them about 8 track tapes, but they put their earphones back on, turned up the Walkman volume, rolled their eyes, and went back to Brittany and Garth. The one who remembered records chugged away, moving to a rap beat.

We didn't have a fireplace to hang stockings, so we just pinned them to the couch. They were just socks out of our drawer. The individualized, decorated specials were for another generation. An orange in the toe, a small toy, then an apple in the heel, and hard candy on top. A candy cane always stuck out the top. Somehow one or two of those chocolate covered cherries always worked their way into the toe of the sock and got scrunched into a gooey mess.

Christmas church services are a tradition in our family. Nothing can match a candle light ceremony with carols. One part of our family follows the Danish tradition celebrating on Christmas Eve. Another allows one present on Christmas Eve, saving most for the next morning. Others "scramble" opening as many presents as they can in the shortest time, then taking time to admire all gifts. It is interesting to see each family incorporate traditions from both sides of the family while adding some of their own.

I'm sure we've enjoyed many brown Christmases, but holiday memories always seem snowy and cold. Photographs, home movies or videos help fix certain images and times in our memory banks. But the time to enjoy them passes quickly. Kids, who wanted a teddy bear, then CDs and a Walkman, decide a set of dishes or silverware would be nice. Before long the teddy bear and toy cycle starts again with the next generation. Christmas blends traditions and new experiences into a unique mosaic. Don't let time spin by too quickly. Don't let the buying and preparation stress occupy us so much that we forget what a magical, mystical, memorable time Christmas can be.

PRESIDENT LINCOLN'S MILITARY TRIBUNALS

By: Terry A. Del Bene

Even at a time when the Middle East is in flames and we are involved in an undeclared war against terrorism, much of the national attention has turned to the issue of trying terrorists with military tribunals. The announced decision by the Bush administration has been extremely controversial and in this controversy both sides have, as is so often the case, cloaked their arguments with the historical record. It is little wonder that the military tribunals during the American Civil War have played heavily in the arguments pro and con. It is not my intent to enter into the fray as to whether military tribunals are the right solution for what to do with captured terrorists. The President has spoken and the military will follow his orders.

Such commissions have been part of American History since the Mexican War. The original tribunals were meant to provide a legal system in occupied territories where the local system of law and order had collapsed. However, each generation which faces an emergency seems to redefine the use of such institutions and ours is no different.

In most cases the tribunals (also known as Military Commissions) held during the Civil War had little in common with our current situation. Attacks by international terrorists upon the United States are significantly different than the secession of several states from the Union. The Southern Confederacy claimed it had legitimately seceded from a government viewed as tyrannical. The Federal Government felt that it was waging a war against rebellious citizens and not the citizens of another country.

President Lincoln used his constitutional prerogative of declaring that a state of rebellion was in progress. This allowed him to suspend certain protections such, as the writ of habeas corpus. Essentially citizens of the nation could be detained without charge or council for an indefinite period. The Civil War period saw the incarceration and detention of thousands of political prisoners. Had the war continued longer and the President not been assassinated it is possible that the Chief Justice of the Supreme Court might have found himself with a view of the beach at Dry Tortugas.

President Lincoln had a very complex situation to deal with. As portions of the seceding states were occupied by Union soldiers they came under martial law. Since the local legal institutions were considered disloyal, military tribunals were necessary, at least until all the judges and magistrates were allowed to take a loyalty oath and reassume their duties.

The Army muddled through as best it could, but the issue kept growing in complexity. Clearly the Northern view was that those bearing arms against the nation were traitors and should be dealt with accordingly. However, Southern prisoner of war camps contained tens of thousands of Northern prisoners. These men would have been subject to retribution for any punishments imparted on the Southern prisoners in the hands of the Union. It was a weighty problem what to do with these men and their supporters.

EXECUTION OF THIRTY-EIGHT INDIAN MURDERERS AT MANKATO, MINNESOTA.—FROM A SKETCH BY MR. BERMAN, OF ST. PAUL.—[SEE PAGE

Engraving of mass execution of Sioux tribal members in Mankato, Minnesota from *Harper's Weekly Magazine* in 1862. (Photo courtesy Terry Del Bene)

The Official Records of the War of the Rebellion (Series II, Volume V, pages 671-682) contain an interesting document, General Order 100 dated May 10, 1863. This document is a series of instructions for the government of armies in the field. Basically it is a set of guidelines for implementing martial law. The document begins to sort out some of the complexity of how to deal with various levels of involvement in the rebellion. Hence, there are prescriptions for dealing with prisoners of war, hostages, slaves, spies, war-traitors, messengers, partisans, war-rebels, scouts, and armed prowlers. For example, partisans "are public enemies and, therefore, if captured are not entitled to the privileges of prisoners of war, but shall be treated summarily as highway robbers or pirates." Many of the categories carry a summary death sentence. Along with this are instructions as to how to handle cases of high treason, assassination, and a variety of other crimes.

Most of the military tribunals convened during the Lincoln administration involved American citizens (by the Northern definition). However, there were cases where military commissions were held to deal with citizens of other sovereign nations. The most famous of these occurred in 1862. It all started over a dispute over eggs and turned into one of the most brutal of America's "Indian Wars" in history. The summer of 1862 would see several tribes of mainly Sioux Indians burning out hundreds of farms. Settlements, such as New Ulm, were put under siege. The Indians at first managed to get the upper hand against the army and came close to capturing a U.S. military post. Make no mistake about it, the events in Minnesota were about as brutal and inhumane as any war has been.

General John Pope was sent from the east to stabilize the situation. He declared, "It is my purpose to exterminate the Sioux if I have the power to do so... They are to be treated as maniacs or wild beasts, and by no means as people with whom treaties or compromises can be made (letter of September 28, 1862). By the time Pope arrived things were already beginning to draw to a conclusion. Sioux resistance seemed to sputter and die almost of its own volition. The Sioux surrendered in large numbers... creating the question... what comes next?

The citizenry of Minnesota had little doubt what came next. There were several hundred fresh graves of their friends and families crying to be avenged. The army had to turn their efforts to keep the citizens from lynching the Sioux in custody. A military commission was empowered to "...try summarily the mulatto, mixed bloods, and Indians engaged in the Sioux raids and massacres..." The commission went about its business with a will and tried roughly 400+ Sioux in a period of six weeks. The final day of the Commission's work saw roughly 40 individuals tried. Of the 400+, fully 303 were convicted and sentenced to death. Many others were handed stiff prison sentences.

The trials necessarily were hurried affairs. There was no recognition that the individuals in question were from sovereign nations then at war with the United States. They were treated as brigands It is not clear if the defendants even knew they were on trial. One of the accused, though fluent in English, was under the impression the hearing was to decide to hold him in detention a little longer. He did not know he was on trial for his life. Some of the Sioux slept through their trial or had to be awakened from a proceeding which they little realized had great meaning to them. There are concerns as to whether the translator was able to do a competent job. The request for council for the accused was turned down and none of the defendants had representation. Witnesses were coerced to speak against individuals with offers of lighter sentences. The transcripts clearly represent the casual rules of evidence where one witness was sufficient to convict and there was no means to examine the story of the witness. In some instances Sioux who tried to prevent depredations were condemned on the testimony of the people they had helped save. Many trials lasted but a few minutes... hardly time to read the charges and specifications before handing out sentences.

President Lincoln had learned by this time that Military Commissions of the period often were more zealous than fair. He had given orders that all death sentences were to be reviewed by the President. In this instance he felt that the court had not completely established guilt of many of the condemned. However, local politicians had already put him on the alert that if he commuted all the death sentences that the people of Minnesota would take the law into their own hands. Of the 303 death sentences Lincoln passed on the recommendations for execution for 38. Most of the 38 were charged with rape as well as murder.

On a snowy Christmas Eve of 1862 these 38 men would hang together in Mankato. This is the largest mass-hanging in American History.

Here in the 21st Century the events of 1862 in Minnesota seem far away in space and time. We have all but forgotten these events as new events fill our lives. The Sioux still remember. Perhaps the struggles of these long-dead people can remind us to take care that our own thirst for revenge does not consume us as well.

Tell our friends that we are being removed from this world over the same path they must shortly travel. We go first, but many of our friends may follow us in a very short time.... When my children are grown up, let them know that their father died because he followed the advice of his chief, and without having the blood of a white man to answer for to the Great Spirit." (Hdainyanka shortly before his execution on Dec. 24, 1862).

"[I] am satisfied in my own mind from the slight evidence on which those are condemned that there are many others in that prison house who ought not t be there, and that the honor of our Government and the welfare of the people of Minnesota, as well as that of the Indians, requires a new trial before unprejudiced judges - (Reverend Thomas Williamson November 24, 1862).

GR HISORIC PRESERVATION COMMISSION: WHO WE ARE AND WHAT WE'VE BEEN UP TO

By: Ruth Lauritzen

The Green River Historic Preservation (GRHPC) is a group of five people who volunteer their time to serve on this city-appointed commission. Members are Terry Del Bene, Bill Duncan, Marna Grubb, Ruth Lauritzen and Bill Thompson. The GRHPC receives a small budget each year from the Green River City Council to implement projects designed to raise public awareness and appreciation of historic resources in our community. While relatively small, the budget is much appreciated and envied by other Historic Preservation Commissions around the state who receive no funding at all.

Though generally appreciated by the public, our projects and actions have occasionally been criticized by some for being too interfering, and by others for not being proactive enough. Commission members are well-meaning citizens who aren't out to change the world, but they like to think their efforts make a difference in the community's understanding and appreciation of its history and resources.

The commission has three long-term projects it has committed to maintain. The first of these is the monthly publication of the "Echoes From the Bluff" column. These articles have been well received and have been most enduring of our projects.

Second is the continued publication of historical brochures including *A Guide to Historic Green River* and *Nature's Art Shop*. Both of these brochures have been reprinted several times at the request of the City and the Chamber of Commerce and have proven useful in the promotion of Green River.

The *Green River Gems* program is the third on-going project for the commission. Each year the commission has added buildings or historic features to this honorary local register of historic places and and has mounted a small plaque on or near each feature to designate the honor.

Other notable projects have also been completed. The public is educated about historical buildings on the *Green River Gems* roster by a series of slides, which show before the film at the local movie theater. The Star Twin cooperated with the commission for this project as a public service.

The commission has hosted two historic preservation-related conferences in Green River. The first, an annual Certified Local Government conference, was held in the spring of 2000 and a series of preservation programs held as part of the Wyoming Association of Municipalities meeting occurred in June of 2001.

The GRHPC contributed to the renovation of the Old Post Office into the new home for the Sweetwater County Historical Museum in two major ways. The commission, with the approval of the City Council, donated all profits from the sale of the the book, *Echoes From The Bluffs*, to the Sweetwater County Museum Foundation for use on projects related to the building. The GRHPC and the City of Green River also sponsored a Wyoming Historic Preservation grant for around $20,000.00 to pay for historic rehabilitation on the building.

Two signage projects were also undertaken. The GRHPC was reponsible for purchasing the signs marking the Lincoln Highway through Green River. The Lincoln Highway was the first paved transcontinental highway in the United States. The commission also was a sponsor of a Millennium Trails grant, which funded the creation of two markers telling the story of the Cherokee Trail which passed through this area in the nineteenth century. These signs are in place along the trail route through town.

Finally, the production of a video about Green

Contractors install a replica door on the Sweetwater County Historical Museum in 2001. The door was funded by a Wyoming Historic Preservation Grant and is nearly identical to the historic door, using original hardware and similar construction materials wherever possible. (Photo courtesy Sweetwater County Historical Museum)

River was completed in the fall of 2003. The commission worked with Brian Madland and his students in the technology department at Green River High School to put together the production, which included both historic and modern images of our city. The video, *Green River: Wyoming's Best Kept Secret*, won first prize in the category of non-professional video productions from the Wyoming State Historical Society in September 2003.

Above: Producer Brian Madland accepts a first place award for the production *Green River: Wyoming's Best Kept Secret* from Governor Dave Freudenthal and Wyoming State Historical Society President Dick Wilder in September of 2003. (Photo courtesy Wyoming State Historical Society)

The Green River Historic Preservation Commission is known as one of the most active in the state. We are proud of all we have accomplished and are grateful for the support of the Mayor and Council and citizens of Green River. We always welcome the interest and input of concerned residents. We can be contacted by writing to the Green River Historic Preservation Commission, City of Green River, 50 East 2nd North, Green River, Wyoming 82935.

THE JACK "IMMORAL" OF THE HILLS

By: Bill Thompson

How to best utilize some 1,000 square miles of Federal land known as the Jack Morrow Hills has been the subject of public meetings, editorials, and letters to the paper for quite some time. Arguments for and against proposed uses are on record and well documented. But finding material relating to the actual Jack Morrow is another story. There is little authentic record of him. It is safe to say that almost no one in Sweetwater County knows about Jack at all. This is ironic for a guy who covered such a vast region with his unscrupulous ventures. Ironic too is that this area with its awesome and inspirational beauty honors the name of a notorious hard drinking murderer, a high-bracket swindler and a common thief. Morrow Creek and Morrow Canyon in Sweetwater County also perpetuate the name of this wily braggart and boaster. After hearing of some of his exploits, local Game Warden Bill Rudd suggested the modification of Jack's last name which is used in the title of this article. So who was this Jack Morrow whose name is so honored?

It was in the 1850s that Morrow became known in the Ne-braska and Wyoming Territories. From Omaha to the mountains and mining towns his wild excesses with money and his notorious drunken sprees were legendary .... fueled by his arrogant rodo-montade. He began as a teamster hauling freight to the mountains for the government. The teamsters were known as "bull-whack-ers". With their whang-leather tip lashes they could nip the hide off a steer just like a knife. Jack could make his pop like a rifle. Armed with a long "gad" and his lash Jack would walk on the dust-free side of the team. The most dangerous man in the group though was the wagon-master who was boss. His major job was to prevent theft from the wagons. "He was king .... and carried a revolver or two..." His face-offs with the whackers were frequent. The wagons were loaded full with drawn curtains to make it difficult to steal anything. But sly Jack worked at it, adding to his wealth by "tapping" his freights. On trips from Omaha to Denver or to Salt Lake City he would steal part of the load and hide it for later retrieval. One time Morrow drunkenly related how he got his start. "I came from Missouri and got to whacking bulls across the plains; after a while I got onto a government train loaded with ammunition and sold it to the ranchmen, filled the boxes with sand, and screwed them down. Then before we got to Laramie I had a rumpus with the wagon-master and he pulled a pistol and I skinned out for somewhere else and nobody got onto it. I never heard a word from it ever afterwards, but I sold a big lot of ammunition." True or not, it was unwise to question Jack's stories.

Using his ill-gotten funds Morrow then went into partnership with Alex Constant, an old trapper for The American Fur Company. Due to the wagon trains and stages on the Oregon and Overland Trails their trading post at Doby Town near Ft. Kearney (Neb) was very prosperous. Later, after robbing his partner, Jack fled westward to the junction of the North and South Platte River. There, in 1860, Jack Morrow built his famous Junction Ranch. Also started near there that same year were the Boxelder Creek Mail and Pony Express Station.

In contrast to the sod ranch houses with sod roofs, Jack's ranch was two-and-a-half stories high and sixty-feet long. It was built entirely of cedar logs including the roof. Soon warnings were passed back along the trail for emigrants to go around the ranch as many met with "misfortunes". In response, Morrow then dug a wide and deep trench across the route. Traces of it are still visible today. He also extended a half-mile dike from the ranch to the river forcing the emigrants to pass his ranch. Jack stocked his ranch with "some bad Indians" and renegade whites. Several hundred Sioux and several white squaw men were kept in moderate comfort near his ranch! In return for rations, liquor and goods from Morrow's trading post, they stampeded emigrant stock and ran off the herds for him. Even by doubling and tripling the guards when this section of the trail was reached it was rare for a wagon train not to lose a few animals if not the entire herd. Jack often would sell previously stolen stock to emigrants as replacements. Woe to the former owner if he indicated that he had much money for he was later robbed on up the trail.

Morrow became a rich man who intimidated a wide territory. He continued to charge outrageously high prices for provisions needed by the travelers on the Oregon and Overland Trails. Due to the wagon train cattle thefts, his herds grew many times larger than the neighboring ranches. Once a year he would bring his long line of freight wagons to Omaha. Piled high with bartered furs and buffalo robes, buffalo meat and beef, they presented quite a show for Jack's swaggering ego. Morrow's easiest money though came from cedar trees in Moran Canyon near his ranch. He sold two thousand at a time for telegraph poles. The land and the cedars were not his. No problem. Threats kept others from cutting logs there. His Indians only attacked other woodcutters.

When Jack's ranch became financially secure (surprise!) he expanded his field of operations. He utilized his knowledge gleaned from years as a whacker between Omaha, Denver and Salt Lake City. He was one of the first to realize how easy it was to mine the surface deposits of lignite coal in Wyoming Territory. He established an operating coal mine near Black Butte a year before the arrival of the Union Pacific and the "Hell on Wheels" towns. It was in such a town named Benton west of Black Butte that Jack had his picture taken by photographer Arundel C. Hull. At the time he was under contract for 25,000 cords of wood to be cut between Green River and Black Butte. Later another one was taken of him in Green River, Wyoming Territory. Morrow's knowledge of the good stands of timber facilitated his contracts for the hundreds of thousands of feet of cord wood and railroad ties. It seems probable that much of the timber and coal he utilized was on land granted

Jack Morrow is pictured sitting on the barrel in Benton, Wyoming. (Photo reproduced from *Shutters West* by Nina Hull Miller)

to the Union Pacific. No matter. He ran ads in the Cheyenne and Laramie papers and in *The Frontier Index* (a newspaper on wheels) for woodcutters and for delivery of ties to the track.

Later he drunkenly boasted of overcharging and short-counting on these railroad contracts. A common way for him to cheat the UP was arranging the cordwood and ties in stacks with a hollow center. . . cribbing.

Another simultaneous financial operation of Jack Morrow's at this time was a mule freight train running between

A photo supposedly taken in Green River shows Jack Morrow standing just left of the telegraph pole. (Photo by Arundel C. Hull, reproduced from *Shutters West* by Nina Hull Miller)

Laramie and Salt Lake City which passed through some of the territory now bearing his name. "These activities made him a frequent traveler to the end of the railroad." As this gave him more opportunity to cheat and swindle on shipments and contracts, Jack spent less time on harassing the emigrants passing near his distant ranch. His hold on the Indians there slipped some too. The well-stocked ranch was left in care of his trusted foreman Hewey Morgan. Morgan never did wholly like stealing from the travelers (but not strong enough for him to quit his lucrative job). He was a versatile and trusted bookkeeper and salesman for Junction Ranch. Morgan oversaw Jack's other enterprises as well. Jack put unlimited trust in him as Morgan took complete control when Morrow was in one of his frequent drunken spells.

Junction Ranch grew to include a row of sleeping huts known as "Pilgrim's quarters." "Pilgrim" was derogatory slang used by the locals to describe a newcomer to the plains (John

Wayne where are you?). Back east the word was Greenhorn" and farther west it was "Tenderfoot." The huts and the third story of the ranch house were rented to overnight stoppers. The upper floor of the ranch house was divided into rooms, but the cross logs had not been sawed out for doors. In going from one high-priced room to another one had to crawl over six feet of cedar log wall! These rooms and huts were usually full as travelers had to get out of the weather. Morrow was such a jerk in his "ways of doing business that quarrels and arguments with Pilgrims, wagon bosses and stage passengers were everyday occurrences."

Eugene Ware the Commander of the military post at Fort Mcpherson some 15 miles from Morrow's ranch related some of his experiences there as a dinner guest. Using field glasses on the way to Jack's ranch they saw an Indian's head peering over the ridge at them. He "scudded away and disappeared." Later at Morrow's they were told that the Indians were keeping constant lookout for Jack from "Sioux Point" even in bad weather. Sometimes they warned Morrow of surprise visitors by sending up "fire arrows." Ware's group arrived after sundown and Morrow acted "two-thirds full". He brought out Champagne and began dinner. " It was broiled antelope heart, baked buffalo hump, fried beaver tails, a regular pioneer banquet." Later a fine-looking and well-educated young gentleman recited poetry for the group. His Indian name was Wa-pah-see-cha (bad matches). He was trying to work into the stock business. (Many years afterward Ware met up with him in Ohio. He had become a prominent minister.) While the horses were being saddled Jack delt out hands of faro bark. Ware states that there were no big losses for anyone. Getting Ware aside, Captain O'Brian whispered to him that he suspected Morrow of trying to get a government contract with their post. Later Ware was approached by Hewey Morgan who wanted to know if Ware could get a contract for Morrow to furnish the Post. The price offered was so umeasonable that Ware immediately turned him down. Each member of the party had been spoken to about the proposed contract. " This whole proceeding was so raw that none of us ever made any visit again to Jack Morrow. Captain O'Brian was an honest man, and was very indignant."

Oddly enough, there came a time when Jack's infamous ranch became an asset to the area. In 1864 the Sioux Indians were pulled into the Cheyenne War. Along the Platte, valley ranches were looted and burned. Some whites were killed. Because of its strong construction and substantial size, the neighboring ranchers gathered there and fortified Jack's ranch with sod walls. For months at a time troops would be stationed at Fort Morrow receiving their supplies from Fort Cottonwood. These troops and Morrow's close association with several hundred Sioux and his status as a "squawman" were major factors why the ranch was not attacked. Junction Ranch became the open line of communication along the Platte. Later his Indian wife died and Jack married a white woman. She was described as "refined, modest, neatly dressed and seemed rather out of place." There is no record of Morrow having children.

It is hard to believe that the other ranchers along the Platte were unaware of Jack Morrow's unsavory and repugnant methods of acquiring wealth. His distasteful reputation was wide-spread over an astounding area. No doubt though his neighbors were grateful for the protection afforded by his ranch during the Indian outbreak. Probably they were impressed by his wealth also. But it is amazing to me that, on election day in September 1866, he was made County Commissioner of Lincoln County, Nebraska Territory!

Jack Morrow retired from his ranch in the late 1960s and moved to an opulent home in Omaha. There he concerned himself with government contracts, general speculation, booze and braggadocio. One writer states that, "his brazen arrogance never failed him and his wealth continued to increase through his contracts and the poker games he played with visiting Congressmen." As in earlier days he bragged about his "scurvy tricks", his killing a man named Murphy in a gunfight and the multiple contract swindles he had pulled. His favorite though was "a poker game in which he won sixty thousand dollars from the members of a committee sent out from Washington to investigate irregularities in government contracts." There are two things to point out here... those were 1860 dollars! And whom do you think the committee was sent out to investigate anyway? Heh.

In one high-class gambling establishment a drunken Morrow whipped out his six-shooter and accused the dealer of cheating and demanded his lost three thousand dollars. Booze prevented him from recognizing the dealer as the owner! Harris, the owner, quietly counted out the money which Morrow pocketed. Morrow accepted a drink while Harris stepped into the next room. Suddenly reappearing with two revolvers he snarled, "Jack you had the drop on me, but now I have it on you. Put the money and your gun on the table and if you make any attempt at gunplay I will kill you or one of my men will." A red-faced Morrow " burst into a loud guffaw, declaring that he had only been joking anyway, but he did as he was ordered." Harris replied that he wasn't sure it was a joke until he had his own guns in hand. Jack finished his drink and left after Harris told him to come around the next day to get his gun when he had sobered up. In spite of his subsequent besotted blustering, Jack's rapid capitulation caused some to doubt his courage in an actual face-off. "The bad whites and Indians he kept under obligation did many a nefarious chore for him. His arrogance and bullying needed only their backing." Described in his younger days as a "tall, raw-boned, dangerous-looking man, wearing a mustache, a goatee on his under lip" his years of dissipation took their toll. Luxurious living, gambling and excessive drinking consumed his wealth faster than he could replace it. The shirts on which he wore his famous enormous diamond began to look soiled. "Prolonged debauches finally undermined the rugged constitution that had survived so many years of abuse, and in 1885 the erstwhile dapper, notorious thief and swindler died in poverty".

Many years later revisiting the plains, Eugene Ware wrote," I went up to where Jack Morrow's ranch stood; I found near its site a house in which people were living in much comfort, surrounded with trees and smiling gardens; they were Swedes, **they had never heard of Jack Morrow, and had lived there 18 years!** (emphasis mine). "The entire valley of the river was a mass of fine farms, and about all I could recognize in the landscape was the Sioux lookout".

Jack Morrow was an amazing man and a fascinating character to research. It is regrettable that he chose to use his brilliance and high-energy intelligence for such a depraved life-style which disintegrated into ignominy. This author muses on what positive contributions Jack might have made to his communities and to society in general had his focus been otherwise. But he was a thug, a forerunner of the Capones. As Terry Del Bene said to me, "He was the Tony Soprano of his day."

For Further Reading:
The Civil War or The War of the Rebellion
The Indian War of 1864 - Eugene Ware
Shutters West - Nina Hull Miller (picture of Morrow)
The Internet Search Machines

Thanks to Paul Miller, Terry Del Bene and the SW County Museum staff for their help on the Jack Morrow story.

THE WAY IT WAS: GREEN RIVER 1941

By: Marna Grubb

Life in the small community of Green River was nearly normal in 1941, with citizens unable to know that December 7th would make a big change in their lives and that of the world.

Although, in reviewing issues of *The Green River Star*, I find in January 1941, Steve Nitse, assistant state director and Green River chairman of the Greek War Relief Assoc., had already collected $1,200 to be used by the civilians in war-stricken Greece.

Also in January, I found that a letter had been received from a young girl in England expressing gratefulness for the aid which Americans were giving to England civilians during German air raids over England when she lost all her clothing. She had received one of the many hand-knitted sweaters from Green River.

January, 1941, had been ushered in with temperatures plunging to 21 degrees below zero as reported by William Hutton Jr., government weather observer in Green River.

The Isis Theater was advertising Gary Cooper in *The Westerner*, with the latest Paramount News, Color Cartoon and Community Sing.

Some of the larger ads for businesses included Y-Bing Cafe (home of good steaks and chops), Utah Power & Light Company (ready to do our part in the National Defense Program), Tomahawk Pharmacy (bottle of Wild Root for 79 cents), Piggly Wiggly Food Store (2# of lard for 19 cents), Red Feather Cafe & Garden (Delicious Food! Expertly Cooked! Reasonable Prices! Fine Liquor!), State Bank of Green River (oldest bank in Sweetwater County), Penneys (white goods sale, sheets $1.00), Mrs. E. A. Gaensslen Ladies' Shoppe (just arrived, suits, dresses, hats), Castle Rock Baking Company (fruit-filled coffee rings for 20 cents), Shanghai Cafe (excellent food), Green River Electric (Jimmy Yates was advertising Flat Plate Ironers for $124.95), White Brothers O. P. Skaggs Food Store (1# Schillings coffee for 25 cents), Green River Mercantile (ladies winter coats for $8.90, snow suits for $1.59), Up-to-Date Store (Steve Nitse advertising 3# can Spry for 54 cents), Meadow Brook Dairy (gallon delicious Meadow Brook ice cream for $1.25), Kemp Motor Company (1938 Deluxe Ford $599), Moedl Drug Store (Lifebuoy, 3 for 19 cents), Grant's Beauty Salon (shampoo, finger wave, manicure for $1.50), and Covey's Little America (coffee shop and Palm Room for banquets).

Town Council meetings showed William Rogers as Mayor and Council members were E. A. Elliott, Lyman Fearn, George Cottle and H. Hermansen. Mayor Rogers was returned to office in the May election, and Joe Desmond replaced George Cottle as Councilman. Chris Jessen was Marshal and Roy Cameron was Fire Chief.

Editor of *The Green River Star* was Raymond M. Davis, with Mrs. Raymond M. Davis as Business Manager. Later in the year, Arne Oja was Business Manager.

In February, Dr. Sudman had the Green River CCC Camp under quarantine due to an epidemic of flu that had about 40 out of 195 men down at one time. The buildings at the camp had been stained spruce green and were now being trimmed in white.

The 10th Annual Southwestern Wyoming District Basketball Tournament was held in Green River on March 5, 6, 7 & 8 with 18 teams competing. The Green River Wolves, winner of 5th place, placed one player, Howard Braden, on the all-tournament team. Tony Katana and Jimmy Reese were placed from Rock Springs.

In April, it was announced that 125,000 ties would be floated down the Green River in May to the tie booms in Green River in the final tie drive to be conducted by the Standard Timber Company.

The ties were waiting at LaBarge Creek for high water expected about May 1.

The Highway Commission appropriated $170,000 for reconstruction of a 10-mile stretch of the Lincoln Highway immediately west of Green River to eliminate several dangerous curves on which fatal accidents had occurred. Work commenced in the Fall.

The April 26 edition of *The Rock Springs Daily Rocket* had headlines of the British troops leaving Athens under a constant blasting attack of German bombers after battling gallantly for 20 days against the Nazi blitz driving nearer to this ancient city.
In a message from Tokyo, the Japanese were of the opinion that the United States would soon be engaged in open hostilities with Germany. It was admitted that this would pose a grave question for Japan because of her commitment to Germany and Italy un-

der the three-power pact.

Back to *The Green River Star*, Green River residents okayed a $125,000 Bond Issue by a vote of 234 to 44 to construct a new high school in Green River to replace the one which had burned down in October of the previous year. Excavation began in May for the Lincoln High School.

Announcement was made in June that the Green River CCC camp would be abandoned in July.

In July, Robert D. Pike, a nationally-known consulting chemical engineer from Pittsburgh, reported that a "great chemical industry" could be developed in Green River. Pike revealed that it is the site of the world's largest trona deposits. Trona was said to be the name used to describe a deposit containing sodium carbonate and sodium bicarbonate.

On August 3, a veritable cosmopolitan hotel on wheels, the sleek new 17-car streamliner "City of Los Angeles," entered service between Chicago and Los Angeles, traveling through Green River.

In September, the "Big Boy" world's largest and most pow-erful locomotive began operating over the Union Pacific Railroad lines on regular runs through Green River. It met the need for greater speed and pulling power to handle freight loads over the mountain grades of Wyoming and Utah.

December 7, 1941 - the Japanese bombed Pearl Harbor. Wyoming Governor Smith moved swiftly to place Wyoming on a full war-time basis and actions were taken to prevent any acts of sabotage. Immediately, all alien Japanese in Wyoming were required to register with law enforcement. Sweetwater County youths swamped the recruiting offices.

PRESIDENT ROOSEVELT'S "NEW DEAL" BROUGHT ABOUT CCC CAMP GREEN RIVER:

Franklin D. Roosevelt was president of the United States from 1933 to 1945. He took office in the height of the "Great Depression." To turn things around, he came up with the "New Deal" and bill after bill was passed.

The CCC (Civilian Conservation Corps) was formed at this time which put over three million young men and adults to work in the 1930s and 1940s.

Eventually there were camps in all states– over 2,650 camps performing more than 100 kinds of work.

In 1941, the need for training the CCC was being questioned when unemployment had practically disappeared and defense came first.

Announcement was made in June of 1941 that the CCC Camp Green Riiver would be abandoned in July. (Sweetwater County Historical Museum photo)

GREEN RIVER'S CCC CAMP

Green River's CCC Camp was located southeast of the railroad tracks and can be seen in the 1938 photo below.

CCC Camps throughout the United States were formed in the 1930s to provide work for millions of young men and adults as President Roosevelt tried to bring the nation out of the "Great Depression."

Some of their accomplishments nationwide included 3,470 fire towers erected, 97,000 miles of fire roads built, 4,235,000 hours devoted to fighting fires, and more than three billion trees planted.

Outstanding contributions were made in the development of recreational facilities and parks.

There were 7,153,000 man-days expended on other conservation activities. These included protection of range for the Grazing Service, protecting the natural habitats of wildlife, stream improvements, restocking of fish, and building small dams for water conservation.

(Sweetwater County Historical Museum photo)

In 1941, the need for retaining the CCC was questioned as unemployment had practically disappeared. Congress abolished the CCC by July 1, 1942. Green River's Camp had already closed the summer of 1941.

Many chose to remain in the towns near their camps. They married, raised families, and put down their roots. Others took their brides back to their home areas, returning as confident and successful individuals.

Green River CCC Camp, Co. 678 recruits in 1939. (Sweetwater County Historical Museum photo)

SPRING GAMES

By: Bill Duncan

Del bounced around outside of the circle, firing his shooter like a pump action Red Ryder B-B gun. "Evers!" He cried, "Get out of my damn way, Evers!" My favorite marbles flew outside the bull ring scratched in the dirt and into his cloth bag, first my clear cherry, then my favorite bulls-eye agate, then the amber cleery. Every marble that I had anted up now belonged to Del.

Experts like Del shot with their shooter cradled on top of their index finger, thumb cocked to propel the missile marble at blazing speeds to knock the target out of a circle, off the line or into a hole. Novices like me shot with the shooter perched perilously in the crook of an index finger with neither the speed nor accuracy.

My favorite game, "holes" anted marbles in the center hole with four holes equidistant from it, like the five on dice. In kind of a marble croquet we would go around the outside holes, knocking opponents out of the field while making the round. The first one around got to keep the marbles in the middle hole. Our playground looked like someone had thrown a Yatzee in fives. Holes pocked soft parts of the playground in the same pattern.

Marbles had their own language. The player who said "Evers" first could dictate some of the rules. I liked to say, "Evers, slips go over," first, so I could reshoot one that just dribbled away from my hand. Fudge wasn't something to eat, it meant "snudging" your shooting hand over the line. "Uppers" or "ups" meant you could put your shooting hand on top of the wrist of your other hand for added height and velocity. It was possible (probable) for me to forget my homework for the day, but never my marble bag.

Although a few girls could shoot marbles as well as boys, most girls played jacks. The game involved bouncing a squishy rubber ball and picking up little several pointed jacks while the ball was still in the air. The games progression picked up one more jack with each throw. If you were really good, you could do "pigs 'n pen", "horses over the fence", and "'round about." Technology gave poorer jacks players an extra lift when Super Ball came out. These brightly colored gems could bounce at least three times as high as the old, soft, red rubber ones.

May was the peak of the playground sports season in grade

school. Games required speed and agility or power and strength. Tag-based games like tag, shadow tag, drop the handkerchief, run sheepie run, duck duck goose, red light green light, fox and geese (usually a snow game), and steal the bacon gave the quick, agile kids a chance for success. Brute power games that required breaking lock hands or hitting someone with a ball like red rover, pump pump pullaway (pom pom pullaway), crack the whip (sometimes an ice skating game), or dodge ball and tether ball gave stronger kids an edge.

Annie Annie over (ante I over) was one of the few games that combined skills and was a team game to boot. We threw a ball over a house roof, much easier in the bungalow days, crying "Annie Annie over." If the ball didn't go over, the throwers cried "Pigtail" and threw again. The other side caught the ball and ran around to the other side of the house, trying to hit members of the other team with the ball.

Nothing is more delicious than the soft, spring, Green River nights just after the sun goes down. It's the kind of evening where your mother makes sure you have a jacket, but you hang it on a bush so you can run faster while playing Kick the Can. The can, a battered tomato or vegetable soup can, sat in the middle of a street intersection. "It" kicked the can first, and then the others tried to kick the can before "it" tagged them.

Up until about 15 or 20 years ago, Green River kids (usually girls) chalked Hop-scotch patterns on the sidewalks or on the paved parts of the playgrounds. They then threw rocks into the nearer squares before hopping out to pick the rocks up. The winner was the one who could throw her rock farthest, hop out without touching any line, pick up the rock and get home without hitting a line or falling on her nose. Earlier game rules called for the pebbles to be kicked out of the grid with the hopping foot.

In those days before half-pipes, skate boards or even in-line skates, roller skates clamped on the sole of your shoe. A key, hung on a string around the neck so you wouldn't lose it, tightened the clamps so that the leather strap fit snugly over your foot and the buckle at your ankle was tight. Alton Hermansen tells of skating around the (Green River) Merc block because the sidewalk surface was the best there. A fast surface was at a premium since most streets were dirt, and sidewalks and curbs were in short supply.

Green River had indoor rinks a couple of places over the

years. One was at the Expedition Island building and another was south of Convenience Corner. But nothing could compare to those early summer evenings after the stores had closed and the pedestrians had gone home. It was a fast, smooth track "under the arc lights" around the Merc block until mothers called, blew whistles or rang bells summoning skaters home.

Before Little League, uniforms, coaches and adults, we played baseball workup. We negotiated (argued, bullied, gave-in) positions. At each out, players progressed from the outfield to third base, around the infield to catcher and pitcher. After the out the pitcher joined the batters. If you hit and got around the bases, you could bat again.

If teams needed chosen, yesterday's kids relied on hands up the baseball bat, or rhymes like one potato-two potato, and enie, meanie, minie, mo. Numbering-off seemed to be saved for teacher-directed activity.

Jumping rope has survived, thanks to PE classes and Jump Rope for Heart. Some jumping rhymes have survived like "A is for Alice" and "Mother May I." Double Dutch (two ropes at the same time) has also survived on the playground.

Increased safety concerns means today's playgrounds lack teeter totters, merry-go-rounds, and hard balls. Plastic has replaced wooden and metal equipment. Slides and monkey bars are safer and have softer landing areas.

Today's kids play good and bad pokemon or power puff girls. They act out skits from movies like Harry Potter or Power Rangers, much more complex than the old war games or cowboys and Indians, isn't it? Soccer has replaced kickball most of the time. Basketball hoops abound both at home and at school. But if you look closely on the lawns adjoining summer baseball and fall football games, you can see kids playing tag, pick up football, or chase.

Speedy, agile kids still excel at grab and chase tag games. Stronger ones wrestle or wrench the item of another's grasp. But more youngsters are interested in hand-held video games than playing catch. Marbles are just something their parents talk about.

And what's happened to Del McOmie? He was still winning, only now he was doing it in the State Legislature as a Fremont County representative.

IN DEFENSE OF FREEDOM

By: Terry Del Bene

Warriors! You are defending religion, the country, and freedom! I am with you. God is against the aggressor. (Tsar Alexander 1812)

How odd it is here in 2002 with our country in a struggle against terrorists to reflect on the historical records regarding the motivations for soldiers to fight. The above quote is attributed to Tsar Alexander as he prepared his country to throw back the invasion of the armies of Napoleon I, Emperor of the French and his European allies. Napoleon had previously declared the campaign to be the start of the Second Polish War and ostensibly had set his armies in motion to liberate Poland from Russia and to crush the Tsar's influence in eastern Europe. It is curious that two of the most despotic individuals on earth chose to couch their struggle in terms of freedom and liberation. It was not by accident.

Freedom as we understand it in 21st Century America did not exist within the borders of Imperial Russia or Imperial France. The Russian serfs would have to wait roughly 50 more years before they would be emancipated (at least in name). Some say the struggle in that country is still in progress. Subjects of Imperial France had a few rights. However these were being crushed under Napoleon's continuing demands for conscripts and money to prosecute his seemingly endless series of wars. In 1812, the only democracy on the planet was a struggling and young government called the United States of America, then at war with the British Empire. The only democracy had a major flaw, slavery was legal. The conflict of having slavery within a free country would almost destroy the nation. The depth of the contradiction is perhaps best characterized by the speech below.

What, to the American slave, is your Fourth of July? I answer: a day that reveals to him, more than all other days in the year, the gross injustice and cruelty to which he is the constant victim. To him, your celebration is a sham; your boasted liberty, an unholy license; your national greatness, swelling vanity; your sounds of rejoicing are empty and heartless; your denunciation of tyrants, brass-fronted impudence; your shouts of liberty and equality, hollow mockery; your prayers and hymns, your sermons and thanksgivings, with all your religious parade and solemnity, are, to Him, mere bombast, fraud, deception, impiety, and hypocrisy-a thin veil to cover up crimes which would disgrace a nation of savages. There is not a nation on the earth guilty of practices more shocking and bloody than are the people of the United States at this very hour. (Frederick Douglass speaking July 4, 1841)

As the above indicates, the issue of what constituted freedom would play large in American politics through the middle of the 19th century. Freedom seems to appear most in foreign speeches in the context of warfare or during the many liberation movements of the period.

The issue before us is one of no ordinary character. We are not engaged in a conflict for conquest, or for aggrandizement, or for the settlement of a point of international law. The question for you to decide is, "will you be slaves or will you be independent?" Will you transmit to your children the freedom and equality which your fathers transmitted to you or will you bow down in adoration before an idol baser than ever was worshipped by Eastern idolators? -(Jefferson Davis, President of the Confederate States of America 1862)

After decades of sectional squabbling over the issue of slavery and its management the nation split in 1860. The resulting war was America's most costly. The issues of liberty and freedom played large for the participants on both sides. Abraham Lincoln seized upon the idea of freeing the slaves only after it was clear the war was bound to be a long one. The emancipation issue did much to aggrandize the Northern cause from a Constitutional argument to a fight for liberty. Similarly the Confederate government sought to couch the war as a struggle for freedom from the tyranny of a government it had cast off. Below is a quote from Jefferson Davis in 1862 which makes claim that the Northern cause was extra-legal, conquest-based, and even against the rules of civilization. All this was said at a time when the North essentially was keeping one-hand tied behind its back in prosecuting the war. The excesses of Atlanta and the marches through Georgia and South Carolina were yet years in the future.

You have been involved in a war waged for the gratification of the lust of power and of aggrandizement, for your conquest and your subjugation, with a malignant ferocity and with a disregard and a contempt of the usages of civilization, entirely unequalled in history. Such, I have ever warned you, were the characteristics of the Northern people--of those with whom our ancestors entered into a Union of consent, and with whom they formed a constitutional compact. Jefferson Davis 1862

Alexander Stephens, Confederate Vice President, presented some of the more frank speeches about the nature of the Confederacy. In his famous "cornerstone speech" he indicates that the Confederacy is built upon the fundamental truth that the races were not equal. In subsequent speeches he turned to a theme that the Confederacy was similar to the fledgling United States in its patriotic fervor "with the same spirit animating the breast of the people; devotion to liberty and right, hatred of tyranny and oppression." It is difficult to conjure the image of those seeking to keep an entire people in bondage indicating that they were doing so out of a hatred of oppression. Yet, this was a common view at the time and has its supporters to this day.

The American leaders (as with Tsar Alexander and Napoleon before them) recognized that soldiers and the populace are inspired by thinking they are sacrificing their all for freedom and liberty. The historical record is filled with examples of these motivations being used to inspire the participants in wars. World leaders such as Lenin, Hussein, Hitler, Mao, Sharon, Arafat, Castro, and many others have all played forms of the liberty card in their attempts to inspire their people. It appears that any group which brings a different way of life, language, religion, or even a different system of government is considered a threat to freedom; even when that freedom is the liberty to live under an autocratic dictator or comes at the cost of liberties for another population. It seems no matter how undemocratic or oppressive the system the leaders recognize the great importance of liberty to their people. This pattern will continue through our current conflicts and, no doubt, will be a characteristic of future disputes. So, why do people sacrifice and fight? For freedom of course. It is the most precious commodity on the planet... keep it always in your heart.

SEPTICEMIA AND SNAKE OIL: MEDICAL CARE IN EARLY GREEN RIVER

By: Ruth Lauritzen

Gravelle Drug in the early 1900s. After founder George G. Gravelle, Sr.'s death in 1878, the business was operated first by his widow, Martha and later by his son George G. Gravelle Jr. (P2hoto courtesy Sweetwater County Historical Museum)

The history of medicine is a tale of suspicion being slowly overcome by science. At the beginning of the nineteenth century the standard practice for healing involved bloodletting with leeches or suction cups, blistering of the skin with hot plasters and purging by inducing vomiting. Often times the cure was considered worse than the disease and the medical profession was, understandably, viewed with great suspicion.

Through much of the nineteenth century formal medical training was haphazard at best. Medical schools had very elementary admission requirements and courses were extremely brief in comparison to accepted practices today. There was very little regulation and just about anyone could call himself a doctor.

George Gideon Gravelle, Sr. was a pharmacist by trade, but oft-times served as community physician in the early days of Green River. (Photo courtesy Sweetwater County Historical Museum)

Most of the trained physicians kept to the settled parts of the United States and so the situation in the rural West was even more difficult. An article, which appeared in the *Laramie Weekly Sentinel*, Laramie City, Wyoming Territory dated July 10, 1876, reported a story which illustrated this situation in Green River. It reports that "Dr. Gravelle, though only professes to be a druggist and chemist, is compelled to do all the medical practice in that region, which gives him his hands full."

This would have been George Gideon Gravelle, Sr. who had come to Green River from South Pass shortly after the establishment of the town and opened an apothecary shop. The story continues:

> While at Green River we were requested to call to see a poor fellow who had been hurt by a train. He was a young man, twenty-five or thirty years of age. He belonged to the "Genus" tramp. Was trying to beat a ride on the train and was discovered; as the train was being stopped to put him off, he attempted to jump, was caught by a wheel and had the whole calf of his leg torn off.
>
> He was taken to Green River and deposited in the jail as the best accommodations they had. There was no doctor, and he had no money to send for one. Mr. Gravelle did what he could for him. When we entered the room where he lay, the stench from his wounded leg was intolerable, and when exposed we found the crushed limb alive with maggots.
>
> It was too late to do anything for him. The poor fellow was con-

scious of his approaching end and terribly anxious to see a priest, but one could not be procured. He died that night before we left the town.

Incidentally, Gravelle did not long outlive the unfortunate young man. He died in 1878 of a kidney ailment, leaving a widow, Martha Baker Gravelle, to carry on with the business which she did until her death in 1910.

By the 1880s the entire field of medicine was undergoing a change. Medical schools were beginning to require a standardized three-year course of study and had instituted entrance exams. Medical practice was becoming increasingly based on scientific fact. The real causes of disease were being discovered and accepted, and advancements in anesthesia and surgical methods and new drugs such as salicylic acid, (later refined into aspirin) were making the medical profession just that, more professional and treatments more reliably helpful. This in turn increased the public's respect for physicians and faith in their abilities.

Green River's earlies physicians were those brought in by the Union Pacific Railroad. Many of their names are lost to history, but the stories of some of them have been preserved. Dr. John H. Gilligan was born and took his medical training in Ireland. He came to Green River in the early 1880s as a UP contract physician. He continued in this capacity until 1888 when he went into private practice. He married in 1891 to Martha Rebecca Baker who, interestingly enough, was stepdaughter to George Gravelle, Sr.

John H. Gilligan was an early contract physician for th eUnion Pacific Railroad and maintained a practice in Green River for most of his life. He also took an interest in community affairs, serving as Mayor. (Photo courtesy Sweetwater County Historical Museum)

They left Green River for a time, eventually returning in 1913. He maintained an active practice here until 1939 when he retired at age 80. His interests also went beyond medicine. He was a sheep rancher and mayor of Green River in 1901-02. A newspaper article of unknown origin in the files of the Sweetwater County Historical Museum tells of his life at his 90th birthday in 1946.

> Gun battle wounds, injuries from runaway horses, range and early day railroad accidents, gave way during his time to treating injuries from speeding automobiles and and more modern causes. Acute indigestion has become appendicitis, extreme forms of la grippe the dread influenza–and the town of straggling dirt streets is a small city of paved streets, with modern buildings. The tiny railroad trains of his first days have given way to freights of 100 or more cars, to streamliners and high speed conventional trains drawn by locomotives as long as some of the passenger trains of those days.

Gilligan died June 30, 1949 in Green River.

A husband and wife team of physicians began their employment with the Union Pacific Railroad in 1896. Dr. Jacob Hawk was born in Mahaska County, Iowa and received his degree from the College of Physicians and Surgeons at Keokuk, Iowa in 1882. He was Railroad Surgeon at Green River and District Surgeon for the Oregon Short Line as well as serving as County Health Commissioner, County Physician and Examinging Surgeon for the selective draft in Sweetwater County. He also served in the state legislature and as mayor of Green River for three terms. He had business interests as well, serving on the board of directors of the First National Bank of Green River and, with Mr. Tom Welsh, built the Tomahawk Hotel, the name of which is a combination of the two investors' names. He died in May of 1925 at the age of 68.

Dr. Charlotte Gardner Hawk served as Assistant Railroad Surgeon at Green River for 29 years, from 1896 to 1938. Dr. Charlotte, as she was known, graduated from Northwestern University and studied medicine in New York. She practiced for eight years in Denver before coming to Green River with her husband. Stories of her experiences were told in a previous column. At one time the Hawks ran a four-bed hospital in the basement of their home on the corner of 1st East and 3rd North (present locaiton of the parking lot for City Hall). An ad in a 1907 *Wyoming Star* reports that the two physicians could be contacted by leaving a call at a local drug store. This apparently was common practice as a similar statement appears in another physician's ad, a Dr. E. Crawford who was also practicing in Green River at the same time.

The second floor offices in the Morris Mercantile building, (located at 1st West and Railroad Avenue prior to its destruction by fire in 1917) were also home to several doctors's offices. Information about these men can be gleaned from advertisements in the local newspaper. Dr. B. G. Benson opened his practice in Green River in 1891. His ad states he was "...late of Heidelberg, Germany". His hours of business are given as "9 to 11 a.m. 2 to 4 and 7 to 8:30 p.m."

A January 6, 1911 advertisement tells of the opening of the practice of Dr. A.C. Kelly.

> Dr. A.C. Kelly who but recently opened an office in the Morris Block graduated from the Medical Department of the University of Illinois, after which he was Resident Physician of the St. Elizabeth Hospital, Chicago, Illinois, coming to Wyoming, was in charge of the Wyoming General Hospital at Rock Springs for two years before opening his office in this city. The doctor has a beautifully furninshed office, equipped with all the latest instruments necessary in the profession of Physician and Surgeon, doctor ready to wait upon them in a most satisfactory manner. Calls received by telegraph, phone or letter will always receive the doctor's prompt attention.

Other aspects of medical care can be gleaned from various sources. In a 1976 *Green River Star* article, long-time resident Eleanor Gaensslen Schofield recalled the "pest house," an old house that stood at the approximate location of the U.S. Bank building on present day Uinta Drive.

> That's where they used to take smallpox and diphtheria victims. There were three or four doctors in town., but they couldn't do anything. No one wanted you in town with such a contagious disease so they took you to the pest house where you either lived or died.

If the advertisements in the newspaper are any indication, there was also a thriving trade in patent medicines. These medicines were available by mail order and from traveling salesmen. The purveyors of these colorfully-named concoctions, "Kickapoo

Indian Oil" and "Balsam of Myrrh" for example, claimed their products could cure everything from cancer to arthritis, and restore lost hair and "manhood" as well as develop a poorly-formed bust. These products generally contained a large percentage of alcohol as well as morphine, cocaine, and other opiates.

The passage of the 1906 Pure Food and Drug Act created the Food and Drug Administration (FDA) and gave it authority to regulate foods and drugs and required content labels on food and drugs. According to the FDA, this "...resulted in the demise of the patent medicine industry". However, a 1907 issue of the *Wyoming Star* shows ads for Lydia E. Pinkham's Vegetable Compound to "...prevent serious derangement of the whole female organism," and "Ballard's Snow Liniment", a "quick and permanent cure for Rheumatism, Cuts, Sprains, Wounds, Neuralgia, Headache, Old Sores, Corns, Bunions, Galls, Bruises, Contracted Muscles, Lame Back, Stiff Joints, Frost Bite, Chilblains, Ringbone, Pollevil, Burns, Scalds and ALL THE ILLS THAT FLESH IS HEIR TO." It appears that the Pure Food and Drug Act may have changed the patent medicine industry, but it was far from gone.

Though there may be problems in the modern health care community in Green River, these are nothing compared to the conditions encountered in the town's early days. In the event of sickness or injury we are at least assured the presence of a physician and the local convenience stores carry many more effective medications than would be in a doctor's bag of the late nineteenth century. George Gravelle, Sr. could only wish he had it so good!

NIGHTMARE AT AH SAY

By: Bill Thompson/Duke Yowell, guest author

My guest author is Duke Yowell. He and his wife Mollie are covered in Echos vol.1, pgs 247-9 by Marna Grubb. Welcome Duke.

The date was December 6, 1905, and as derailments go it didn't amount to very much. However, the eight freight cars that left the track effectively blocked the Union Pacific main line in Echo Canyon, east of Ogden, Utah, long enough for First and Second No. 10, No. 6 and No.2 (The Overland Limited) to reach the first station west of the blockade. The track was eventually cleared and the four delayed trains moved eastward, just a few minutes apart, racing into the night toward what was to become one of the worst train wrecks in Wyoming history.

At that time the final player in this tragedy moved into position on the siding at Ah Say, between Green River and Rock Springs, Wyoming. Westbound freight train Extra 1658 had received orders to take the siding at Ah Say and to stay there until First and Second No. 10, No. 6 and No. 2 had passed.

It was after midnight, December 7, 1905, when the four first class trains left Green River running ten minutes apart with right over opposing trains. First and Second No. 10 and No. 6 passed the siding at Ah Say without mishap. At this time the gravest of mistakes was made. After three trains had passed Ah Say, the engineer on Extra 1658 gave the signal to move out onto the single track, heading west. The head brakeman opened the switch and the train left the siding. The conductor was in the caboose and had only checked three trains by, but concluded he was wrong and that the engineer was right. Without a second thought he allowed the train to continue. Extra 1658 was moving west at fifteen miles per hour when, approximately 1 mile east of Wilkins Station and on a curve, Extra 1658 west struck passenger train No. 2 head on. No. 2 was speeding to pick up time and was traveling about 50 miles per hour. A local newspaper, *The Rock Springs Miner*, later reported heavy fog had prevented the engineer on No. 2 from seeing the headlight on Extra 16513 West.

The story broke in a special dispatch from Cheyenne to the *Omaha World-Herald* in Omaha, Nebraska, with great impact. This was followed by reports from the *Cheyenne Leader* and the *Rock Springs Miner*. Other morning newspapers all over the country shocked and horrified their readers with the graphic word of the tragedy. Telegraph operations copied the dots and dashes releasing the story to an entire population whose attention hung on every word.

According to the *Omaha World Herald*, the Overland Limited was running at full speed in an effort to make up time, and the freight train had attained high speed down the hill. The crash was terrible; the big locomotives literally plowing through each other and the cars behind carrying death and destruction with them. The mail cars, combination baggage/dynamo and buffer car and the dining car following were crushed like eggshells and the first ten or twelve freight cars, all heavily loaded with Pacific coast mer-

Train wreck at Ah Say, a rail siding between Green River and Rock Springs, in 1905. (Photo courtesy Stimpson Collection, Wyoming State Archives)

chandise, were transformed into kindling wood in seconds.

The electricians, the dining car cooks and three postal clerks were picked up and carried along by the splintered cars and mass of broken and twisted iron to death or horrible injury.

The engines of the two trains, freight cars, the baggage, mail and dining cars and one Pullman car of the Overland Limited were derailed and piled in a heap, with the exception of the Pullman car which rolled down the embankment. In the latter car were the passengers who were injured. A gas tank under the dining car exploded and set the wreckage on fire. The baggage, mail and dining cars were consumed in the fire and with them the cremated bodies of eight of the dead. None of these could be identified. It was thought that one of the mail clerks was not in the mail car at the time of the collision. Immediately after the wreck a person was reported to have fled the scene heading south toward the badlands and the mountain. This was never confirmed.

The darkness of the night lay heavily upon the wreckage leaving 10 dead and 18 injured. The Coroner's verdict, issued a few day later, contained the following conclusion:

> After viewing the bodies and place of accident and hearing the testimony of the witnesses, do find that the deceased persons came to their death about 2:20 AM, December 7, 1905, at about one mile east of Wilkins Station, Sweetwater County in the State of Wyoming on The Union Pacific Railroad, and we find that the freight engineer and freight brakeman came to their death from injuries received by collision. The remaining 8 came to their death either by direct injuries received from the collision, or by fire resulting from the collision.

In a few days following the disaster, three of the remaining eight burned bodies were identified and were taken to their homes for burial. The remaining five were placed in separate caskets, given a brief funeral and buried in the Rock Springs cemetery. A memorial stone was placed at the site of their internment bearing the following inscription:

In God's Care
Six unidentified Victims Of
The Willkins Train Wreck
December 7, 1905

It is noted that the inscription reads, "six unidentified victims", whereas the news releases accompanying the coroner's verdict said five burned bodies were buried. The brother of one of the mail clerks spent several days looking for the remains of his brother. He was not successful but did find his brother's watch. His U.S. Mail key remains missing. It was also reported that Union Pacific train No. 2 carried $90,000 in gold and that another body was found under the coal from the freight train. These reports were considered to be without foundation.

When the burned-out baggage car was opened, rescue forces were confronted with a macabre scene! The bodies of two women, one from Washington State and one from Santa Barbara, Calif., were being transported east for interment. The two bodies had been entirely cremated by the fire. The two husbands were escorting the bodies. One returned to Washington and the other continued on East.

According to the *Cheyenne Daily Leader*, dated Friday, December 8, 1905, the point at which the wreck occurred should have been equipped with automatic block signals, which were to have been installed by December 1st, but the work was delayed. The article further stated that had these signals been in place it would have been impossible for the accident to have occurred.

In conclusion:

1. Ten died in the wreck.
2. Of these 10--two (the freight engineer
and fireman) died from the collision, while the remaining eight died from the fire.
3. Of the eight burned bodies, three were identified and were taken to their homes for burial.
4. The remaining five unidentified remains were placed in separate caskets and were buried in the Rock Springs Cemetery.

In the final analysis, observations will be made, questions will be asked and conclusions will be drawn. However, these are the foundations upon which mysteries are made and we must not dwell too long on them. They must remain no more than an afterglow of the fires of our imagination.

God Bless-May they rest in peace.

THE WAY IT WAS: GREEN RIVER 1945

By: Marna Grubb

The citizens of Green River experienced a roller-coaster year during 1945 with extreme sadness along with great joys.

In reviewing 1945 issues of *The Green River Star*, I find that World War II took center stage. Each week the front page was covered with photos and news of local servicemen and women; some were injured, taken prisoner, reported missing, killed in action, while others were seeing action in France, Germany, the Battle of the Bulge, Italy, Iwo Jima, Guadalcanal, and various other fronts in the South Pacific. Green River was represented all over the world, leaving an emptiness at home, but also a feeling of pride.

In Green River, everyone was tightening their belts. The February Ration Calendar listed stamps good through March 31: Meats, Fats, etc. – Book four red stamps; Processed Foods – Book four blue stamps; Sugar – Book four stamp 34 good for 5 lbs.; Shoes – Book three airplane stamps 1, 2 and 3; Gasoline – 14A coupons good for 4 gallons, B5, C5 and C6 coupons good for 5 gallons.

Rationing in Green River was handled by Mrs. Margaret Jacobucci who headed up the local Office of Price Administration (OPA). Mrs. Edna Rhodes worked under her upstairs in the old court house.

Tragedy struck on March 5 when five-year-old Gary Widdop was on his way home from kindergarten when his school papers blew out on the river ice. He followed after them. The ice, beginning to deteriorate from the warm spring temperatures, plunged the youngster into the icy waters. His body was not recovered for more than five weeks.

In April, the nation was stunned when President Franklin D. Roosevelt died from a cerebral hemorrhage. He had held the presidency of the United States longer than any other president – 12 years, 1933-1945. Green River Mayor Edward L. Taliaferro directed a two-day period of mourning with all public dancing to be halted and public music boxes to be muted. Flags remained at half mast for one month.

Victory in Europe, V. E. Day, May 1945, was observed quietly in Green River with people expressing their joy that the fighting in Europe was over, but at the same time expressing their fears with the war in the Pacific.

Go carts were a fun way for local boys to spend the afternoon in the mid 1940s. These were home-made from wooden boards, wheels and a rope for steering. Shown in the background is the temporary housing made available for returning World War II servicemen. These were known as the Vets Apartments and were short-lived. At the top of the street is the Washington Grade School. (Sweetwater County Historical Museum/Proctor photo)

Then tragedy struck again. In June, the waters of the Green River took two more lives when an 88 degree heat wave sent two girls and others to the sandy beach on the south side of Island Park. Jane Valencia, 15, and Lucy Gomez, 21, were wading far out on the beach in high spring runoff water when they were suddenly swept from sight. Searchers recovered Jane in 40 minutes and Lucy in an hour and a half, but attempts to revive the girls were unsuccessful.

Hostilities with the Japanese ended on August 14 after the dropping of atomic bombs over Hiroshima and Nagasaki. On September 6, 1945, victors and the vanquished gathered on the U. S. battleship Missouri in Tokyo Bay to complete Japan's surrender. Three years, eight months and 26 days after Pearl Harbor, the war was over.

Green River celebrated with continuous blasts from locomotive whistles, roundhouse whistles, the Air Raid warning siren on the social hall and church bells. Special services were held at the local churches to give thanks.

Servicemen and women began jamming the rails seeking to get home by Christmas. Railroad coaches were lettered with "Thank God – We're Loose," "Dischargees!" and "On our way home – for good or worse." Many were hitchhiking.

Armistice Day in November turned into a day of appreciation for Green River citizens to join hands in welcoming home veterans who were already home and to send welcome to those who were still to arrive. There was a parade, a football game, barbecue for adults at the Social Hall and youths at the Masonic Temple, a free picture show at the Isis Theater, and dances at the high school gymnasium and Social Hall.

A memorial service was held at the high school auditorium to pay memorial tribute to those from Green River and outlying communities who had laid down their lives. Those listed on the Honor Roll were: Paul Andrews, Donovan Astle, Darrell Barnhart, Dick Behunin, Robert Bramwell, Floyd Hoover, Bert Jensen, Melvin Likes, John Logan, Ernest Pelser, Lafe Potter, Howard Schultz, Guido Sebastian and Jerry Tripp. Tech Sergeant Jesse Stewart was preparing a story of his life in the prison camps of Japan.

A message from Harry Foster of Green River's PAY N' SAVE said it all. "Let us be thankful that we attained a decisive Victory – that freedom and decency still live – that America was untouched by destruction – that we had a united will to carry on – that we had leaders of great vision – that we had men and women of courage. Let us never forget, however, that we barely attained the victory! Let us never forget that Germany was a few months behind us in developing the atomic bomb. Let us never forget that on innumerable occasions in both wars, our battles were won with very slender margins."

THEY DON'T MAKE KRUMBLES ANYMORE

By: Bill Duncan

The soggy Wheaties in the bowl in front of me were not going away. I pouted. I whined, "Mom, why don't we ever have Krumbles?" In one breath she answered, "Eat-your-cereal-or-you'll-be-having-it-for-lunch-they're-not-on-the-shelf-anymore."

I checked the next time she sent me to Dell's Market. Cheerios, Wheaties, Puffed Wheat and Rice, All Bran, ...but no Krumbles. I still miss the dark, narrow ribbons of malty tasting crunch.

Actually, any cold cereal was a treat. Usually we ate hot cereal: Zoom (I was sure it was mostly sawdust); what my Dad called "spotted dog" (his way of making Cream of Wheat more tasty by adding raisins); Wheat Hearts (tasty lumps of goodness—my favorite--and not available anymore either); or oatmeal.

Grandmother Duncan loved her oatmeal. Grandfather cooked it overnight in a double boiler at the back of the wood-fired kitchen stove. She would dip a tablespoonful of liberally sugared oatmeal in a teacup of sweet cream, then pop it into her mouth with great enjoyment. But, I doubt she would have bothered with today's cereal and milk bar that sandwiches "milk" between two layers of sugarcoated cereal. Nor would she have given a second look at the seventeen or so different oatmeal flavors on today's shelves. "Porridge is good as it is, especially with cream and sugar," she often told me.

Hurry and bustle have changed today's breakfast choices. We can fix an Instant Breakfast drink, frozen Breakfast in a Bowl, Tang, Instant Oatmeal and two minute Cream of Wheat. Is that quicker than instant? Now we can rush through breakfast to stand in line waiting for a double latte or cinnamon cappuccino.

Does any body else miss Black Jack gum besides me? Clove flavor has been replaced by "Ice", strongly reminiscent of Vicks Vapo-Rub. Chewing Pepsin-flavored gum aided digestion. My wife's favorite, Teaberry, occasionally makes a momentary appearance among the boxes of gum flavors that have stood the test of time: Spearmint, Doublemint and Juicy Fruit.

I miss Spudnuts--a raised, potato-flour circle of goodness for just a nickel. Glazed or sugared – it didn't matter. Two of us could ante up 30 cents each and scarf down the baker's dozen after school. Enough to hold off the hunger pangs until supper. Today's kids drooling over Krispy Kremes will never know the pleasure of Spudnuts plunged in and out of the hot grease, dipped through the glaze, dropped in the bag and popped into your mouth with assembly line speed.

Speaking of sweet things, every kid had a store to stop by on the way to school. It might have been the Handy Store or Johnson's Variety on the North Side or Hilltop or Kalivas's on the South Side. We could get huge chunks of banana or grape taffy for just a penny. Round, multi-colored candy pellets, held in by a small cork, filled realistic glass cars and guns. We wore huge wax lips as a joke, then chewed them later. Kids bought small wax bottles filled with flavored sweet syrup to drain and chew at recess.

Candy cigarettes (white with a red tip, no filter) gave us a chance to act more grown up. We found refreshment in an envelope of Lick-Em-Aid. A nickel's worth of bubble gum or an all day sucker lasted until after school (Spudnut time).

Remember when Log Cabin Syrup actually came in a cute metal "log cabin" container? The pour spout was the chimney on the end of the can. Lard came in ten lb. buckets. Every family had a "fat can" on the stove to keep grease in until time to fry the next batch of chicken, potatoes, or steak.

It's socially acceptable nowadays to carry a plastic water bottle with you to class, concerts, ball games, church and most anywhere else. When I was little and we were starting a car trip, my job was to soak, then fill the canvas water bag. It hung outside of the car on the rear view mirror or from the hood ornament in front of the grille. Drinking today's flavorless (even if it's juiced or sugared) water from a plastic bottle can't compare with taking the cork out of the metal hole at the top of the bag to let the cool water run down your throat and shirt front. Now that water had character.

One of my bosses used to tell me, "Things aren't as good as they used to be...and maybe they never were." I don't miss some of the personal hygiene products. Remember dipping your fingers into a glass tub of Mum or Arid to apply underarm deodorant? And how about tooth powder? Getting the proper amount out of the slot atop the metal can was a challenge. I was taught to pour the powder into the palm of my hand and then swipe it up with my toothbrush. Wasn't it faster to just pour it directly on the toothbrush? Some people I know talk longingly of missing McClean's toothpaste. An older friend wishes Ipana were still available.

Burma-Shave cream came in a tube. The company was famous for entertaining motorists with rhyming, humorous signs. They were always in a series of four or five white on red signs along side the highways--the last sign always had the Burma-Shave logo. "Listen bud,....these signs....cost money....so roost awhile....but don't get funny." Guys only needed to squeeze the right amount of Burma-Shave onto their fingers, spread onto the face and enjoy a "smooth, refreshing shave" with a Gillette double-edged safety razor. After scraping and rinsing, men slapped their faces with some stinging, alcohol-laced, perfumed, aftershave lotion, like Aqua Velva, Old Spice or Hai Karate. Men also used their fingers to apply Vitalis, Brylcream ("a little dab'll do ya') to their hair or Butch Wax, a perfumed, stiff jelly that made "crew-cut" hair stand straight up.

My brothers and I love to reminisce about the time you could get a set of china dishes if you bought enough oatmeal or soap because the dishes came right in the box. Tom and I talk of the colorful art on the end of orange crates and wonder where bushel baskets went. Bob and I discuss the evolution of beer cans from church key to push tabs to pull tops. We look anxiously for the white Double K nut cases with the heat lights, carousels of cashews or mixed nuts with a scale on top.

Of course modern store shelves are filled with new, wonderful products—but only those that sell well. You can eat a different TV dinner each day of the month. You can start your day with a different breakfast each morning of the year.

But they don't have Spudnuts. With their mega shelves and massive floor space, wouldn't you think there might be room for a box or two of Krumbles?

ON THE CHEROKEE TRAIL NEAR GREEN RIVER

By: Terry A. Del Bene

Green River and Rock Springs 1850

Those of us who travel the Interstate 80 corridor would have had trouble recognizing the place in the mid-nineteenth century. The convergence of the highway, railroads, and countless other developments through the past decades have transformed this area. Let us travel this area for two days in 1850. As far as history goes these might represent the original echoes from the bluffs.

Our correspondents are William Minor Quesenbury and James Mitchell. These men and their companions pioneered one of the Cherokee Trail routes to the California gold fields. Both men started their trek with companies emigrating from the Cherokee Nation in Indian Territory. I have kept the original spelling of the texts. For those not used to nineteenth century documents, if you read the text aloud you should be able to grasp the meaning. You will also note that the rules of punctuation were looser. Many sentences have no punctuation. Capitalization is unruly and occasionally a word is omitted.

Our travelers have split off from the slower moving wagon trains and are in search of a more direct route to the gold fields. They were impatient to get to the gold fields before all the good mining claims were taken. In fact, they would arrive about a month earlier than the wagon trains. They provide some of the earliest written accounts of the Green River and Rock Springs area. Additionally Quesenbury provides us with the earliest known drawings of the palisades of the Green River.

The party in which our two diarists are members spent the night of July 2, 1850 somewhere near Point of Rocks. They had just traveled up the Bitter Creek and had stopped along the way to sketch the Haystacks and Man-and-Boy Butte. The route they would establish partially would be followed in the 1860s by the Overland Trail. Our correspondents were having difficulty in finding good grass and water. They had to divert to the Haystacks to get good water from the snow pack. The romance of their adventure was wearing thin. Quesenbury wrote in his diary of the trip along the Bitter Creek, *"I am now writing in a country dreary and desolate, and from appearances waterless for a great distance, but whilst I write a number of mosquitoes are singing around. They must have been blown by a great western breeze to this place. (July 2, 1850)"*

Diary of James Mitchell July 3, 1850: *"Started Soon west again over a hilly Sandy nacid country full of curious bluffs Some of them with a little cedar on them though mostly nacid about 2 oclock we found water bad again we could scarce hold out animals when we come to it. crums broke loose and plunged in & had to be haled out with ropes not one blaid of grass could be Seen about here and we left without cooking Some of our men had eat nothing Since yesterday & ar complaining of hunger we Soon got to good grass and water worse then ever So bad that we were afraid to drink it or let our horses drink of horses graised under a Snowy mountain not than 4 or 5 miles distant they returned with Snow in their pans & good water in their Jugs. they reported good grass and water and wood under the Snow we went up and camp here our poor horses filed up here with good water & grass and we cooked to do us a day or 2 prepairing for another Scarcity of water & grass which we flt the next day."*

Diary of William Quesenbury July 3, 1850: *"We got up and saddled our animals as soon as it was light enough to do so. Struck out W. our old course. The country became no better as far as water was concerned. Passed some remarkable scenery of rocks but we were in no condition to enjoy such things.*

At one o'clock we came to a miry little stream of alkai water. Watered my animals with Crum's bucket. Ate a snack with Mr. Mitchell. There was no grass on this branch, so we left after we got out animals across which we had difficulty in doing. After travelling three or four miles our course was stopped by a bluff. Turned N. and found a going down place. Stopped at the bottom and grazed our horses for a little while, but came on and found good grass a little further over.

Took off our packs. There is water below this place about a hundred yards, but Mr. Mitchell who tasted it thinks it a mixture of every thing vile, -alum, copperas, arsenic etc. He says it is too mean to drink, to taste, or even look at. Ford and three others, Crum included have gone to some snow banks on a mountain. S.W. They have taken jugs, and expect to reach it in a mile and a half.

Whilst searching for the snow men, Mr. Mitchell lost his pistol which we found after a short hunt in the grass. Presently the snow men came back. The bank was four miles off. They brought two jugs of water and a pan or so of snow. They reported a camping place above, to which we went, finding there good wood, and tolerable water and grass."

Our two correspondents describe an area with poor water and little grass. It appears that they tried to find water in the areas between present-day Rock Springs and Superior but had to resort to a side trip to Quaking Aspen Mountain to keep themselves and the animals watered. The abundance of snow in July suggests that the winter of 1849-1850 likely was a wet one. Yet there is little water around. Perhaps the uplands received an exceptional snow cover while the basins remained relatively dry The camp of July second probably was near the Sulfur Springs near Point of Rocks, exacerbating the need for good water.

Those of us who travel the modern highway systems rarely leave the immediate corridor. Almost all needs can now be provided at travel plazas. It is astonishing to many to realize

July 4. 1850.

Near Green River

Sketch of rock formations near Green River done by William Quesenbury. (Photo courtesy *Omaha-World Herald Quesenbury Sketchbook.*)

Quesenbury sketch. (Photo courtesy *Omaha-World Herald Quesenbury Sketchbook.*)

that the emigrants passing through this area in the nineteenth century would travel so far afield to find things as simple as potable water and good grass. The emigrant trails here truly have wide corridors of use far beyond the silent ruts we now visit to commemorate the passing of these adventurers.

Diary of James Mitchell, July 4, 1850: *"we Started over a bad rocky mountain all our horses could do to get down it I lost my pistole going down it & had to go back and clime it again after it we found a good cold Spring under the west Side of this mountain but too Soon in the day to benefit us we continued our corse among the mountains west as near as we could the country curiously bluffed and all a Sandy & Salty foundasion we pased on the high lands large groves of Juniper in the evening we got to a Stree runing west without grass or watter fit for use crusted with Salt and Some poisones matter we continued down this Streem west among cliff juting up to the river So that we had to clime larg Steep hills Sometimes from the Streem on the account of these cannions on the Streem being impasable we had a plain Indian trail to gide us late in the evening when we were on a high hill we could see this Streem imtyed into a larger Streem we supposed the larger to be the mary river though when we got to it found it to be a larger Streem than we expected runing South. All agreed it must be green river fine grass was here in the river bottom and good water & wood."*

Once again Mitchell had dropped and retrieved his pistol.

Losing and regaining lost property, be it a coat or a pistol, seemed to be a recurring theme for this party of emigrants. Mitchell describes the rough terrain in the vicinity of Baxter Peak leading down to the palisades of the Green River. Having just come through hundreds of miles of land with poor water, the issue of water quality was foremost in the mind of Mitchell and his companions.

While heading west through the rough terrain the travelers are saved much wasted effort by the discovery of a path created by the first inhabitants of the area. This handy Indian trail would lead them to the current location of the City of Green River. While there Quesenbury would produce the earliest surviving sketches of Tollgate Rock, Kissing Rock, and the immediate area.

Diary of William Quesenbury- July 4, 1850: *"The Glorious Fourth! Dry times with us. Left early, going over rolling ground as usual. Went down a high steep slope. After going about a mile and a half– Mr. Mitchell discovered that the mare had shaken off his pistol again. I turned back with him and found the pistol about two thirds up the steep slope we had passed. Found our men at a spring in the high prairie on the side of a slope. The spring was exceedingly cold, clear, and pure. Rested here a few minutes, and then went on. Dreary prospect ahead.*

Travelled several miles down a hot, dry valley which was tolerably in our course, Struck over a ridge and came to another valley running W. with water in it. Followed on several miles and came in sight of a stream running apparently E. It seemed from the high lands where we were to be small– not more that twenty steps across.

Descended the highlands to the stream and camped. Before we had been here long several began to suppose we were at Green River."

This diary entry describes the trip from Quaking Aspen Mountain to the vicinity of the City of Green River. While camping here Quesenbury took the opportunity to draw several of the prominent features of the palisades of the Green River. Many other artists would follow in his footsteps. His images depict the palisades with little vegetation and many large birds flying above. One image depicts a scattering of Cottonwood Trees mixed in with the brush along the banks of the Green River.

It is not only artists who would follow in the footsteps of these adventurers. The Overland Trail would follow much of the route blazed by this party.   Soon the railroad would come, followed by the Lincoln Highway, and followed yet later by Interstate 80. How easy it is to forget the handful of would-be gold miners stumbling their way to-and-fro through the landscape we now consider home. We are most fortunate that a few paragraphs have survived the decades to remind us of our past.

SANTA CLAUS: THE MAN, THE MYTH, THE LEGEND

By: Ruth Lauritzen

The secular side of Christmas is peopled by many figures including toy soldiers, nutcrackers and elves in pointy shoes, but the preeminent figure is Santa Claus. Who is this man we all know so well and where did he come from?

There are major differences between the American Santa and older European figures of the main man of Christmas. One of the earliest European personifications was St. Nicholas, a Christian saint who is usually represented by a figure wearing a bishops' hat and vestments with a cross on his chest and carrying a shepherd's staff. Another form was Father Christmas, as he was known in England or by his German name of Weihnachstsmann. This figure was represented as a slender old man with stern facial features. He was frequently dressed in fur-trimmed knee-length coats of blue or green or black. He visited the homes of children on Christmas Eve, bringing not only toys and goodies for the good children, but also delivered and decorated the Christmas tree. Another contributor to the modern Santa was the figure of Sinterklaas, the Dutch interpretation of St. Nicholas, which was brought to the United States by the early Dutch settlers in New England. Also in the mix is Christkindle or Kris Kringle. Literally translated this means "Christ Child" and represents the Spirit of Christmas. In addition to the Santa form, Christkindle is also represented as a benevolent dwarf, elf or fairy. In this probably lies the roots of the tradition of Santa's helper elves.

The Santa Claus we know in America today was first immortalized by writer Clement Clark Moore in his poem "A Visit From St. Nick". Moore was born in 1779 as the only son of Benjamin Moore, president of Columbia College and bishop of the Protestant Episcopal Church in New York. He was a graduate of Columbia College and earned a Master Degree from there in 1801. He maried in 1813 and this poem was written in 1822 as a Christmas gift for his children.

Santa's fur clothing, rosy cheeks, twinkling eyes and "nose like a cherry" were described in loving detail as were his white beard and belly which "...shook when he laughed like a bowl full of jelly."

> He was chubby and plump, a right jolly old elf, And I laughed when I saw him, in spite of myself...

The poem also describes his arrival on Christmas Eve with his sleigh and "eight tiny reindeer" and his habits of entrance via chimney and leaving gifts for good children.

Moore's words were later given life by one of the most famous illustrators of the era, Thomas Nast. Nast immigrated to the United States from Germany in 1846. He showed early promise as an artist, but was forced to leave art school at age fifteen to support his family. This he did by working as an illustrator for *Lesley's Weekly*. He first came to prominence when he joined the staff of *Harper's Weekly Magazine* in 1862 and took the job of Civil War correspondent. Nast was well known for his political cartoons. He is responsible for several symbols in American political life including the Democratic donkey, the Republican elephant and even Uncle Sam. But it is his images of Santa Claus that he is most famous for. His multitude of drawings of Santa Claus that he completed for *Harper's Magazine* were compiled into a book called *Thomas Nast's Christmas Drawings for the Human Race* which was published in 1890.

The modern American view of Santa Claus was shaped by the work of Victorian artist, Thomas Nast.

Regardlesss of his origins (German or Dutch, Christian or pagan); his description (young or old, fat or thin, red coat or black); and even his habits, (gifts left wrapped, or unwrapped, prefers sugar cookies or chocolate chip); Santa Claus represents the fun of Christmas. He is the spirit of giving and a favorite of parents whose otherwise unruly children are as good as gold during December...at least until Christmas morning.

LINCOLN HIGHWAY CONNECTED
THE ATLANTIC TO THE PACIFIC

By: Marna Grubb

Green River and Rock Springs were two of the towns through which the Lincoln Highway traveled in Wyoming.

On July 1, 1913, the Lincoln Highway Association was organized at Detroit, Michigan, with the objective of procuring the establishment of a continuous improved highway from the Atlantic to the Pacific, open to lawful traffic of all descriptions, without toll charges, and to be a lasting memorial to Abraham Lincoln.

An announcement was made on September 14, 1913 of the route from Times Square in New York City to Lincoln Park in San Francisco, covering 3,380 miles, the first transcontinental highway. It traversed 12 states: New York, New Jersey, Pennsylvania, Ohio, Indiana, Illinois, Iowa, Nebraska, Wyoming, Utah, Nevada and California. A route change in 1928 added West Virginia.

In 1913, with the coming of the automobile, the original Lincoln Highway route through Green River had been across the railroad tracks at Elizabeth Street (later known as North First East) and Railroad Avenue. Automobiles often had to wait long intervals at the crossing while trains were passing or being switched. Travelers then had to cross the Green River by going south over the old wagon bridge built in 1910 and west on the Overland Trail road, up Telephone Canyon to the Peru hill. This was reported to be one of the worst stretches on the Lincoln Highway in the state.

In 1922, the Wyoming State Highway Department built a new highway bridge across the river west of Green River. The Lincoln Highway was then routed west through town past Tollgate Rock to the new bridge across the Green River. This highway became known as U.S. Highway 30 in later years.

In 1928, the Lincoln Highway was marked coast to coast by concrete posts set by the Boy Scouts. The posts, which featured Lincoln medallions, contained directional arrows.

The Lincoln Highway Association then dissolved in

1935 after the publication of the story of the Association's great achievement in the book, *THE LINCOLN HIGHWAY: The Story Of A Crusade That Made Transportation History.*

In October of 1992, the Lincoln Highway Association reactivated at a meeting in Iowa. Many have become interested in learning more about the Lincoln Highway. Therefore, the Association is currently involved in projects for promoting the Lincoln Highway as a tourism destination. Such projects include dedicating the Lincoln Highway as a "Historic Highway" and some as "Scenic Byways," the posting of Lincoln Highway signs and directional markers, publishing Lincoln Highway maps and driving guides, performing surveys of historic sites and structures and developing Lincoln Highway Interpretive sites.

The original Lincoln Highway route went west of Green River up Telephone Canyon, south of Green River. It was reported as being the "worst stretch" on the Lincoln Highway in Wyoming. (Postcards-as-art, Kathryn Cummings photo, Wyoming 1920)

Covey's Little America filling station was located on Highway 30, and the former Lincoln Highway, near Granger, Wyoming. After the hotel building burned in a fire of undetermined origin in 1950, the popular tourist attractiopn was moved to its new location on Interstate Highway 80. (Sweetwater County Historical Museum photo)

MURDER IN THE SAGE

By: Bill Thompson/Steve DeCecco, guest author

My guest author, Steve DeCecco, graduated from UW with a BS in Wildlife Management, came up through the ranks in the Wyoming Game and Fish Department and is Wildlife Supervisor stationed in Green River since 1997. His article deals with a game warden who was stationed in Rock Springs in 1919. Welcome Steve.

From 1899 to 1910, there was one State Game Warden in Wyoming. In 1911 the Commission was created and four Assistant Game Wardens (regional) were appointed as well as an undetermined number of Deputy Game Wardens.

The period when John Buxton worked (1919) was during the fledgling days of wildlife conservation in Wyoming. Game herds were being protected from exploitation (market hunting and poaching) and fisheries propagation was charging ahead.

In 1919, William T. Judkins was State Game Warden. There were six Assistant Game Wardens and 27 Deputy Game Wardens. Department records list John Buxton as one of the Assistant Game Wardens and he was stationed in Rock Springs. He is not listed in the 1918 annual report so we assume he served less than a year.

John Buxton was the first of three Game Wardens to be murdered in Wyoming. He was mortally wounded while contacting two young men who were hunting in violation of game laws just north of Rock Springs.

John Buxton was born on September 23, 1888 in Cincinnati, Ohio or Iowa, depending on the source. His family moved to Rock Springs when he was nine years old. After finishing school he worked as a miner for Union Pacific Coal Company. During World War I he entered the military and was assigned to an artillery unit but the war ended before he was to be sent overseas. After his discharge from military service, he married Jennie Roberts and they had a baby girl. Sometime in 1919 Buxton was commissioned as an Assistant Game Warden (often referred to as a Deputy Game Warden). Little information remains about

Buxton's short career but it was in the performance of his duties that he met his demise on September 14, 1919.

Newspaper reports have some conflicting details but the elements of the tragedy have been preserved. *The Rock Springs Miner* reported on Sunday afternoon, September 14, 1919, John Buxton and his pregnant wife were returning from E Plane, a small mining camp north of Rock Springs and discovered two boys hunting. Contrary to that report, *The Rock Springs Rocket* stated that Buxton received a report that some boys were hunting in the hills north of town and Buxton and his wife drove from Rock Springs towards E Plane to investigate.

Upon approaching E Plane, about five miles from town and three miles east of what is now Elk Street, Highway 191, Buxton heard the shooting and observed the two young men. Warden Buxton left his wife in the car and approached the suspects, later identified as Joe Omeyc and John Kolman. The two newspaper reports listed Omeyc's age as either 17 or 19. He contacted the two and told them that hunting season was closed and that they would have to go to town. After taking a 30-30 Savage rifle from Joe Omeyc, Buxton started walking back to his car. The suspects were behind him and Omeyc cursed the warden and shouted he was not going to town. Buxton turned to walk back to the boys. As he approached, Omeyc drew a .38 caliber revolver that was concealed and shot at Buxton. Omeyc fired three shots but it is assumed the first shot struck John Buxton in the lower chest, above the stomach. Buxton shouted to his wife to get his gun and get help. Omeyc and Kolman ran off toward a nearby railroad spur. Jennie Buxton either ran to E Plane or her shouts summoned Walter Ferguson who came to their aid. Ferguson helped Jennie get John into the car and drove him to the hospital. John Buxton died before medical treatment could be rendered. Warden John Buxton died in the performance of his duties nine days before his thirty-first birthday.

The suspects were found hiding in a railroad coal car by Sweetwater County Sheriff Stoddard and Deputy Sheriff Partitt. The suspects were arrested without incident and transported to jail where they both gave accounts of the event.

Funeral services for the slain warden were held on September 18, 1919 at the home of Buxton's brother Ralph. The news-

John Buxton. (Photo courtesy Wyoming State Archives/ Wyoming Game and Fish Department)

papers reported that the funeral "cortege was one of the longest ever seen in Rock Springs with a line of automobiles reaching from the hospital to the railroad on C Street." John Buxton was survived by his wife and daughter and, shortly after his death, another daughter was born to him and his wife.

His youngest daughter is still living and has lived her entire life in Rock Springs.

Joseph Omeyc was charged with second degree murder, found guilty and sentenced to twenty years in prison on March 17, 1920. Omeyc was paroled four and a half years later but, after a parole violation, returned to prison and remained until 1931, serving only eleven years of his sentence.

Wildlife law enforcement techniques, procedures and training have changed considerably since John Buxton's death eighty years ago. What hasn't changed is the inherent risks involved with law enforcement and the dedication of Wyoming's wildlife officers. Although Assistant Game Warden John Buxton's wildlife protection career was measured in just a few months, he is remembered as a dedicated wildlife officer. *The Rock Springs Miner* recalls,

> "Since his appointment, he has been most faithful in carrying out the duties of his office, so much so that he lost his life while in their performance. He was a genial, courteous man and was liked by all who knew him."

No Wyoming Game Warden, past or present, could hope for a finer epitaph.

THE WAY IT WAS: GREEN RIVER 1950

By: Marna Grubb

Fifty-three years ago, Green River began the year quietly, as reported by *The Green River Star*. Many held open houses at their homes. Others welcomed the new year at the various night clubs in the area, such as Andy's, the Log Inn, the Purple Sage and the Covered Wagon.

Memories of the previous winter were fresh in their minds. In January of 1949, snow and high east winds had piled snow 10-to-14-feet deep, halting road and train travel. Six passenger trains were held in Green River stranding approximately 1200 people for several days. Food demands taxed the local business houses. The large herds of antelope in the Red Desert country east of Rock Springs were frozen to death. It was considered the worst storm since 1888.

In 1950, things warmed up about 30 miles west of Green River as reported by *The Green River Star* of January 5. A fire of undetermined origin destroyed Covey's Little America hotel. The building also housed a café and bar. The buildings were scheduled to be moved to a new location, since the new highway between Green River and Lyman bypassed the famous "oasis" on Highway 30.

Also in January, President A. E. Stoddard of the Union Pacific Railroad Company in Omaha announced that 35 or more coal-burning locomotives would be converted to oil because of the three-day work week imposed by the coal miners and to insure the railroad against harassments and "continued shutdowns" of its Wyoming coal properties. Miners in Rock Springs had posted "NO CONTRACT – NO WORK" signs on Union Pacific mining properties and had refused to show up for work at the Stansbury mine. Stoddard declared that the railroad was left with only one course – that of converting more locomotives to oil.

In March, the Green River Wolves basketball team was undefeated until they reached the finals at the District Basketball Tournament held in Green River. They were "dumped" by the Rock Springs Tigers in the championship game, 31 to 26. The

Wolves were coached by James Weir.

On May 4, The Green River Star reported over a foot of snow had fallen over night. Editor and publisher of *The Green River Star* was Joe McGowan, Sr.

Also in May, the new census figures were disclosed. Green River's official population was 3,177, an increase of 537 from 1940.

With the arrival of summer, Green River was preparing for their annual Fourth-of-July celebration. Bill Hutton, one of the city's pioneer residents, was quoted as he described past celebrations. Hutton reminisced that in 1897 many events were held during Independence Day – one was a bicycle race down Main Street, then only a dirt road. The prize was three silver dollars which he informed were "quite a bit in those days." Celebrations were usually conducted by volunteer firemen. He remarked that he and Emil Gaensslen "opened the day by climbing to the top of Castle Rock at daybreak and hoisting a big flag and firing our six-shooters." The morning events included a race between the town's hose cart and the Union Pacific's hose cart. The only form of firefighting at that time was a hose cart pulled by the volunteers. The celebration also included horse races, foot races, sack races, three-legged races, wheelbarrow races, softball games with teams from adjoining towns, and a big parade.

In the evening, dances were held in the Opera House (on Railroad Avenue) and later at the Island Park after a bridge was built to the Island and an outdoor pavilion was constructed. Fireworks were popular.

Back to July 1950, contractors were preparing to break ground for approximately 100 new homes in the Man's Face Addition. Five foundations were to be poured each day, with houses to be completed in 60 days.

The shortage of housing had become a problem with the announcement that Westvaco Chemical Company planned to expand its operations west of Green River and would be in need of housing for construction workers and employees. Westvaco officials, from New York City and Newark, California, met at Little America with Green River Mayor Frank Wilkes, town council and civic leaders.

This was another review of history in the making!

A fire of undetermined origin destroyed Covey's Little America hotel, cafe and bar in 1950. This was shortly before they were to be moved from their location on Highway 30, and the former Lincoln Highway, to a location on the new Interstate 80 highway several miles east between Green River and Lyman. (Sweetwater County Historical Museum photo)

TAKE ME TO THE MOVIES?

By: Bill Duncan

When production companies make today's movies, they target people who grew up on video games, violent television, blatant sex, and "reality shows." I find myself out of the "demographic target area", settling for two star (out of four) films and wondering why Ebert's thumb points up on so many bad movies. I anxiously look to see what is playing in the local theaters. Why can't I find a movie that catches my fancy?

If video rental houses had to survive on my business, they would have gone broke long ago. Oh, I look. I comb the new releases and rifle through the classic section. I read the title and flip the case over to the back trying to catch the essence of the movie. But I seldom find anything suitable to take home to watch with mother.

I miss the old classics I used to watch on the Cine-o-rama screen. Gordon McRae and Shirley Jones were bigger than life in *Oklahoma* and *Carousel*. And there will be just one John Wayne – ever. Then there were all of those funky horror shows (like *The Blob*) we snuggled to at the drive in. Another era gone.

Now don't get me wrong. I laugh at Ben Stiller, idolize Renee Zellweger, think Gwyneth Paltrow can handle Shakespeare, and marvel that Richard Gere can sing and dance. But I also felt excited watching Gene and Roy ride. I fell in love with Virginia Mayo and Susan Hayward. I think the epitome of a love story is Kim Novak and William Holden in *Picnic*.

I find fuzzy-footed, hirsute men, wizards and witch academies ludicrous. I'm bored by endless battles of zooming video images. Maybe that's because I didn't make the jump from Pong to Playstation 2. As far as movies topics are concerned, I feel as invisible as a guy dressed up in a plaid suit standing against a plaid wall. Nobody makes movies for my age or interest group anymore.

I long for the days when we stood in line at the old Isis, dime and pennies clutched in our hand, waiting for the Saturday afternoon matinee. The afternoon's entertainment included previews, a double feature, a couple of cartoons, a newsreel, and a serial. If I could squeeze another nickel out of Mom or Dad, I could enjoy a box of popcorn. On those rare days when I got a quarter, I could plan on picking from the jars full of colorful penny candies or even splurge for a dime Sundae after the movies at Ecklund & Cottle's confectionary on the corner next to the theater.

I most remember the westerns starring Charles Starrett with Smiley Burnett. Smiley had a white horse with a black ring painted around his eye. Some afternoons, Hopalong Cassidy or the Lone Ranger and Tonto solved mysteries, captured the bad guys, or found the missing person.

The cartoons were Mickey Mouse and Donald Duck, Woody Woodpecker, and Popeye. Newsreels kept us current on events of the day, the economy or the war, and were great examples of propaganda. Serials were weekly installments of mysteries where the hero was put into jeopardy, then saved. Each week a crisis was solved and a new one created.

Can you imagine singing in a movie theater? While the sound system played the melody, a yellow ball bounced on the projected syllables in time to the rhythm. We sang about how far it was to Tipparary, claimed to be a Yankee Doodle Dandy like George M. Cohan, or sang America the Beautiful. Most songs were campfire songs, the kind sung while gathered around the piano or what we sang in our car since we didn't have a radio. I can't imagine whole audience participation on an Eminem rap or oooing and ahhhing to a Brittany Spears' ditty.

Golly, there has to be something better than the TV sitcoms and dramas. I'm neither a survivor nor a watcher of reality shows. I tire of the overacted soap operas that run afternoon and evening. TV sports are OK if I can mute the rabid announcers and still tell what is happening. Maybe I'll take another look at the classic section of the rentals. Suppose they have anything featuring Charles Starrett and Smiley Burnett on DVD?

TRAVELING WITH SIR RICHARD F. BURTON

By: Terry A. Del Bene

In the summer of 1860 the Overland Stage carried a most remarkable character through southwestern Wyoming. The man in the coach was Richard F. Burton, a man who would have sufficient accomplishments and adventures for several lifetimes. He traveled the world extensively, studying a variety of cultures. He translated the *Arabian Nights* into English. He would discover the source of the Nile River. He was nothing short of an exceptional chronicler of people and places.

In 1860 Burton was traveling to the Valley of the Great Salt Lake. Burton had made a habit of studying holy cities and he had come to the Rocky Mountains to study Salt Lake City and the Mormon Church. On his journey through Wyoming he provided some of the best descriptions of the landscapes and the people which had ever been penned. These were published in 1862 in his book *The City of the Saints*.

Let us pick up with Burton in his reminiscences of August 21st. His stage had crossed the South Pass the evening before. Stage travel was several times faster than wagon travel. The overland stage would cover almost as much territory in a day as an oxen-powered wagon train would cover in roughly a week. By contrast the same distance can be covered by automobile on paved roads in almost two hours.

> At the Pacific Creek, two miles below the springs, we began the descent of the Western water-shed, and the increase of temperature soon suggested a lower level. We were at once convinced that those who expect any change for the better on the counterslope of the mountains labor under a vulgar error. The land was desolate, a red waste, dotted with sage and greasbrush, and in places pitted with large rain-drops. But, looking backward, we could admire the Sweetwater's Gap heading far away, and the glorious mountains which, disposed in crescent shape, curtained the horizon; their southern and western bases wanted, however, of the principal charms of the upper view: the snow had well-nigh been melted off... We kept them in sight till they mingled with the upper air like immense masses of thunder-cloud gathering for a storm.
>
> From Pacific Creek the road is not bad, but at this season the emi-

grant parties are sorely tried by drought, and when water is found it is often fetid or brackish. After seventeen miles we passed the junction of the Great Salt Lake and Fort Hall roads [Parting of the Ways]. Near Little Sandy Creek- a feeder of its larger namesake- which after rains is about 2-5 feet deep, we found nothing but sand, caked clay, sage, thistles, and scattered fragments of campfires, with large ravens picking at the bleaching skeletons, and other indications of a halting-ground, and eddy in the great current of mankind, which, ceaseless as the Gulf-Stream ever courses east to west. After a long stage of twenty-nine miles we made Big Sandy Creek, an important influent to the Green River; the stream then shrunken, was in breadth not less than five rods, each + 17.5 feet, running with a clear, swift current through a pretty little prairillon, bright with blue lupine, the delicate pink malvacea, the golden heliathus, purple aster acting daisy, the white mountain heath, and the green Asclepias tuberosa [milkweed], a weed common throughout Utah territory ..
[Farson] We halted for an hour to rest and dine; the people of this station, man and wife, the latter very young, were both English, and of course Mormons; they had but lately become tenants of the ranch, but already they were thinking as the Old Country people will, of making their surroundings "nice and tidy.

We prepared for drought by replenishing all our canteens- one of them especially, a tin flask, covered outside with thick cloth, kept the fluid deliciously cold- and we amused ourselves by the pleasant prospect of seeing wild mules taught to bear harness. The tricks of equine viciousness and asinine obstinacy played by the mongrels were so distinct, that we had no pains in determining what was inherited from the father and what from the other side of the house... At last, being "all aboard," we made a start, dashed over the Big Sandy... and took the right side of the valley, leaving the stream at some distance.

Rain-clouds appeared from the direction of the hills: apparently they had many centres, as the distant sheet was rent into a succession of distinct streamers. A few drops fell upon us as we advanced. Then the firery sun "ate up" the clouds, or raised them so high that they became playthings in the hands of the strong and steady western gale. The thermometer showed 95 degrees in the carriage, and 111 degrees exposed to the reflected heat upon black leather cushions. It was observable, however, that the sensation was not from the height of the mercury, and perspiration was unknown except during severe exercise... The heat, however brought with it on evil- a green-headed horsefly, that stung like a wasp, and from which cattle must be protected with a coating of grease and tar. Whenever wind blew, tourbillions of dust coursed over different parts of the plain, showing a highly electrical state of the atmosphere. When the air was unmoved the mirage was perfect.... A sea lay constantly before our eyes, receding as we advanced...

After twelve miles' driving we passed through a depression called Simpson's Hollow, and somewhat celebrated in local story. Two semicircles of black still charred the ground; on a cursory view they might have been mistaken for burnt-out lignite. Here, in 1857 the Mormons fell upon a corralled train of twenty-three wagons laden with provisions and other necessaries for the federal troops, then halted at Camp Scott awaiting orders to advance... As at Fort Sumter, no blood was spilled... They still boast loudly of the achievement, and on the marked spot where it was performed the juvenile emigrants of the creed erect dwarf graves and nameless "wooden" tomb- "stones" in derision of their enemies.

Burton describes an event from the Utah Campaign of 1857. It is of interest that a mere three years after the actual event, at which no one injured, that local legend had children commemorating the casualties of the "battle" with grave markers. This legend appears to have survived into the present. The actual site of the wagon burning appears to have been destroyed when Highway 28 was built.

As sunset drew near we approached the banks of the Big Sandy River. The bottom through which it flowed was several yards in breadth, bright green with grass, and thickly feathered with willows and cotton-wood. It showed no sign of cultivation; the absence of cereals may be accounted for by its extreme cold; it freezes there every night, and none but the hardiest grains, oats and rye, which here are little appreciated, could be made to grow.

We are now approaching the valley of the Green River, which,... appears formerly to have filled a far larger channel. Flat tables and elevated terraces of horizontal strata- showing that the deposit was made in still waters- with layers varying from a few line to a foot in thickness, coimposed of hard clay, green and other sandstones, and agglutinated conglomerates, rise like islands from the barren plains, or form escarpments that butress alternately either bank of the winding stream...

Advancing over a soil alternately sandy and rocky- an iron flat that could not boast a spear of grass- we sighted a number of coyotes, fittest inhabitants of such a waste, and a long, distant line of dust, like the smoke of a locomotive, raised by a herd of mules which were being driven to the corral..."

Burton here noted an encounter with a Pony Express rider. The party was now but a few miles from the Green River

Within five or six miles of Green River we passed the boundary stone which bears Oregon on one side and Utah on the other. We had now traversed the southeastern corner of the country of Long-eared men, and were entering Deseret, the Land of the Honey-bee.

At 6 30 P.M. we debouched upon the bank of the Green River.... The ground about had the effect of an oasis in a sterile waste, with grass and shrubs, willows and flowers, wild geraniums, asters, and various cruciferae. A few trees, chiefly quaking asp[en], lingered near the sation, but the dead stumps were far more numerous than live trunks. In any other country their rare and precious shade would have endeared them to the whole settlement; here they are never safe when a log is wanted. ... We supped comfortably at green-River Station, the stream supplying excellent salmon trout.

Burton continued his account of the day with additional prose on the Green River Station and the environment. When he visited the river was described as being at a record low 330 feet in width. He reported the width expanded to 800 feet in the wetter cycle. His observations continue to be important glimpses into Wyoming's past.

We are fortunate today to be able to trace Burtons's trip of August 21st in less than two hours. Modern Highway 28 cuts a path through the country described so eloquently by Burton. There are interpretive sites along the trail at Pacific Springs, Plume Rocks, Parting of the Ways and the Little Sandy Crossing. There are interpretive stops along Highway 28 at "South Pass Overlook," False Parting of the Ways, Farson, Simpson's Hollow, "Pilot Butte Overlook," and Seedskadee. Large portions of the trip still look much as described by Burton.

WILD RIDE: THE PONY EXPRESS YESTERDAY AND TODAY

By: Gary Perkins, Exhibits Coordinator,
Sweetwater County Historical Museum (Guest author)

On June 5, 2003 at 7 p.m. at the Sweetwater County Library in Green River the Sweetwater County Historical Museum hosted a program on the Pony Express. This was held in conjunction with an exhibit at the museum on the 100th Anniversary reenactment run of the trail in 1960. Green River resident Donald "Duke" Yowell loaned the museum parts of his uniform and other commemorative items he received during his participation in the run. Gary Perkins, Exhibits Coordinator put together the exhibit and it was so good and full of local information that I asked him to submit it as an Echoes article. I hope you enjoy it! – Ruth Lauritzen

The Pony Express was a commercial venture of the Russell, Majors, and Waddell Freight Company. On April 3, 1860, the first Pony Express riders left St. Joseph, Missouri, and Sacramento, California, each carrying mail destined for the other end of the route. Westbound mail took just nine days and 23 hours to reach Sacramento. The last relay rider heading east arrived in St. Joseph 11 days and 12 hours after the eastbound mail had started.

The mounts used were not ordinary ponies, but the fastest and most fleet American horses obtainable. The organization consisted of 80 riders, 400 men to tend the way stations, and 420 horses stationed at 190 stage stops. The Oregon/California Trail route was used from St. Joseph to the western slope of South Pass, where it bent in a southwesterly direction, passing through Sacramento, crossing the high Sierras between Nevada and California. Total distance of the route was about 2,000 miles.

Each rider had a run from 30 to 75 miles depending on the terrain, with a change of mounts every 10 to 15 miles. Originally it cost $5.00 per half ounce to send a letter. Later on, this fee was reduced to $1 per half ounce. Letters were written on the thinnest tissue paper available and rolled in pencil rolls to save space. The mail was wrapped in oilskin and placed in four boxes of hard leather that were fastened to a large leather skirt, or mochila, that fitted over the special saddles.

The fastest run ever made was the combined relay carrying

Lincoln's Inaugural Address to Sacramento in the unbelievable time of seven days and 11 hours. Robert H. "Pony Bob" Haslam chalked up the longest ride, 380 miles in 36 hours, when he found his stations burned by Indians and continued until he could relay the mail to another rider. Another time "Pony Bob, " slumped over his saddle unconscious, was found on a horse that had carried on to a relief station. "Pony Bob," carrying election returns of Lincoln's election, had been shot with several arrows, one of which shattered his jaw. This ride covered 120 miles in only eight hours and ten minutes, from Smith Creek to Fort Churchill, Nevada. Haslam was 22 years old– small, muscular, tough and daring. His salary amounted to about $125 per month.

The Pony Express was put out of business by the telegraph in 1861 and mail was hauled on overland stages after that time. However, the riders of the Pony Express thrilled the nation with their great and dangerous rides, maintaining their schedule in all kinds of weather, and in the face of Indian attacks and other hazards.

In 1960 the **Sweetwater County Sheriff's Mounted Posse** was honored to be picked as the county riders for the one-hundred-year anniversary re-enactment of the Pony Express ride. For the re-enactment, 32 riders were used, 16 westbound and 16 traveling eastward. The Uinta County Sage Riders Posse passed the mail sack or *mochila* to the Sweetwater County riders at the Ham's Fork Pony Express Station near Granger at 11:37 p.m. on July 23, 1960. The relay riders, galloping for five-mile stretches, traveled most of the 80-mile route in darkness. The next moring the last Sweetwater County rider handed the *mochila* off to the Sublette County riders at 8:05 a.m. at the site of the Dry Sandy Pony Express Station east of Farson. Two hours later and another Sublette rider handed off his *mochila* to a Sweetwater County rider at the Dry Sandy Station and the relay continued westward.

Sweetwater County Sheriff's Mounted Posse

Sweetwater County consists of over 10,000 square miles of mostly rough and rugged terrain that poses a difficult problem for search and rescue. Until the Sweetwater County Sheriff's Mounted Posse was formed in 1955 by Sheriff George Nimmo, it was difficult to organize an effective search of the backcountry. Searches by volunteers tended to be haphazard and ineffective–occasionally the searchers got lost and had to be rescued themselves. With the formation of the Mounted Posse the sheriff assumed control of all searches and was able to use his posse in a more effective manner.

Although the posse members were sworn in as special deputies, they had to provide their own horses, equipment, and uniforms. The men spent many hours in the saddle looking for people lost in the desert or stranded by bad weather on the back roads of the county. Sometimes the people were found in time, but sometimes the rescue came too late.

It was not all hard work though, for the posse also performed at fairs, rodeos, and parades. The unit diligently trained to perfect their mounted equestrian drill routines. The organization was also a social one and cookouts, trail rides, and dances were held for posse members and their families. The posse earned the

The Sweetwater County Sheriff's Mounted Posse was the predecessor to the modern Search and Rescue. (Photo courtesy Sweetwater County Historical Museum)

county much goodwill and brought fellowship to its members.

The Sheriff's Mounted Posse was replaced by the Sweetwater County Search and Rescue organization in 1962. The new organization primarily uses four-wheel drive vehicles for its searches.

Duke Yowell and his horse "Shorty" in their official portrait for the Sweetwater County Sheriff's Mounted Posse. (Photo courtesy Duke Yowell and the Sweetwater County Historical Museum)

WYOMING'S FIRST GAME WARDEN

By: Bill Thompson/Jay Lawson, guest author

*This is the first of a two-part column by guest author Jay Law-
son, wildlife division chief of the Wyoming Game and Fish Department
He writes a series of articles for the* Wyoming Wildlife News. *This
one is of particular interest for those in this area. Thank you, Jay.*
Bill Thompson

For those who study the history of wildlife conservation in
Wyoming, the bleakest period in terms of declining game species
is the era from 1870 to the end of the 19th century. Opportunities
to preserve dwindling populations were lost at every turn, market hunting and indiscriminate shooting by settlers occurred in
a free-for-all atmosphere. The last remnants of many elk herds in
the smaller mountain ranges and foothills were wiped out. Migratory traditions among many bighorn sheep herds were lost
with the elimination of sub-populations; and, despite protests in
certain quarters, the last group of 25-30 wild bison in the Red
Desert of southwestern Wyoming were shot in 1889.

It was during this time that immigrant Albert Nelson arrived in Wyoming. Born and raised in Sweden, he had served in
the Army and studied at an agricultural college where he worked
extensively with horses. As a boy, he was fascinated by a Swedish
translation of James Fenimore Cooper's "The Leather Stocking
Tales," and longed to see the American wilderness.

After taking passage on a German freighter, he landed in
New York in 1883. He rode an empty freight car to Nebraska, was
discovered and kicked off the train, worked in the hay fields a
short time, then hopped another train to Rock Springs, arriving
just weeks short of his 24th birthday.

Albert's knowledge of horses served him well in the wild
west, and he soon found work as a cowboy. His granddaughter,
Dena Nelson-Stilson, allowed me to copy an 1889 portrait of Albert in those early years. He is decked out in full cowboy regalia,
including embroidery on the flared cuff of his gloves and a Colt
.45 on his hip.

Much of the range was still open in those first years, and Albert roamed from Brown's Hole to South Pass. He became an accomplished hunter and crack shot, with many a chuck wagon cook relying on him to keep the outfit supplied with fresh game meat.

At some point in the late 1880s, Albert partnered up with an older fellow named Billy Bierer. The two of them hunted, trapped, and prospected along the Wind River Mountains, and decided to homestead on the East Fork of Green River in 1888. Luckily, they laid in a supply of game meat and staples, for the ensuing winter was horrific, killing the majority of livestock and big game in much of the state. Since they had shared their supplies with neighbors, Albert and Billy soon depleted their own stores and were forced to snowshoe 70 miles to Rock Springs, returning with heavily laden toboggans.

Albert became a consummate outdoorsman, and sought out every opportunity to make his living in the open. He began guiding hunters and taught himself taxidermy; he was soon quite proficient, and hunters began bringing him their trophies for mounting.

In the fall of 1894, Albert and Billy trapped in the Jackson Hole country, building a small cabin on Flat Creek. They had success hunting and trapping, and since they liked the country, they decided to homestead.

In early July, 1895, a posse appeared at their cabin to enlist them in an effort to apprehend Indians from Idaho who were killing elk for their hides. Albert offered to go along on his first of many experiences related to wildlife protection. After apprehending the Indians on the upper Green River, the posse seized 211 hides. Several Indians were taken to Evanston for trial, but were later released due to vagueness about jurisdiction and the unclear language of early game laws. (see: Ward versus Race Horse 1896, by Bill Thompson in *Echoes From the Bluffs Volume I*, page 201.)

Albert filed for a homestead on the Gros Ventre River and began building a cabin there. He resumed his big game guiding and taxidermy work, and his reputation for quality hunting trips and trophy mounts soon brought him some fascinating customers.

The Harrimans and John D. Rockefeller Jr. were among his clients, as was the famous author Ernest Thompson Seton. Seton was so impressed with his taxidermy specimens that he tried to persuade him to relocate with a big firm of New York taxidermists. Albert declined.

Noted artist and photographer, J.E. Stimson, took numerous pack trips with Albert in search of wilderness subject matter. He also taught Albert photography and film development.

Another interesting client was the painter Carl Rungius. The two men became fast friends, and Rungius took every opportunity to ride the hight country with Albert. On one trip, Rungis broke his leg near the head of the Green River. Albert packed the artist as far as Saouth Park and a doctor was summoned from Jackson. Arriving with whiskey on his breath, the doc set the leg and applied a cast in a hurried fashion. When he departed, Rungius asked the other hunters if they thought his leg had been set straight and none of them felt it had.

Albert cut off the cast and ground it up; then the other men pulled the broken leg and separated the break so he could reset the bones. They then dissolved the Plaster-of-Paris and Nelson used it to apply a new cast.

The leg healed perfectly, and several months later a packing tube arrived in the mail along with a letter from Rungis. Thinking it was a calendar, Albert forgot to even take it from the post office. On his next trip, the post mistress reminded him it was still there, and when he opened the package it contained an original

Albert Nelson. (Photo courtesy Wyoming State Archives/Wyoming Game and Fish Department)

painting of a bull elk. Albert's granddaughter, Dena, showed me the picture, and it is a fine example of Carl Rungius's big game illustrations.

At the age of 39, Albert met Sara Avila Allen, who had come to Jackson's Hole in 1896 with her parents. Here was a woman after his own heart - she loved to hunt, ride and dance; they were soon married.

In 1899, Albert Nelson was appointed the first state game warden by Governor DeForest Richards. His appointment was endorsed by many notable citizens and sportsmen of the state.

Yet Wyoming's new game laws were generally held in contempt by those holding on to frontier traditions. Albert made numerous arrests and rode horseback to trials across the state, including several in Cheyenne. But the courts turned a blind eye to the continued slaughter of big game and Albert was unable to obtain a single conviction for wildlife crime. After three frustrating years, he resigned.

Adversity often brought out the best in Albert; an illuminating example is the time when his young daughter, Anna, was injured in a fire. The local doctor told them there was little to be done, but Albert sterilized one of his razor-sharp taxidermy knives and carefully cut away infected skin and proud flesh. It was a horrific task for a parent, but his daughter lived through the ordeal and had minimal scarring. Anna, at 94, still lives in Jackson, and I doubt that you could find anyone who has more reverence for a father.

After giving birth to seven children, Avilla passed away on December 4, 1913; she was only thirty-four years old. This changed Albert's life in a dramatic way. Since he was determined to keep his children together, he sold his ranch and moved to Kelly. He opened a taxidermy shop, and between making a living and caring for seven children, had time for little else.

He was obviously heart-broken after losing his wife and best friend and would never have interest in another woman. His daughter, Anna, told me that he was still a handsome fellow and loved to go to the dances in Jackson; but he had lost the love of his life and had no desire for romance.

Albert's troubles continued when, in the spring of 1927, the natural dam which had formed Lower Slide Lake on the Gros

Ventre River gave way and washed out the town of Kelly. The flood claimed six lives and destroyed every business, including Albert's taxidermy shop.

After relocating to Jackson, Albert worked until his mid-80s, at that time being the oldest practicing taxidermist in America. He carved many beautiful ornaments from horn and antler, including a pair of tall lamps with spiraling branches and leaves along their bases, each perfectly carved from thin sections of antler.

Fortunately, Albert lived to see wildlife protection become a reality and game herds recover throughout the state. He was able to teach his children and grandchildren how to hunt, fish and get along in the woods. He remained active until his death at the grand old age of 95.

Reprinted with permission from the September/October 2002 issue of Wyoming Wildlife News

THE WAY IT WAS: GREEN RIVER 1960

By: Marna Grubb

In 1960, the buzz words in Green River were "Flaming Gorge" and "Trona".

In January of 1960, it was announced that clearing work on the Flaming Gorge reservoir site south of Green River was scheduled for the summer.

Also in January 1960, Stauffer Chemical Corporation outlined plans for a multi-million dollar trona plant northwest of Green River. They were waiting on mining permits to be received on the Seedskadee project. Employment of 300 to 350 personnel was anticipated.

Some were even predicting that Green River may, in the near future, be the trona-producing center of the nation. The U.S. Geological Survey estimated that Green River's trona reserves exceed seven billion tons. Intermountain Chemical, a subsidiary of Food, Machinery & Chemical Corporation, at Westvaco, had been the sole Wyoming producer of natural trona in the area.

Of course, our small town was having its own problems. Adrian Reynolds in his *Green River Star* editorial of March 10, 1960, commented that "At best, you must admit our streets are lousy and growing worse day by day because of the frost going out of the ground. Every member of the administration knows what is needed: the rebuilding of block after block of street. The problem is that of finance. We had heard some persons criticizing the town administration. That criticism we believe is unwarranted as the laws of Wyoming concerning town financing tie the hands of town administrations. So the town dads have a real problem. AR"

Also, after a curfew recommendation to town administration from the Green River Parent-Teacher Association and comments, for and against, from the public, *Star* Editor Adrian Reynolds gave the following comments in his "Chewin' the Fat" of March 10, 1960: "...don't get me wrong...a curfew ordinance has a definite place, and does give police a checkrein if it is needed...

if parents don't take the leadership and responsibility, then who will?...a child raised without work or activity for busy minds and hands, and without home guidance can hardly be expected to grow up with any responsibility toward society or family. AR" A curfew ordinance was adopted in April 1960.

The Green River Star in May 1960 reported that a jury in the

Excavation for the Flaming Gorge dam and reservoir took place in 1959-1960. Placing of concrete took place from 1960 to 1962. It was completed in 1963, taking five years to build. It is an arch-type, concrete dam. (Sweetwater County Historical Museum photo)

Natrona County District Court was hearing the case of the State of Wyoming vs. Stephen E. Rallis of Green River. Rallis, a Green River tavern operator, was charged with aggravated assault upon F. R. Schofield, Green River town attorney. The jury found Rallis guilty of assault with intent to kill. Rallis was sentenced to a term of four to five years in the state prison saying that it had taken into consideration the convicted man's health conditions.

In the spring of 1960, the water outlook for the Green River Basin was reported as slim. Forecast on the Green at Fontenelle was 70 percent of normal.

The Riverside Outdoor Swimming Pool, located by the bridge to the island, opened for the summer season on June 15 under the management of Leo Sunada. Bathing caps were required.

Pony Express Days was the theme for the annual Fourth-of-July celebration. The celebration committee announced that "If you haven't donned western wear...if you aren't growing a beard or haven't obtained a shaver's permit for the privilege of remaining clean shaven, then you are fair game for the Green River celebration committee's vigilantes." Chairman Ed Lewis advised that they were starting to pick out the culprits to be tried in kangaroo court, with the prospect of facing a "firing squad" as the penalty.

The headlines in *The Green River Star* of August 25, 1960, announced that concrete would soon be pouring into the Flaming Gorge Dam. At the aggregate plant where approximately one million yards of sand and gravel was to be produced within the next two years, stockpiles were beginning to assume mountainous size. Arch Dam Constructors, prime contractor, prepared to go on continuous operations as soon as the serious work of concrete production started at the concrete batching plant high on the walls of Red Canyon above the dam site.

In September, Stauffer Chemical Corporation broke ground for trona development 21 miles northwest of Green River. Plant completion was expected in two years.

Forty-three years later, in 2003, the buzz words in Green River were still "Flaming Gorge" and "Trona".

THE ROOD FAMILY

By: Bill Duncan
Green River Historical Preservation Society

The Bert Rood family poses for a family portrait sometime during the mid-1920s. Anne (Neilsen) a Danish native, William Albert "Bill", Walter "Wally", Henry (the oldest), Charles "Dutch", and Albert "Bert" Rood, who originally came from Wisconsin. (Photo courtesy the Rood family)

Albert Rood, his wife Anne (Neilsen), and his four sons homesteaded about seven miles above Big Island on the northeast side of the Green River in 1919. His four sons ranged from 15 to 5 years old. Bert and Anne, a Danish native, had moved around the Utah, Idaho, and Wyoming area for some years after making their way west from Wisconsin. Bert was 55 years old when he homesteaded on the Green and Anne was 37.

Life was hard. Roods cut logs upriver and floated them down to the house site. The river flooded every season occasionally covering pastures and fields. Winter temperatures were bone-chilling. Indians continued to pass by on their traditional migratory routes, sometimes asking for handouts. Beef, sheep and horse prices dropped after World War I. Like most of the homesteaders during this time, the Roods worked for other ranchers to scratch out a living. Town was a long day's wagon ride away. Today, a sagebrush corral held together by steel cable and a few derelict buildings mark the homestead.

Before long, Roods moved into Green River. They found a cozy house at 285 North and 5th East. Bert became a teamster, working for a time at the Green River Sand and Gravel Plant. He earned extra money working for the Union Pacific carting cinders in a wagon across the river to dump them on the other side. Bert and Anne's four sons graduated from Green River High School An infant son, Andrew, had died when he was 2 weeks old.

Henry, the oldest, began work at Stockgrowers Mercantile in Rock Springs. He later worked at retail clothier Nan Thompson before retiring. He died in 1985 at age 81.

Like many other Green River young men, Charles "Dutch" worked for the railroad. He spent most of his life in Ely, Nevada,

The Rood family home still stands at 285 North 5th East. Although no longer in the family, it is still well-maintained and tidy. (Photo courtesy Bill Duncan)

and died in 1983 at age 73.

Wally, the youngest, worked for the UP Employees Club. He served in Italy with the US Army during WWII. Wally was frost-bitten during the winter of 1944 and suffered from it the rest of his life. He started again with the railroad after the war, moved to Stauffer (now OCI) and worked as a bartender at the Green Gander. Old-timers remember his dry wit and a speech impediment that were part of his personality. Wally died at age 61 in 1975.

Bill (William Albert) is remembered for the jaunty way he wore his hat and the respect he earned in the community. Bill started out working for the railroad as a call boy at age 14. Before a UPRR hotel and lacking a facility like the Oak Tree Inn, railroaders stayed at rooming houses around town. They were called to their trains by young "call boys" like Bill.

Bill was an outstanding high school athlete, excelling in both football and basketball. Later, he played baseball at Evers Field with the company teams. According to *The Green River Star* he was still actively playing city league softball when he was 41. He was a coach and manager for the Green River American Legion Junior Baseball Team at one time, too.

While still in high school, Rood worked his way up to assistant yard master. After graduation, he began as a sheet metal apprentice. Bill Rood worked 49 years as a railroad sheet metal worker. He was a shop steward and always heavily involved with the Sheet Metal Workers Union. Like most repairmen, he could weld and had a vast mechanical knowledge. He was with the UPRR for a total of 52 years.

According to his son Henry, Bill was proud of being able to dismantle a huge, rotary snowplow that had never worked. "He made it run and, as far as I know, it is still running today," Henry said. Another memorable incident concerned breaking through the huge drifts that towered over the 13 ft. tall rotary plow, to open up the stranded Atlantic City Iron Ore Mine.

Cleonne (Lutrell) and Bill were married in Green River on July 18, 1937.

Bill served Green River as an elected Justice of the Peace for 17 years while he was still working for the UP. Legislation later changed this office to Municipal Judge. He was district director for the Democratic Party. Bill was active in civic affairs, serving as Lions Club secretary/treasurer for over 20 years. In his almost 30 years as a Lion, he was a zone chairman and the District Governor. When the Union Pacific had their own Fire Department, Bill was their chief for a time. He died in 1974 at age 66.

Bill's two sons, Bill Jr. (William Arthur) and Henry, put their mark on the community. Bill worked as a crane operator when the Jim Bridger Plant was being built. After a career in construction, he owned and operated Rood's Custom golf club shop. He was one of the first local businessmen to bring custom hats and sports gear with local logos to the community. Bill died in 1989.

Bill loved traveling to watch his sons play sports. His sons are Craig Rood, Mike Rood and Rick Rood. Craig and Mike work at OCI and Rick works at SF Phosphates. They are all GRHS graduates.

The Rood legacy of public service continues today. Craig has served as chair of the Flaming Gorge Days celebration and is still on the planning committee.

Bill (senior's) son, Henry, is a city councilman whose term ends in 2005. After graduating from Lincoln High School (GRHS) in 1965, Henry was drafted while a student at Casper College.

He served in Viet Nam in 1966 and 67. Adrian Reynolds, then the editor and publisher of *The Green River Star*, gave Henry some note paper and asked him to write his observations while serving as a finance dispersing clerk in Long Binh. Henry's diary proved lively reading including his time in Binhoa Province just before the Tet offensive. He was cut off and surrounded until relieved by units of the 2nd Cavalry and the 101st Airborne.

Henry returned to finish his Associate of Arts degree at Casper College. He succeeded his Dad, Bill, as Justice of the Peace in 1973 and held night court until 1974. "This was the boom times and the days of the 55 mph speed limit," Henry remembers with a grimace. When the State Legislature determined that the local judge should be a lawyer, Henry could no longer serve.

Henry has held a variety of jobs in the trona industry. He was the owner and operator of HD Enterprises, a pipe, valves and fittings firm. He served a time in the Air National Guard and traveled widely. Henry's son Robb Rood is the editor of the

Altoona Herald Press in Altoona, Iowa.

Today, Henry services and repairs Bunning Transfer's equipment. He looks forward to retirement so he can fish and spend time at the family cabin on the Big Sandy, not too far north of where his grandfather homesteaded on the Green 84 years ago.

The author is indebted to Henry D. Rood for the facts and photo of his family.

THE OTHER SEPTEMBER 11TH

By: Terry A. Del Bene

Let us whisper about forbidden things...

The cool of the morning gave way to the heat of the desert afternoon. The travelers were relieved that they now had a protective escort through this part of Zion. The caravan divided into three groups all with an armed compliment of men to keep away the savage hosts which had beset the weary travelers for the past four days. Surely these men were sent from heaven to save them. The travelers no longer needed to carry weapons now that they had been rescued. Some wondered why their saviors had disarmed them when there was still danger about. After the parties had traveled a half hour the procession stopped. It is reputed that a leader of the escort called out, "Halt! Do your duty to Israel." At that signal, the children of Israel slew the gentiles. Men, women, and children spilled their life's blood into the sands. Some say young women were raped. The only ones spared were 17 children, though other children were murdered along with the adults. They say it was over in a few minutes. When the dust cleared there were roughly 120 corpses left to feed the vultures and the wolves. Visitors to the site reported seeing bits of bone and hair from the hapless victims years after the massacre.

One might think from telling of this event that it is just another example of senseless violence and religious zealotry from the Middle East. It might surprise the reader to learn that the event in question happened just a few hours drive from Green River in the year 1857. The event described is the Mountain Meadows Massacre, one of the most controversial events in the history of the American West. So controversial is this topic that to even bring up the subject could label one as "anti-Mormon". Though this reaction is misguided, it is somewhat understandable as anti-Mormon forces have used Mountain Meadows as a rallying cry for decades. The misuse of the history on both sides has affected our ability to study and understand the event as history.

Let us whisper about these things together. Maybe by

whispering we can help to let in light to disperse the dark mists which surround this event.

American history is filled with the tales of massacres besides that at Mountain Meadows. Who could forget the Waxaus, the Levels, Lawrence, Fort Pillow, the Moravian Missions, New Ulm, Lancaster, Boston, Paoli, Sand Creek, Ludlow, Rosebud, My Lai, Bear River , Kent State, the Utter Disaster, Wounded Knee, Columbine High School, and a host of other massacres? Odds are that most people have probably only heard of a few of those massacres. Books and films freely discuss and interpret many of these massacres. They are for the most part things of the past. They are thought impossible to happen in anymore. Why is it that Mountain Meadows still needs to be whispered about?

The answer is that Mountain Meadows in not a single event. The horrific crimes committed to a peaceful wagon company between September 7th and 11th in 1857 were in many details comparable to those of any of the other massacres. One group brutally murdered another outside a condition of "honorable" combat. What sets Mountain Meadows apart from the remainder is the cover-up and how it has kept the issue alive.. Fear of repercussions for the events of September 11, 1857 set off a coverup perhaps unprecedented in American history.

To understand the event we need to put it into an overall historical context. The emigrants massacred were within a territory which thought itself to be at war with the United States. The undeclared war (or rebellion depending upon one's interpretation) is referred to as the "Utah War." This is a little-known chapter in American history where Utah Militia and the U.S. Army actually exchanged a few shots as one-third of the U.S. Army was in transit to Utah to build a new post and relieve Mormon Church President Brigham Young as acting territorial governor. President Buchanan had underestimated Young's reaction to the news that he was being replaced and Federal troops were going to back it up. Territories have no legal standing to bar the movement of Federal troops within their borders but legality was not the issue.

Young placed the territory on a war footing and prepared to repulse an invasion. He issued an order to the commander of the U.S. troops to stay out of Utah. He attempted to rally Native

American warriors to attack the army. Defenses were established. Arms were stockpiled. The Utah Militia (a.k.a. Nauvoo Legion), numbering almost as many men as the entire U.S. Army, was called to arms.. Blistering rhetoric filled the temple. Trading with emigrants was restricted.

While these events were in action, the U.S. Army was unaware that it was about to enter a war zone. The illusion of a peaceful transfer of troops was shattered when Utah Militia forces struck a dragoon camp near South Pass and shortly thereafter burned several supply wagon trains near the Big Sandy River in Sweetwater County. With all its potential for destruction, the Utah War was a relatively bloodless affair, except for the events at Mountain Meadows. A peace was negotiated in 1858 and a new territorial governor was installed without a major military action. A blanket amnesty was granted by Buchanan for the rebellious acts of the previous year. The events at Mountain Meadows were not common knowledge at that time.

The coverup started with a series of diversions intended to place the blame away from the perpetrators of the crime. Mountain Meadows was an act involving deception, betrayal, violence, murder of children, murder of women, theft, and possibly rape. Such a heinous breech of civilized warfare needed some kind of explanation. The massacre could not be listed as an act of war and needed to be explained to the watching world. Poor handling of the public relations could create a crippling blow to church prestige. It needed to be ennobled and sugar-coated. The wheels of the spin-doctors whirled furiously remaking the event and its participants. So effective was the deception that coverup had taken on a life of its own. The wheels continue spinning into the 21st century.

The Coverup

The deed done and the Utah War over, the American public began to howl for justice. Pandora's box had been opened. The murder of 120 travelers was not taken lightly and the lack of closure on the issue tainted the relations between the Federal Government and Utah Territory. The stench of the Mountain Meadows corpses hung heavy whenever Congress considered bills affecting the territory. Initial attempts sought to place the blame elsewhere and hope this resolved the matter.

Bad Indians

> Nearly all of that company were destroyed by Indians. That unfortunate affair has been laid to the charge of the whites. (Brigham Young writing of the Mountain Meadow Massacre in 1863).

Many of the perpetrators had disguised themselves as Indians. In fact, the hapless victims thought they were under attack only by Indians when they agreed to be escorted out of danger by the Utah Militia. There may have been a few Indians present especially in the early stages of the siege but it clearly was run top to bottom by the Utah Militia and its command system. The surviving children remembered the Utah Militiamen washing off their war paint after the massacre.

However, the initial blame went to the Indians. Such barbarity could only have come from savages. Some accounts indicated that the Utah militia killed only the men and that the Indians present killed the few women and children that were murdered. Other accounts make it clear that the militia participated in the less honorable actions of killing women and children.

> The plan was for the Indians to kill the women and children and the white men of the posse to kill the men of the emigrants, but owing to some of the white men of the posse failing to kill their men, the Indians assisted in finishing the work. There were about 150 Indians present. (Eyewitness Nephi Johnson affidavit about the Mountain Meadow Massacre).

The degree of the participation of Indians was (and still is) highly exaggerated to make the event less horrific. The accounts include participation of at least one Indian leader who had been dead for three years at the time of the massacre. The Native Americans claim that their participation in the event was peripheral, at best, with just a handful of their warriors in the vicinity. In any case their participation was at the behest of their white allies. If Nephi Johnson is to be believed there was clear intent to include children and women in the murders.

Bad Emigrants

> In the fall of this year, a large company of emigrants passed through our quiet settlements. They made threats, and swore that Johnston's Army was coming from the East and they from the South and would kill every Mormon in Utah. (Perry Liston 1857).

As that story unraveled, the blame was shifted to the emigrants. Stories were told that the emigrants had threatened the Utahans as they traveled. Stories arose that they were impolite. Some claimed that the emigrants had played a role in the murder of church founder Joseph Smith. Some said the emigrants had poisoned a spring, killing livestock and a young man who consumed the meat. None of the stories stand up to scrutiny and appear to be a pattern of post-massacre fabrications.

The Liston example above is fairly typical of the kind of testimony which was collected after the massacre to justify that the murder victims were bad people deserving of death. As is usually the case with such attempts to remake the truth, the stories rarely stand up to scrutiny. In this case the emigrants are supposed to have referred to "Johnston's Army". If the emigrants knew of such a force (which did not leave Missouri until months after the emigrants were already on the road) they would not have called it "Johnston's Army." The original commander of the force was General Harney. When Harney stayed behind to resolve some of the "bleeding Kansas" issues, the force was commanded by Colonel Alexander until Harney's replacement joined the force in October (after the massacre).

For a moment let us assume that the Liston account, and those like it are completely accurate. Even in the wild west, being rude and threatening are not considered sufficient grounds to waylay an entire wagon train, kill those who made the threats, kill those who made no threats (including children and women), and confiscate their property.

Bad Brigham

As tales of the massacre received attention from the American public and justice system, the issue turned to one of whether Brigham Young had ordered the massacre. Young exercised exceptional control over his followers and it defied reason and common practice that such an act could have been done without his consent or direction. The crushing of the Morrisite sect's attempt to break away from the Church in the early 1860s demonstrated that Young was capable of ordering violent retribution against his opponents. It was clear that until there was closure to the events of September 11th, the relations with Washington would remain strained. Someone would have to pay for the murders.

Young orchestrated an increasingly more complex cover up. Young has provided contradictory accounts of what he knew of the massacre. Carefully kept diaries of Utahans often have 1857 ripped out, hence purging the observations of those who might have witnessed the events. The ranking leader present at the massacre was John D. Lee, Young's adopted son and part of his inner circle. Young apparently even offered up John D. Lee as a sacrifice. After two trials John D. Lee was convicted of murder. He was executed by a firing squad at the site of the massacre on March 23, 1877. He went to his grave claiming that he was the scapegoat for Brigham Young. Standing by his coffin and awaiting execution Lee lashed out at Young.

> I studied to make this man's will my pleasure for thirty years. See, now, what I have come to this day! I have been sacrificed in a cowardly, dastardly manner. I cannot help it. It is my last word. It is so. Evidence has been brought against me which is as false as the hinges of hell, and this evidence was wanted to sacrifice me. (John D. Lee, moments before his execution.)

The ghosts of Mountain Meadow apparently drew little solace in the execution of but one of the killers, as the issue continued to haunt those associated with it for decades to come. In the third installment the restless spirits are not done with us yet as the controversies spill into the 20th and 21st centuries..

The Coverup That Would Not Die

One would think that having executed one of the murderers that the coverup would end there. However, Mountain Meadows has many secrets yet to reveal. In the summer of 1999 a mass grave containing the remains of 28 people was unearthed at Mountain Meadows. Under Utah State law such discoveries of human remains normally are examined by scientists. However, Utah Governor Mike Leavitt ordered reburial of the remains shortly after they had been retrieved. The scientists were given 24 hours notice to surrender the remains for reburial.. The tradition of cover-up had jumped from the 19th Century into the 20th. Researchers Shannon Novak and Derina Kopp managed to perform some analysis and photograph the remains before the completion of analysis was curtailed by political forces. Much more could have been done to study the population of emigrants. However, the Governor apparently was afraid that it would bring too much attention to an event which remains unspeakable.

The bones tell a chilling tale of the mechanics of the murders. Three of the bodies were children under the age of ten, whose skulls had been bashed in. Another middle-aged female had suffered the same fate. A second female also had numerous skull fractures. Seven of the men had gunshot wounds to the head. Some of the bodies had been bludgeoned and then shot.

Imagine holding the battered skull of a child between the ages of three and five in your hand. What possible roll could this innocent have played in the purported reasons for the massacre? The child was not killed by a stray shot. He or she was killed by a deliberate blow. A child of this size could only be recognized for what it was, an innocent. Yet the death blow was delivered with sufficient force to deform the bone. These revelations may be the unspeakable things which the Governor may have been trying to keep from surfacing.

The coverup refuses to die; but die it must. Juanita Brooks, the pre-eminent chronicler of the Mountain Meadows tale could not use all the material she had gathered for her book on the massacre. According to Brooks there was interference from church officials with her intellectual property, even going so far as to stifle a proposed motion picture project.

> The same motives that caused 19 Muslims to crash airplanes into buildings full of strangers led God-fearing Christians to murder 120 men, women, and children at Mountain Meadows in 1857. (Will Bagley speaking in 2003).

Recent popular books by Will Bagley *(Blood of the Prophets Brigham Young and the Massacre at Mountain Meadows)* and Jon Krakauer *(Under the Banner of Heaven)* serve to take the discussion of how religion-inspired murders occur. Bagley's book has harvested numerous awards including the Caughey Book Prize of the Western History Association, Best Book of the Westerners International Annual Award, Western Writer's of America Best History Spur Award, and the Caroline Bancroft History Prize. Bagley (a member of the Mormon Church) does a masterful job of reconstructing the events of 1857 and after. According to Bagley's research, there is abundant evidence pointing to Brigham Young using the concept of blood atonement to pull off mass murder. In response, it appears there will now be an official and definitive history. This research apparently is in progress. Will this be a continuation of the tradition of cover-up? Initial statements published to date lead us to suspect that old habits die hard. The attacks on Bagley's book serve only to remind all that the coverup is alive and well. The quality of Bagley's work makes it difficult to go back to the way things were.

> This is not a time for recrimination or the assigning of blame. No one can explain what happened in these meadows 142 years ago. We may speculate, but we do no know. We do not understand it. We can only say that the past is long since gone. It cannot be recalled. It cannot be changed. (First President Gordon Hinkley, September 11, 1999).

President's Hinkley's eloquent words deal exceptionally well with the act of 1857. Would that the speech included direction to open the records and put an end to the decades of covering up the details, for that has overshadowed the crime itself. If we really wish the ghosts of Mountain Meadows to rest in peace then the tradition of covering up the facts needs to end. The coverup gives life to the story far more effectively than the event itself.

We have only whispered of unspeakable things here. Our whispering was not done to injure any person, group, or faith. The whispering is intended to provide a call for changing the dis-cussions of Mountain Meadows from an emotional flash point to one of dispassionate history. The young child with the battered skull deserves to be remembered as the unfortunate victim of a hate crime and not as a pawn between forces bent upon spinning the web of history in a fashion which best suits their needs. After all, like all of the other massacres it could not happen today.

JACK O' LANTERNS AND OTHER JOLLIES: OLD-TIME HALLOWEEN CELEBRATIONS

By: Ruth Lauritzen

Once the excitement of starting a new school year wanes, one question burns in the hearts of children everywhere–"What am I going to be for Halloween?" Halloween, one of the most beloved of childhood holidays, has its beginnings among the ancient peoples of Europe. The harvest celebration of Samhain (pronounced "sow-en") marked the new year for the Celtic peoples. According to tradition , the last night of the year, October 31st, the spirits of all those who died the previous year wandered the earth. In order to avoid these spirits, the Celts made offerings of food and drink and build bonfires on sacred sites.

As Western Europe came under Roman control beginning in the 1st century A.D., some of these traditions were adapted and absorbed into the conquering people's seasonal observances. When Christianity spread through the Ottoman Empire the same process continued. Elements of pagan celebrations were incorporated into Roman Catholic Church traditions in order to attract converts. Two Christian holy days are closely related to Halloween. Established in 835 by Pope Gregory IV, All Saints' Day, a holy day to honor Christian saints, was celebrated on November 1 and All Souls' Day was established in the 10th century to be observed on November 2 for the purification of the spirits of the dead. The term "Halloween" is a corruption of All Hallows Eve, the night before All Hallows Day or All Saints' Day.

The custom of Halloween was brought to the United States through immigrants from the British Isles, primarily the Irish. The exceptions to this were the New England Puritans who rejected the celebration as a Catholic and pagan custom. By the time Green River was settled in the mid-1800s most of the traditional Halloween customs were well-known and practiced in the United States.

Certainly the young people of Green River embraced them readily. The November 5, 1909 *Green River Star* reported on a "Halloween" party sponsored by the M.O.M. Club. This was a club of young women who, despite their rather tongue-in-cheek name, (it stood for Miserable Old Maids), had a very active social life if the newspapers of the time are any indication . The party was held at the Carnegie Library, (the Circuit Court building) and included appropriate decorations, a supper and seasonal activities listed as follows:

> The evening's amusements consisted of various Halloween games, dancing, singing and ghost stories, the latter being told by the young ladies with the view of the young men taking pity upon any young lady without an escort, and their little schemes worked to perfection, as not one member of the club had to wander home alone.

Games were a big part of many Halloween celebrations and most had to do with the practice of divination or fortune telling. One game specificially mentioned in the same 1909 *Star* article, the fate cake, was quite an elaborate one. The fate cake "... contained various prizes, each of which represented some fate for the one that secured it..."

The process for making the cake is described in the *Little Colonel's Holidays* by Annie Fellows Johnston in the chapter entitled " A Halloween Party". This is one of a series of books for girls which were very popular around the turn of the last century and contains a snapshot view of Victorian girlhood.

> When the guests had all arrived, they were taken into the kitchen. Under the ban of silence (for the speaking of a word would have broken the charm) they stood around the table, giggleing as the cake was concocted, out of a cup of salt, a cup of flour, and enough water to make a thick batter. A ring, a thimble, a dime and a button were dropped into it, and each guest gave the mixture a solemn stir before the pan was put into the oven...Then the fate cake was cut, and everybody took a slice to carry home to dream on. "Eat it the last thing before you retire," said Miss Allison. "Then walk to bed backwards without taking a drink of water or speaking another word tonight. It is so salty that it is likely you will dream of being thirsty, and of somebody bringing you water. They say if you dream of its being brough in a golden goblet you will marry into wealth. If in a tin cup poverty will be your lot. The kind of vessel you see in your dream will decide your fate. Ah, Walter got the button in his slice. That means he will be an old bachelor and sew his own buttons on all his life." Anna More got the dime, and Eliza Hughes the ring, which foretold that she would be the first one in the company to have a

wedding. The thimble fell to no one, as it slipped out between two slices in the cutting. "That means none of us will be old maids," said little Elise.

Bobbing for apples was also a way of predicting marriage. The one who first bit into an apple was declared the first to be married in the coming year. In a more complex version of the game, the names of the group of marriageable females were inserted into apples to be bobbed for by the men and vice versa. The bobber was to say the following verse before making his or her bite:

Witches and wizards and birds of the air,
Goblins and brownies, all lend me your care,
Now to choose wisely for once and for all,
And ever your names in praise loudly I'll call.

Green River children dress up for a Halloween party around 1940. (Photo courtesy Sweetwater County Historical Museum)

Another marriage divination game had participants walking down the cellar stairs backward with a candle and a mirror. The face of your intended was supposed to appear in the mirror held by the seeker.

Apple peeling also had divination purposes. One game decreed that the longer the unbroken peel, the longer the life of the one who cut it. Another practice saw the unbroken peel tossed over the shoulder. The initial it formed when it came to rest was of the person's intended mate.

The tumbler test had those seeking their fortune blindfolded and led to four water tumblers. One of the tumblers was filled with blue water (the source suggests using laundry bluing for color), one filled with soapy water, another filled with clear water, and finally, one with no water at all. The seeker was invited to dip his fingers into one of the tumblers to determine his fortune. If his fingers went into the clear water, he would marry a rich and beautiful woman. Soapy water meant marriage to a poor widow. A future famous author would touch the blue water, and to dip into the empty glass meant that he would die a bachelor.

Decorations of many of the Green River parties described in contemporary newspaper society items included all of the traditional touches of, " ... yellow and black, with bats, black cats, witches, and scary looking pumpkin faces. .. " (Green River Star, November 3, 1911)

Like most of the Halloween traditions in the United States, the Jack O' Lantern can be traced back to European customs. It is probably based on an Irish folktale about a trickster and drunk-ard named Jack. He supposedly tricked the Devil into climbing a tree and then carved the image of the cross on the trunk, trapping the Devil up the tree. Jack extorted a promise from the Devil that he would never tempt Jack again before he was allowed to come down from the tree. According to the story, Jack got his comeuppance when he died and was refused entrance to heaven because of his evil ways, and the Devil wouldn't allow him in Hell due to the trick he played. Jack was doomed to wander in the cold darkness forever with only one ember in hollowed-out turnip to light his way. The practice of using the pumpkin for the lantern originated in the New World where the native gourd was plentiful.

Costume wearing, so much a part of modern Halloween tradition, also had its roots in old European tradition. It dates back to the Celtic rituals during the Sahmain when, in order to avoid possession by wandering spirits, people would dress in ghoulish costumes and noisily parade through the streets. Costume parties for adults were a part of Green River's Halloween scene. A 1919 *Star* article tells of a masquerade ball being held in the Social Hall, while a 1931 party of the 1907 "500 Club," a card-playing group, mentioned that prizes were awarded for the best costumes. The Culinary Workers Alliance #635 of Green River held a costumed dinner and dance in the basement of the Stanley Hotel in 1939. First prize for her costume of a scarecrow was awarded to Mrs. Evelyn Merchant while Mrs. Jack Shaw received second place for her depiction of an old prospector.

Church and community groups sponsored costume parties for children as well. The L.D.S. Primary held a party in 1933 where, "...all the kiddies came in costume". The Sweetwater Aerie #2350 Fraternal Order of Eagles and the Green River Volunteer Firefighters both held children's costume parties in 1952.

The practice of trick or treating was based on ancient traditions as well. The Celts made offerings of food and drink to appease the wandering spirits of Samhain. Also contributing to the custom of trick or treating was the Christian celebration of "souling." For All Soul's Day on November 2nd early Christians would travel between villages begging for "soul cakes", a bread with currents. For each soul cake the beggar received, he promised to say a prayer for the soul of a departed loved one of the giver. According to religious belief of the time, a soul remained in limbo for some time after death and his progress to heaven was sped on by prayers made on his behalf.

Dave Potter, who grew up in Green River in the 1940s and '50s recalled his final year of practicing the time-honored custom of trick or treating in a submission to the electronic newsletter *Lincoln High Mirth and Missives.*

> Although not of any historical importance I thought I would share one of my Halloween experiences. I can't remember whose idea it was for certain but I can probably take ownership. The truth is that Jim Crosson and I were at that awkward age of about twelve. We had started wondering whether or not we were too old to go trick or treating. I can't say how much time it took us to decide to

Green River Historic Preservation Commission

The L.D.S. Primary organization sponsors a circa-1940 Halloween party. (Photo courtesy Sweetwater County Historical Museum)

go "one last time," but apparently not long because we decided we would go two nights–Halloween Eve and Halloween Day. I mean, how neat was that? We could canvas more houses, collect more candy (hopefully Snickers bars) and it all meant heaven in our mouths. Talk about sweets and sickness– we were going to go whole hog that year.

We bought our masks from the five and dime store (Johnson's Variety Store), which is where we always bought them, and as I remember, the long floppy scary rubber ones were hung higher on the walls and the cheaper ones on the counters. I bought the ones I could reach which wasn't very high. We waited for dusk and took off. In a way it was kind of neat because we didn't run into other trick or treaters and had the street to ourselves. All went well for the first handful of houses even though we were starting to talk about the surprised look on some of the faces of the people who answered the door. After another dozen or so houses and hearing some of the people actually ask the question, "Isn't Halloween tomorrow?" we started to lose some of our enthusiasm and could only muster courage to knock on a few more doors before we decided to pack it up and head for home. It wasn't a huge haul but then again, there was always tomorrow night and we certainly wouldn't be going to the same houses. That wouldn't have been right now, would it? We had already had half of a Halloween and a whole one was just twenty-four hours away. The piles of candy in our big salad bowls were already starting to grow and the glue-smelling, slightly moist (around the mouth and nose area) masks could be put away until tomorrow night.

As a sign of the times, in the socially-conscious 1960s there was a great push on for the "Trick or Treat for UNICEF (United Nations Children's Fund)" Many youngsters carried the donation cans on their rounds in order to raise funds for underprivileged children worldwide. In Green River the drive was organized by the Green River Women's Club and was coordinated through local churches. "Through the fun of an evening, our boys and girls raised the equivalent of 2,786 shots of penicillin, each one enough to cure a child of yaws," Mrs. Vern Newman, chair of the local drive stated in a 1960 *Green River Star* article. "The coins they received could mean 5,700 vitamin capsules for children suffering from malnutrition, or the sulfone to treat successfully 139 young leprosy victims for three years."

The "trick" part of trick or treating was always a part of the holiday in America and usually consisted of harmless pranks such as tipping over outhouses and ash cans or soaping windows. However, in Green River of the 1930s, destructive pranks had become a real problem. A 1931 *Star* article described an increase in such activities. "Many auto tires have been injured by spikes being driven into them, some tires suffering deep knife cuts and some property about town destroyed in such a manner that costly repairs will have to be made."

Thus, during that decade the Green River Community Club began to give parties for children who signed a pledge which promised that they would abstain from vandalism and destruction of property in playing Hallowen pranks. A 1939 newspaper article promised, "..a huge bonfire at the softball park in the east end of town where games will be played and gifts distributed to the children... free rides on the city fire truck... a parade of all those participating will be formed for marching to the Isis Theatre, where a free show will be given."

The Man They Could Not Hang starring Boris Karloff was presented at a special midnight showing that same Halloween at the Isis Theatre. It was described as, "Weird... Horrifying... Fascinating... only Karloff, king of horror, could play this terror-packed role! Back from the grave for retribution comes a doctor turned demon, burning with a hate so strong that even the gallows are powerless before the might of his bloodlust."

In 1969 a Green River High School student organization, the National Honor Society, offered a Halloween service as a fund-raiser. A newspaper article announced that "Spook Insurance" would be for sale from members of the Society and their sponsors, Bill Duncan and Barbara Arnold. Buyers of the insurance were guaranteed cleanup and repair of Halloween depredations such as soaped windows, overturned garbage cans, chalked sidewalks and other repairable damages. The cost was 25 cents for car coverage, 50 cents for house coverage and $1.00 for business building coverage with the policy good for labor only.

Halloween is most children's second-favorite holdiay, surpassed only by Christmas. The recollections of those fun times continue to live in adult hearts as well. Dave Potter will forever cherish his memories of childhood Halloweens in Green River.

> The anticipation and excitement of Halloween as a young boy in Green River was always a joy and I believe it was the same for every kid in town. It meant costume parties at the churches, a scary movie at the Isis Theatre, deciding what to buy other "treaters" coming to your house (and of course refraining from eating too many of whatever that was before they came–hard to do), ganging up with neighborhood buddies to actually retrieve those "heavenly Halloween handouts"–and finally, what to wear over your costume. I mean, it could blow, snow, rain, be calm, or all of the above–those were the possibilities. I know one thing for certain, there was never any concern about your haul. It would be tasty and safe. As far as "tricks" were concerned I remember a few car windows being marked with bars of soap. That was the worst of the damage.

THE TRAVELS OF MONTY AND HIS WIFE

By: Bill Thompson

Once upon a time when I was a youth (obviously a long time ago), Mom brought home a version of the following story. She had been with a small group of ladies at a dinner party. A prize was awarded to the person who could complete it most accurately. Mom won with a perfect score. No surprise there... for years Edith M. Thompson was known for her meticulously researched historical articles in the *Casper Tribune Herald (Star)*, her many articles in various outdoor magazines and later for her Award winning book, *Beaver Dick - The Honor and the Heartbreak*. She was a recipient of many historical awards and honors. . . and oh, how much I learned from her. . .

Years later I used this as a teaching aid in my High School and College classes that dealt with Wyoming history and government. Some of you former students might recognize it.

As you read this simple and rather labored story, fill in the blanks with the correct name of the county. They are numbered in order. As an helpful hint, the number in parenthesis is the number of the county. So, time yourself...and enjoy.

Monty 1. (16) and his wife Natty lived in 2.(5) New York. They decided to 3. (23) their apartment and go 4. (21) the train. But, in spite of the fuel shortage, when they reached St. Louis they bought a 5. (12) car and with a 6.(8) of Wyoming, they traveled on. First they came to the 7.(l4) River and 8.(1) exclaimed, "Oh, the river is filled with 9.(4) As they went on they saw 10. (2) Peak and the 11. (22) Mountains. They were most surprised to see a cow with a 12. (9) and on down the road a 13. (17). They saw a statue of General 14. (3) and stopped to 15. (13) with a descendent of Chief 16. (20). After awhile they had to 17. (11) the car because something went wrong. Natty said, "I don't believe a 18. (18) will come along, you are 19. (10) to go and get help." After awhile Monty came back with a mechanic. He found surprising things... there were 20. (15) in the carburetor and 21. (6) in the engine (my apologies to Paul and Darrel Miller). He said, " I'll tow 22. (19) the next town and get it fixed." Which he did. Monty and

Natty liked Wyoming so well that they decided to settle down here and live in the land of 23. (7).

1.   2.   3.   4.   5.

6.   7.   8.   9.   10.

11.   12.   13.   14.   15.

16.   17.   18.   19.   20.

21.   22.   23.

Wyoming's 23 county members are: 1 Natrona, 2 Laramie, 3 Sheridan, 4 Sweetwater, 5 Albany, 6 Carbon, 7 Goshen, 8 Platte, 9 Big Horn, 10 Fremont, 11 Park, 12 Lincoln, 13 Converse, 14 Niobrara, 15 Hot Springs, 16 Johnson, 17 Campbell, 18 Crook, 19 Uinta, 20 Washakie, 21 Weston, 22 Teton, 23 Sublette

DECEMBER 7, 1941: UPRR WOMEN IN THE WORKFORCE

By: Marna Grubb

The Great Depression of the 1930s brought about difficult times in the United States. Then World War II, in the 1940s, triggered an economic boom and a resulting busy time for the railroads. Franklin D. Roosevelt was president of the United States at this time, 1933-1945.

With the demand for high numbers of men in the military, a stream of women began to assume jobs previously performed by men only, and railroad jobs were no exception. Up to this time, many felt that a "woman's place is in the home."

While I was growing up in Green River (1940s), nearly everyone's parents worked for the railroad. Therefore, I contacted a few residents who were employed by the railroad during this period to question them about women entering the workforce for the Union Pacific Railroad in Green River.

One of the residents I contacted was Hiney Krause who began working for the railroad as a "call boy" (a name used for crew callers) in 1923 when he was 14 years old and in the seventh grade. Three years later, he was transferred to the car department. After 50 years of service, Hiney retired in May of 1974. During his years of service he operated the "Big Hook" and operated three different wrecking derricks.

I also contacted Dale "Peg" Morris who began his employment with the Union Pacific Railroad in Green River as a plumber's helper in the B&B Department in 1930. He was 14 years of age. He continued working and going to high school off and on until he graduated in 1936. Dale became a switchman in 1942 and a yardmaster in 1943. He retired in 1976 with 43 years of service, which included a three-year lapse in service during the depression.

Since there was a continuous stream of trains traveling through the center of Green River, townspeople found entertainment in parking by the depot to watch all the activity. When the troop trains would stop for servicing, there would be a big rush across the street to the bars located along Railroad Avenue. Some would still be running back as the trains were beginning to pull away.

Hiney Krause remembered the Embassy having music and a loud speaker inviting the troops over.

Green River's Elsie Lee began working for the railroad in 1943 in the store department and transferred the same year to the yard office calling crews. The crew callers who had been known as "call boys" were now the "call girls." After confusion over the name, it was thought best to just call them crew callers. Elsie was later a billing clerk and ticket agent, retiring in 1982 after 30 years of service.

UP Coach Cleaners posed for this photo in front of the carman's shanty. Hiney Krause's wife, Ada, is shown center front. (Krause family photo)

W. Averell Harriman, visiting UP official at Green River Shops on October 25, 1952, with turntable operator Dorothy Twitchell Holbrook, pipefitter helper Edna Miller, and Mary Buckler. (Sweetwater County Historical Museum photo)

Elsie recalled some of the first ladies working with her as crew callers as Drucilla Rollins, Edith White, Martha Marino, Pat Roche, Delores Torres, Ricci Kirby and Bernice Bahan Barnhart. Bernice later became an engine dispatcher. Also calling were Bertha Ball and Catherine Maher Davis. Mrs. Deardon and her daughter, June Deardon, were both crew dispatchers.

Mary Bahan worked in the storehouse pricing material unloaded from boxcars and later transferred to the yard office. Anna Parvacini worked in the office at the storehouse. Flora Clark, Phyllis Hoover and Mrs. Ellis were clerks in the train dispatchers' office.

Barbara Martin (later Walker) began her career with the railroad in 1943 as a jumbo clerk recording in a "large" book each car on trains arriving and departing. Some of the ladies who

Green River Historic Preservation Commission

worked with her during World War II were Tula Kourbelas and Gertrude Beveridge. Barbara later became a diversion clerk, ticket clerk, rate clerk, payroll clerk and chief clerk.

Some of those in the yard office were Alice Riddle, Ruth Riddle, Melba Deardon, Margaret Berganzo, Lucy Gaston, Hilda Carroll, June Petrie, Shirley Hoover, Phyllis Ginger Stoll Braden, Mary Ann Farrah, Annie Hunter, Esther Rollins (later Spence), Mary Bodine and Georgia Petersen (later Proctor).

Margie Moore Davis was a clerk in the superintendent's office. Lorna Evers was a clerk in the Assistant Superintendent's office upstairs.

During the war years, Edna Miller was a pipefitter's helper at the roundhouse. Dorothy Twitchell (later Holbrook), Evelyn Merchant and Georgia Davis operated the turntable. Stamata "Sam" Curtis and Agnes Walker also worked in the roundhouse.

Hiney Krause advised that his wife, Ada, before they were married had been a coach cleaner. He remembered that some of the other coach cleaners around 1944 were Sophie Hamilton, Nellie Anderson and Bernice Braden. Dorothy Morrison, Wyonne Dailey and sister Beverly Daily Merchant also were coach cleaners.

Hiney reminisced that some of the troops wanted to know how Castle Rock got there. He advised them that "me and my partner took it up there last night!" They also were concerned about where the cowboys and Indians were.

Barbara said that, in the telegraph office during this period, there were PBX operators such as Myrtle Hoover, Mae Joy, Blanche Anderson, Lois Jones (later Robertson) and Louise Overman. Also in the telegraph office were Merle Stoll (later Hermansen), Numa Walker (later Grubb), Vonnie Gilmore Bundy, Jean Neiderheiser and Vera Oberreuter (later Lewis).

Vera Lewis said that things were really rockin' at the Narrow Gauge Bar on Railroad Avenue with dancing being provided for the servicemen while they socialized with local residents. Some servicemen had longer layovers while trains were being switched.

Elsie reminded me that inside the depot, many women were employed at the news stand and the beanery. The beanery served excellent meals to travelers, train crews and other railroad employees. Banquets with nice linens were served upstairs from the beanery in Lynch Hall. In the beanery were Evelyn Kinniburgh, Butch Hodges, Fern Roberts and Vivian Roche. The news stand provided snacks, newspapers, magazines and gifts.

Elsie, Barbara and Sharon Rhodes mentioned that Mrs. Bridget Bussart was one of the first women who worked for the railroad as a clerk beginning in April of 1919 during World War I and continuing into the 1940s during World War II before retiring. Also Lucy Coutts.

This has been just a glimpse at the people and what was happening at the railroad in Green River during World War II. I'm sure I may have misspelled some names or missed mentioning some very special ladies who contributed to this busy period in Green River history. If so, please accept my apologies.

GREEN RIVER MAYORS
1891 - 2003

GREEN RIVER MAYOR, COUNCIL AND POLICE

February 5, 1932
Front row: Mike Maher, Marshal; Bill Evers, Mayor from 1923 to
1935; and Charles Young, Night Police Officer.
Back row: Council members William Mortimer; E. E. Peters, F. O.
Young; and William Rogers. (Chris Jessen family photo)

GREEN RIVER MAYORS
1891 - 2003

HISTORY OF GREEN RIVER GOVERNANCE

Originally founded in 1868, Green River is one of the oldest cities in Wyoming, and has a long history of local government. The *Cheyenne Leader* mentioned the new town in the June 10, 1868 edition, "The city of Green River is laid out about a mile above the stage crossing where the railroad will cross the Green. A city company has been formed with H. M. Hook, Esq., formerly Mayor of Cheyenne and now one of its leading businessmen, as President and Frank B. Gilbert, Esq., formerly of the firm of Gilbert and Sons, Salt Lake City, as Secretary."

From its inception, Green River has always had a Mayor/Council form of government. Unfortunately, very little is known about territorial-era public officials. More complete city records were kept following the town's incorporation under the newly-formed State of Wyoming in 1891. They show the first election was held on July 15th of that year. The first City Council consisted of one Mayor, serving a one-year term in office, and four Councilmen, two serving a one-year term and two serving two-year terms.

This governmental structure remained in place until January 12, 1979 when Green River became a first-class city. The Council changed to include a Mayor and six Council members elected from three wards to staggered four-year terms.

A dramatic change in the way the city was governed took place on September 29, 1980 when Charter Ordinance One was adopted. This established a City Administrator position. The Mayor and City Council retained their legislative authority, but delegated most of the executive authority to a professional administrator who is directly responsible for City employees and operations.

In the one-and-a-quarter centuries since Green River was established, it has grown from a tiny railroad stop to a city of thousands. Mayors and Councils have addressed many issues relating to this growth and development from the purchase of

Green River Historic Preservation Commission

the first jail in 1895 to the massive growing pains of the 1970's boom.

The following pages display some of these remarkable people and their visions for the City of Green River.

MAYORAL HIGHLIGHTS

* Hugo Gaensslen served the longest number of years as Mayor – 13 years (1902-1915).
  Richard W. Waggener is second in the number of years served – 11 years (1971-1982).

* Two fathers and sons were Mayors:
  T. S. Taliaferro and son E. L. Taliaferro
  William Rogers and son T. E. Rogers.

* Three Mayors have had streets named for them:
  William Evers – Evers Street
  Franklin W. Wilkes – Wilkes Drive
  Richard W. Waggener – Waggener Circle.

* Bonnie Pendleton was Green River's only woman Mayor. Pendleton Parkway was named in her honor.

* Several Mayors were medical doctors:
  Dr. J. W. Hawk
  Dr. John Gilligan
  Dr. R. C. Stratton
  Dr. R. J. Stapleton was a dentist.

* Evers Ballfied (later changed to Evers Park) was named in honor of Mayor William Evers.

* Stratton-Myers Park was named for Mayor R. C. Stratton and Council member Carl Myers.

EDWARD J. MORRIS

Edward J. Morris and his twin brother Robert were born on November 8, 1851 in Peru, Illinois. His family came to Wyoming in 1869 and settled at South Pass. His mother was Esther Morris, a pioneer woman of the state, credited as being the author of women's suffrage in Wyoming. She was also the first woman justice of the peace.

Mr. Morris later moved to Green River where he served as

Edward J. Morris
1891-1893 1896-1898

The Morris Mercantile building was located on the corner of West Railroad Avenue and North Cen-ter Street. (Sweetwater County Historical Museum photo)

County Clerk for a number of years. On July 15, 1891, after the town's incorporation under the laws of the State of Wyoming, Mr. Morris became Green River's first Mayor.

He held the first Council meeting on August 3, 1891. The first Council members to serve with him were Dr. John H. Gilligan, Walter S. Powell, Jacob F. Snyder and Thomas F. Carey. Mr. Morris was re-elected in 1892, 1896 and 1897. At the beginning of town government in Green River, the Mayor served a one-year term.

AS MAYOR: Under Morris, the first ordinance adopted was "An Ordinance Adopting Town Seal." Among other ordinances adopted were "An Ordinance Concerning the Appointive Offices of the Town and Prescribing Their Duties and Terms of Office" and "An Ordinance for the Protection of Growing Trees."

THOMAS S. TALIAFERRO, JR.

T.S. Taliaferro, Jr.
1893-1896

Thomas Seddon Taliaferro Jr. was born July 1, 1865 in Virginia. He moved to Wyoming at age 18, later working for the Union Pacific Railroad as an agent.

Mr. Taliaferro was responsible for the construction of the Opera House and several residences. He was president and manager of the Green River Electric Light and Power Company. He also served as President of the 1st National Bank in Green River and President of the Green River Mercantile Company.

In May of 1893, at the age of 28, Mr. Taliaferro was elected Mayor of Green River and re-elected in 1894 and 1895.

After resigning from his position as Mayor in 1896, Mr. Taliaferro became a practicing attorney in Rock Springs in 1900.

AS MAYOR: During his years as Mayor, an ordinance concerning and providing for the construction of sidewalks and an ordinance regarding the cleaning of snow from sidewalks were adopted.

The Green River Fire Department and fire limits were established in 1893. In December of 1894, plans for a park on Railroad Avenue were accepted and carried out.

LATER, on November 16, 1931, the Town of Green River, with a population of a little more than 3000 deemed that "an emergency exists" and passed and approved Ordinance No. 175, which prohibits door-to-door selling. William Evers was Mayor at the time. The ordinance, still referred to as the Green River Ordinance, was drawn up by Attorney T. S. Taliaferro Jr. to "abate the nuisance" of house-to-house canvassing to private homes.

In the 1890s a band shell was built in the Railroad Park located on Railroad Avenue. (City of Green River photo)

ELMER E. PETERS

E.E. Peters
1896-1896

Elmer E. Peters was born April 4, 1861 in Hancock County, Ohio. He attended elementary school in Ohio. In 1844, he moved to Omaha, Nebraska, and was employed for three years by the Union Pacific Railroad.

Mr. Peters moved to Green River on December 31, 1887. He worked as a carpenter for the railroad until 1890. In 1894, he began a lumber and contracting business, which built many homes and businesses in Green River.

Mr. Peters served as Mayor from March 1896 until May 1896, filling the unexpired term of Mayor T. S. Taliaferro Jr.

In 1913, Mr. Peters established the first garage in Green River known as Peters Motor Company.

He passed away in August of 1942.

AS MAYOR: In the brief time Mr. Peters was in office, an ordinance was passed providing for the construction of a bridge across the Green River. The bridge was completed in the late 1890s by Wrought Iron Bridge Company for approximately $2,500.

THE E. E. PETERS LUMBER COMPANY: The E. E. Peters Lumber Company was located at 316 East First North, later known as Flaming Gorge Way. The building is a two-story, wooden-frame structure on the corner of Flaming Gorge Way and North Third East Street.

Alfred Young Jr. had purchased the property from S. I. Field in 1890. Robert Morris purchased the property in 1895. The property was purchased by E. E. Peters in 1904.

This was the first lumber yard, contractor and builder business in Green River. Mr. Peters built and started the E. E. Peters Lumber Company in 1894. Mr. Peters also had a blacksmith shop and stables with hay, grain and feed.

In 1898 he also was selling coal. In 1913, he began repairing automobiles in his blacksmith shop.

In 1916, he sold the lumber business to the Weber Lumber Company and continued in the garage business until 1922 when he built a larger garage to the east. He continued in the storage and second-hand goods business until 1937.

The E.E. Peters Lumber Company store was located at 316 East 1st North Street, later known as Flaming Gorge Way. (Sweetwater County Historical Museum photo)

ROBERT H. LAWRENCE

Robert Lawrence was born in Ohio. He was a manager of the dry goods department of the firm Hunter & Morris. At one time he and a partner managed the firm of Lawrence & Hoadley Mercantile Company.

On May 10, 1898, he was elected Mayor of the Town of Green River and was re-elected in May, 1899. He later served as Town Treasurer

R.H. Lawrence
1898-1900

Green River circa 1897-1899, looking south from Castle Rock. (Chris Jessen family photo)

from 1906 to1910.

Mr. Lawrence enjoyed writing poems and setting them to music. A copy of his song, "Wyoming Rose" is filed with the State Library.

AS MAYOR: While Mr. Lawrence was Mayor, the council adopted an ordinance "Dividing the town of Green River into five wards" and an ordinance "Granting a franchise to the Rocky Mountain Bell Telephone Company the rights to place and maintain fixtures necessary to conduct a telephone business in Green River."

Mr. Lawrence appointed T. S. Taliaferro Jr. attorney for the Town of Green River at a salary of $150 per month.

DR. JACOB W. HAWK

Dr. J.W. Hawk
1900-1901 1917-1921
1923-1925

Dr. Hawk was born November 12, 1857 in Mahaska County, Iowa. He received his degree from the College of Physicians and Surgeons at Keokuk, Iowa, in 1882.

In 1896, Dr. Hawk and his wife, Dr. Charlotte Hawk, moved to Green River. Together they served as surgeon and assistant surgeon for the Union Pacific Railroad.

At the time of their arrival, downtown Green River was two blocks long, consisting of one drugstore, one bank, one Chinese restaurant, one general store, one

The Tomahawk Hotel was named after its two owners, Mr. Thomas Welsh and Dr. Hawk. (Sweetwater County Historical Museum photo)

movie theater and six saloons.

They maintained a four-bed hospital in the basement of their home because the nearest hospital was in Rock Springs. Dr. Hawk also was officer and director of the 1st National Bank of Green River, County Health Commissioner, County Physician and Examining Surgeon.

Green River's Tomahawk Hotel was named after its two owners, Mr. Thomas Welsh and Dr. Hawk.

Dr. Hawk served a total of seven years as Mayor from 1900 to 1901, 1917 to 1921, and 1923 to 1925.

He passed away while serving as Mayor in May of 1925 at the age of 68.

AS MAYOR: Council adopted an ordinance concerning levy and collection of special assessment and tax (1917). A resolution was adopted providing for the construction of a sewer system for the Town of Green River. Signs were provided informing tourists of camping grounds in Green River (1917).

DR. JOHN H. GILLIGAN

Dr. John H. Gilligan
1901-1902

Dr. John H. Gilligan was born in Ireland on September 13, 1856. He completed his medical schooling in Ireland and then came to the United States where he first practiced medicine in Nebraska and Colorado.

Early 1889, Dr. Gilligan came to Green River to practice medicine for the Union Pacific Railroad Company.

Dr. Gilligan was elected Green River's sixth mayor in May of 1901.

In addition to an interest in the medical profession, he also was a sheep man and rancher.

Dr. Gilligan maintained an active practice until he was 80 years old. He passed away on June 30, 1949 at the age of 93.

AS MAYOR: During his administration, a resolution was adopted for a sewage system to be connected with the sewer of the Union Pacific Railroad Company. At that time, sewage was being dumped directly into the river.

Also, an ordinance was passed for the licensing of gambling houses and prescribing the penalty for gambling without a license.

Dr. Gilligan's home was located on the corner of First East and East Second North. (Sweetwater County Historical Museum photo)

HUGO F. GAENSSLEN

Hugo Gaensslen
1902-1915

Hugo Fredrick Gaensslen was born in Chicago, Illinois on September 21, 1869. He attended private schools in Illinois and graduated from Power Business College in 1887. He continued his education at the U.S. Brewers Academy in New York City, where he graduated with a degree of MAB in 1891.

Throughout the years he worked his way upward in commercial circles and eventually became proprietor of "The Brewery" in Green River. He was principal stockholder, general manager, secretary and treasurer of The Brewery until the business was abandoned with the coming of prohibition in 1919.

Mr. Gaensslen was president of the State Bank of Green River, vice president of the Big Island Cattle Company, president of the Green River Livestock Company and vice president of the Green River Mercantile Company.

He was mayor for eight terms from 1902 to 1915, serving 21 consecutive years as council member and mayor.

Mr. Gaensslen died December 22, 1931 at the age of 62.

AS MAYOR: Among the accomplishments while he was Mayor, "Island Park" was completed, a dancing pavilion was built, a bridge placed and trees planted.

The first publication of Town Council Minutes in *The Green River Star* took place.

A resolution was passed providing for the purchase of a cemetery.

Various ordinances which were passed include "Providing where the garbage shall be dumped" (May 1907) and "Requiring cement sidewalks on the principal business blocks" (May 1908).

THE GREEN RIVER BREWERY, the first brewery in the Territory of Wyoming, was built and owned by Adam Braun in 1872. The brewery was located at 46 West Railroad Avenue.

In 1880, Karl Spinner Sr. purchased and operated the Green River Brewery, specializing in bottled beer for family use. Spinner hired Hugo Gaensslen, who held a MAB degree as brew-master.

In 1891, Mr. Gaensslen purchased the brewery, specialized in lager beer and bottled beer was a specialty. The Green River Brewery name was changed to Hugo Gaensslen Brewery in 1891. In 1899, the name was changed to the Sweetwater Brewing Company.

Mr. Gaensslen built a new stone brewery building in 1901. The building was modeled after the Chicago water tower and the stone was quarried locally.

Sweetwater Brewing Company, "The Brewery," was located on Railroad Avenue in Green River in the early 1900s. (Sweetwater County Historical Museum photo)

Charles L. Young
1915-1917

CHARLES L. YOUNG

Charles Young was born on April 4, 1868 in Elgin, Illinois. He came to Green River in the late 1880s at the age of 20.

Mr. Young served as the town's Night Marshal for many years, as well as the Sheriff from 1903 until 1904. He served as Green River's Mayor from 1915 to 1917. During the Depression years, Mr. Young owned and operated the "Candy Kitchen."

He passed away in May of 1944 at the age of 76.

AS MAYOR: An ordinance of interest adopted during his term was "An Ordinance declaring the fast driving of automobiles within the limits of the Town of Green River and the driving of automobiles within the limits of the Town of Green River after dark without lights constitute nuisances, prescribing penalties for committing the same and providing that the same be abated by the Police Officers of said town." This ordinance set the speed limit within the town limits to not exceed 8 miles per hour.

In 1923, under Mayor Hawk, the ordinance was amended and the speed limit was set at 18 miles per hour, 15 miles per hour within the business district.

Town of Green River around 1915, population approximately 1,200. (Sweetwater County Historical Museum photo)

CHARLES NICOLL

Charles Nicoll
1921-1923

Charles Nicoll was born July 2, 1874 in Kerremuir Forfarshire, Scotland. He was educated in the public schools and graduated from Dundee University in 1893. He immigrated to the United States in 1904 at the age of 30.

Following a brief time in Colorado, Mr. Nicoll moved to Green River in 1905 as manager of the Morris Mercantile Company.

On October 1, 1910, he became a naturalized citizen.

In 1916, he established his own grocery and hardware business, later purchasing the Schwartz Men's Clothing Store. He operated these businesses until 1932.

Mr. Nicoll served as mayor of the Town of Green River from 1921 to 1923.

Mr. Nicoll served many years on the school board and was chairman during the construction of the Washington Elementary School.

Mr. Nicoll passed away in January 1943 at the age of 68.

AS MAYOR: Under Mayor Nicoll, *The Green River Star* was appointed the official newspaper (1921).

The Union Pacific Railroad donated $500 for the purchase of a new town fire truck. The fire truck was personalized with the Mayor's name without his knowledge.

The organization of a town police force was established in 1922.

Green River's first motor-driven fire truck was purchased in 1922 from American La France while Billl Hutton was Fire Chief and Charles Nicoll was Mayor. The Mayor had been instrumental in its purchase; therefore, the truck was personalized with his name without the Mayor's knowledge. Fire Chief Hutton is at the wheel with Deputy Sheriff/Volunteer Fireman Chris Jessen at the rear. (Sweetwater County Historical Museum photo)

WILLIAM EVERS

William Evers
1925-1935

William Evers was born February 28, 1885 in Crawford County, Iowa.

He came to Green River in 1909 and became a carpenter with a bridge and general building corps of the Union Pacific Railroad. He later formed a partnership with Victor Smith and Thomas James and established the Superior Lumber Company of Rock Springs.

Three months later, he opened and became manager of the company's branch yard in Green River. He retained that position until the business was turned over to the Overland Lumber Company in 1918. That same year he became general manager of a contracting building business called the Evers Bros. who built the high school, Stanley Hotel, Washington School and Green River Mercantile.

Mr. Evers served as Mayor from 1925-1935. During the 1931 election, Mr. Evers' opposing candidate was Helen Mucho. Mr. Evers received 639 votes to Mrs. Mucho's 110.

AS MAYOR: While Mr. Evers was Mayor, the town bought land south of the river to be held for residential and industrial development.

Ordinance No. 175, which has become widely known as the Green River Ordinance, was adopted. This ordinance, which prohibits door-to-door selling, has been adopted by other com-munities throughout the United States.

Evers Street and Evers Ballfield (later known as Evers Park) were named in his honor.

The underpass beneath the Union Pacific main line through Green River was opened to public use in August of 1937. (Sweetwater County Historical Museum photo)

SAMUEL S. HOOVER

Samuel S. Hoover was born November 3, 1885 in Harrisonburg, Virginia.

Mr. Hoover moved to Green River from Missouri in 1915. He was assistant yard master at the Union Pacific Railroad. In November 1926, he was elected to the State Assembly serving in the 1927 regular session.

Samuel S. Hoover
1935-1939

Mr. Hoover was elected Mayor of the Town of Green River in 1935. He resigned in 1939 to accept the position of State Welfare Director in Cheyenne.

AS MAYOR: The main issue during the first part of Mr. Hoover's term was street improvements.

Safety and convenience features around the Union Pacific Railroad tracks in the center of town were addressed with the completion of an underpass and a pedestrian overpass.

The underpass beneath the Union Pacific main line through Green River was opened to public use in August of 1937. (Sweetwater County Historical Museum photo)

DR. RICHARD C. STRATTON

Dr. R.C. Stratton
1939-1940

Richard C. Stratton was born December 16, 1904 in Sedan, Kansas.

He graduated from Ottawa University and the University of Kansas Medical School at Kansas City, Missouri. His internship was served at St. Mary's Hospital in Kansas City.

After practicing medicine in Lyman for two years, Dr. Stratton opened an office in Green River in 1933.

In 1939, Dr. Stratton was ap-

In 1998, a stage building was constructed at Stratton-Myers Park. It also houses the restrooms, a concession area and storage room. The Flaming Gorge Days concerts have been held at this location beginning around the year 2000. (City of Green River/Roger Moellendorf photo)

pointed to fill the unexpired term of Mayor Hoover. He was then elected in 1939. He resigned in August of 1940 due to the fact that he would be out of town for a year.

During World War II, he was a Major in the U. S. Army Medical Corps and was awarded the Purple Heart and Distinguished Service Cross for his military service.

He returned to Green River in 1945 following his discharge and was appointed Sweetwater County Health Officer, serving in that position for many years.

Dr. Stratton retired from his private medical practice in 1973, although he continued as medical consultant for the mines for a few years. He passed away on March 17, 1977.

AS MAYOR: An ordinance was adopted regulating traffic through the underpass.

A lease was signed with the CCC Camp for furnishing water to Camp DG-76.

The Zehawi Athletic Fields at the Stratton-Myers Complex were dedicated in 1997. They were named in honor of Ahmed Zehawi and his family. Zehawi was instrumental in establishing soccer in Green River. He continued his efforts until the high school adopted a soccer program in Green River. The field offers three soccer fields and three ball fields. (City of Green River/Roger Moellendorf photo)

WILLIAM ROGERS

William Rogers
1940-1943

William Rogers was born December 4, 1862 in Breckonshire, South Wales. His family moved to the United States when he was 8 years old. They settled in Bevier, Macon County, Missouri, where he was educated in public schools and St. James Military Academy of Macon for one year.

Mr. Rogers came to Rock Springs where he worked in the mines for the Union Pacific Coal Company and held various positions with several companies during the next few years.

In 1902, he moved to Green River, having been appointed Deputy County Treasurer of Sweetwater County, serving five years in that position.

He then served as Deputy County Assessor for three years and postmaster for eight years, 1907 through 1915. In 1919 he became cashier of the State Bank of Green River, where he held the position for 25 years, and became vice president in 1943.

Mr. Rogers was a member of the Green River town council for nine years. In 1940, he was appointed Mayor to fill the unexpired term of Dr. Stratton. Mr. Rogers was elected to the office in 1941 and served until 1943.

He and his wife, Isabella Pierce, had three children, Eva, Sarah and Thomas E. Thomas later served as Mayor of Green River in the 50s and 60s.

William passed away April 13, 1953 at the age of 91.

AS MAYOR: During William Rogers's term as Mayor, Sec-tion 1 in the Riverview Cemetery became known as the "Veterans Plot," a section of the cemetery designated for veterans only.

The Social Hall was purchased from the Union Pacific Rail-road for use as a Town Hall.

For several years, the State Bank was located in the Hotel Tomahawk building as shown in the photo above. William Rogers was a cashier at the State Bank of Green River for 25 years. He became vice president in 1943. (Sweetwater County Historical Museum photo.)

EDWARD L. TALIAFERRO

E.L. Tallaferro
1943-1947

Edward L. Taliaferro was born October 13, 1905 in Rock Springs where he spent the early years and received his elementary education.

Upon graduation from Epis Boys High School in Alexandria, Virginia, Mr. Taliaferro entered the banking business. He was president of the First National Bank for many years and co-owner of the Green River Mercantile and Big Sandy Livestock Company.

He was elected Mayor in 1943 and re-elected in 1945.

T. S. Taliaferro, Green River's second Mayor, was Edward's father. Edward passed away September 23, 1987 at the age of 81.

AS MAYOR: During his term as Mayor, the town purchased the land south of the river, which later became the Rancho, Liberty, Valley View, Hutton Heights and Paxton Webb subdivisions.

Ordinance #338 was adopted regulating and prohibiting the maintaining of livestock within the corporate limits of the town of Green River.

When Mr. Taliaferro left office in 1947, the town was $56,000 richer.

RANCHO ADDITION AT GREEN RIVER, WYO.

Green River looking east show-ing newly-constructed homes in the Rancho and Liberty Additions circa, 1950. This land, south of the river, had been purchased while Edward Taliaferro was mayor. (Sweetwater County Historical Museum photo)

DR. R. J. STAPLETON

Dr. R.J. Stapleton
1947-1949

Roy J. Stapleton graduated from Creighton University in 1924 with a degree in Dentistry.

Mr. Stapleton came from Cheyenne to Green River in 1930 to open his dental practice. He continued his practice in Green River for 41 years until his retirement in July, 1971.

Dr. Stapleton served as Mayor from 1947 to 1949.

He was active in civic organizations as chairman of the Green River Promotion Committee from 1959 to 1961, president of the Green River Lions Club in 1942 and chairman of the Green River Airport Committee in 1961.

Upon his retirement in 1971, he and his wife moved to Arizona.

AS MAYOR: Among the ordinances passed was #353 prohibiting gambling in the town of Green River. Also approved was Ordinance #354 prohibiting the sale or use of fireworks within the town of Green River except for public display under a permit from the Chief of Police.

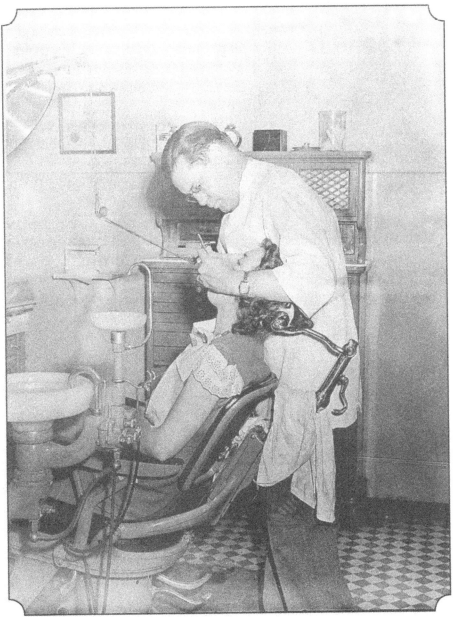

Dr. R.J. Stapleton shown at work at his dentist office located upstairs in the First National Bank building on Green River's East Railroad Avenue. (Sweetwater County Historical Museum/Proctor photo)

FRANKLIN W. WILKES

Franklin W. Wilkes
1949-1955 1959-1963

Franklin W. Wilkes was born September 2, 1914 in Evanston, Wyoming. He attended schools in Salt Lake and moved to Green River in 1941.

Mr. Wilkes worked as a switchman for the Union Pacific Railroad for 30 years, retiring in 1975.

He served as Mayor from 1949 to 1955 and 1959 to 1963.

Mr. Wilkes was a member of the Eagles No. 2350 Post and Golden Hour Senior Citizens.

Wilkes Drive, located in Hutton Heights, was named in his honor.

Mr. Wilkes passed away August 15, 1981 at the age of 66.

AS MAYOR: During his years as Mayor, the town acquired its first packer-type garbage truck and its first pumper fire truck. Also many streets were paved.

A town hall was constructed for the offices of the town government at a cost of $25,000, which was paid in cash.

The Planning and Zoning Committee was established in 1960, along with a schedule of uniform building codes.
A sewer disposal plant was built on the south side of town.

This city hall building was constructed in 1954 while Mayor Wilkes was in office. This was the first city hall building which the Town of Green River had built. Previous to this, they had either rented, leased or purchased buildings to use as a meeting place for the Town Council and to carry on the town business. (City of Green River/Dick Waggener photo)

THOMAS E. ROGERS

T.E. Rogers
1955-1959 1963-1965

Thomas E. Rogers was born October 3, 1894 in Rock Springs.

Mr. Rogers was cashier of the Citizens National Bank in Cheyenne and active as president of the State Bank of Green River. He was a Certified Public Accountant and, at one time, headed the State Board of Public Accountancy.

Mr. Rogers served as Mayor of the Town of Green River from 1955-1959 and 1963-1965.

Mr. Rogers was manager of the Green River Mercantile Company and past president of the Green River Chamber of Commerce.

He passed away in 1970 at the age of 76.

AS MAYOR: One of the resolutions passed while he was in office was #761 changing the name of 1st North Street to Flaming Gorge Way.

Green River Historic Preservation Commission

Green River, 11-10-56, looking north. The newly-constructed Rancho housing can be seen at the lower right, leading the way to further construction south of the river. The shadow of Mansface Rock is in the foreground. (WHD photo)

WILLIAM J. LUZMOOR, JR.

W.J. Luzmoor, Jr.
1965-1969

William "Bill" Luzmoor Jr. was born December 10, 1920 in Lafayette, Colorado, where he attended elementary school. He received his junior high and high school education in Boulder and graduated from the University of Colorado with a degree in Journalism in 1942. He then joined the Marine Corps and served for four years.

After his discharge in 1946, he joined his wife in Hampton, Iowa, where he was briefly employed with the *Hampton News and Chronicle*. From there he moved to Lander, Wyoming, where he worked on the *Wyoming State Journal* for 11 years.

After a brief return to Colorado, he arrived in Green River in 1959 and accepted a position with *The Green River Star*, where he remained for nearly 22 years.

He served as Mayor of the Town of Green River from 1965 to 1969.

Mr. Luzmoor was a Charter member of the Lander Lions Club and a member of the Green River Lions Club. He also was a member of the Golden Hour Senior Citizens.

Bill passed away in May of 1994.

AS MAYOR: The Industrial Revenue Bond issue ($27 million) for the development of Allied Chemical's plant and mine was passed and signed by Mayor Luzmoor.

Also plans for the Evers Field complex were drawn up, Expedition Island was dedicated as a National Historic Landmark, and the "GR" lettering project on Mansface Mountain was completed. The letters are an identifying symbol for the town.

During this period, the town budget exceeded $200,000 for the first time.

The 1869 Powell-Colorado Expedition monument was dedicated at Green River's Expedition Island in 1969. (City of Green River/Dick Waggener photo)

RICHARD D. SCHUCK

Richard D. Schuck
1969-1971

Richard D. Schuck was born on August 8, 1932 in Milford, Nebraska. He received his BS degree from the University of Wyoming and his Master's degree from the University of Wisconsin.

Mr. Schuck moved to Green River in 1959 after accepting a teaching position with School District #2. Dick taught in the High School Industrial Arts Department for 13 years. In 1968, he began the first Building Trades Program in Wyoming. When he left his position at the high school, he became Vocation Director at Western Wyoming College for two years.

Mr. Schuck then became Employment Supervisor for Al-lied Chemical, where he worked until 1981.

Mr. Schuck served as Mayor of Green River from 1969 to 1971.

After building several houses in Green River, he took up construction full time and began Schuck Construction.

Dick is a past president of the Green River Jaycees, past district director of the Wyoming Education Association and served two terms as president of the Green River Lions Club.

AS MAYOR: During Mayor Schuck's term, Green River's first shopping center, the Hutton Heights Shopping Center, began construction and the complete paving of the South Side was accomplished.

The controversial "no-burn" Ordinance #905 was passed during Mayor Schuck's term.

Mr. Schuck served as councilman for four years in addition to being one of Green River's mayors.

The Hillcrest Shopping Center had a grand opening in April 1970. It was located on the west side of Uinta Drive. The Center consisted of Castle Department Store, Hillcrest Drug Mart, and Mr. D's Food Center, all located along the top. As shown in this photo, additional stores had been added down along the side. The name was changed to Hutton Heights Shopping Center in 1974. (City of Green River/Richard Waggener photo)

ROY K. LAKE

Roy "Rosie" K. Lake
1971-1971

Roy "Rosie" Lake was born on May 22, 1904 in Evanston, Wyoming, where he was raised and educated. Rosie moved to Green River in 1947 and worked as a mechanical supervisor for the Union Pacific Railroad. He also was employed with FMC Corporation for some time.

Mr. Lake served as Green River Mayor from May 1971 until he resigned in July of the same year, reportedly due to ill health.

Mr. Lake was well known around Green River for his Christmas spirit as he donned a Santa suit and strung Christmas lights and decorations around his home. This enthusiasm spread to his neighbors, who in turn also lit up Jensen Street at Christmas time.

He passed away July 1985 at the age of 81.

AS MAYOR: In the 1971 election, "Rosie" Lake won election as Mayor by 938 votes to Mr. Schuck's 267 votes. The number of voters set a new town election high. As quoted from *The Green River Star*, "Much of the heavy vote has been attributed to opposition to the new 'no-burn' garbage and trash disposal ordinance recently adopted after several months of controversy over the subject."

Mayor Lake signed assessment district #33 documents to improve Barnhart, Andrews, Bramwell, Monroe and several other streets in that area. This work included extensive paving, curb and gutter, and drainage improvements.

Mr. Lake's residence on Jensen Street was always an attraction each Christmas season as he displayed the many lighted decorations he had made. There would be a special night when he invited Santa to greet youngsters and their parents and candy was given. (*The Green River Star* photos of December 21, 1967)

RICHARD W. WAGGENER

Richard Waggener
1971-1982

Richard W. Waggener was born January 24, 1930 in Green River, to Mr. and Mrs. Edgar E. Waggener. His father was transferred to Cheyenne when Dick was 8 years old. Dick graduated from Cheyenne High School in 1948 and from the University of Wyoming in 1952 with a BS degree in Engineering. He then returned to Green River, accepting employment with FMC Corporation in 1952. He held the position of Project Supervisor at retirement from FMC in 1985.

After retiring, Mr. Waggener spent numerous hours in volunteer work serving on the Hospice Board, Sweetwater County Drug and Alcohol Awareness group, and was a committed member of the Episcopal Church.

Mr. Waggener began his many years with city government with his appointment to the Green River Planning and Zoning Commission in June, 1965. Throughout the next 18 years he served on the Green River City Council as Council President and as Mayor. November, 1978, brought about a four-year term for a mayor, and Mr. Waggener was the first to serve in such a term. He did not seek re-election in 1982.

In 1984, Mr. Waggener became the second Green River citizen to receive the prestigious honor of Distinguished Citizen. Mr. Waggener served in the 1985-86 State Legislature as a Representative from Sweetwater County. Later he continued to be involved in government as Assistant Director of the Wyoming Association of Municipalities in Cheyenne.

AS "BOOM TOWN" MAYOR: Between 1970 and 1980, while Richard Waggener was mayor, Green River skyrocketed from 4,000 to nearly 13,000 inhabitants. The trona industry breathed life into the area. With the boom came many serious problems.

A housing shortage developed. Tent cities and unplanned mobile-home parks sprang up everywhere. The trona-processing companies found themselves forced to construct housing for their employees.

Mayor Waggener was instrumental in the construction of a new city hall building. It was dedicated in December of 1982. (City of Green River/Dick Waggener photo)

To cope with all the demands of city government, Mayor Waggener was instrumental in making a dramatic change in how the city was governed. On September 29, 1980, Charter Ordinance No. One was adopted. This established a City Administrator position. The Mayor and Council Members retained their legislative authority, but delegated most of the executive authority to a professional administrator who would be directly responsible for city employees and day-to-day operations. The city hired its first City Administrator in 1981. This form of government still continues today (2003).

Mr. Waggener was serving as Mayor when Green River became a First Class City in January of 1979.

Chambers in the new City Hall building, December 1982. (Sweetwater County Historical Museum photo)

Trailers crowded into Routh's Trailer Court at the east en-trance to Green River during the "boom" years, 1970-1980. The larger building was a Husky's station and cafe. Across the highway are railroad tracks filled with trona cars ready for shipment or empties waiting to be filled. (Sweetwater County Historical Museum photo)

Bonnie Pendleton
1983-1986

BONNIE PENDLETON

Bonnie Pendleton was born December 18, 1940 in Tryon, North Carolina. She attended her first twelve years of school in Tryon, then attended a liberal arts college in Berea, Kentucky, for two years. She transferred to the University of Wyoming and received her B.A. degree in 1963 and her M.A. degree in 1965 in American Studies.

She taught English and Social Studies at Calloway, Nebraska, for two years and then moved to Lusk, Wyoming, where she taught at the Lusk Jr. High.

In 1974, Mrs. Pendleton moved to Green River with her two children and her husband, who had been hired as high school band instructor. At that time there were no positions available in the English Department in School District #2, so she did volunteer work in the community joining the Garden Club and Women's Club and became involved in civic projects. Mayor Waggener appointed Mrs. Pendleton to the Committee on Downtown Business Development.

In 1980, Mrs. Pendleton became part-time coordinator for the Right-to-Read program where she recruited volunteers to work with illiterate people. The program eventually required her to work full time with two assistants. The program became known as the Adult Learning Center, of which Mrs. Pendleton became the Director.

Mrs. Pendleton was Green River's first councilwoman (1977-1982) being appointed to fill the unexpired term of Walt Goldsmith and, subsequently, became the first woman mayor of Green River.

She was elected mayor in 1982 and served from January, 1983, until December, 1986. She also was elected to head the Wyoming Association of Municipalities board of directors.

She served as President of the University of Wyoming Advisory Board for Graduate Students in Adult Education and on a Governor-appointed position with the State Department of Education Chapter 2 Advisory Committee.

Mayor Pendleton was a strong advocate of beautification projects during her term. A portion of the Uinta Drive beautification project was accomplished with manpower from the City's Parks and Recreation Department laying sod along the west side of the highway. (City of Green River/Roger Moellendorf photo)

AS MAYOR: The initial planning budget and setting of fees and charges for the new Recreation Center were undertaken during her term. The City worked together with School District #2 to help reduce the cost of this joint project.

Mrs. Pendleton was a strong advocate of beautification projects which were completed along Flaming Gorge Way and the west side of Uinta Drive.

In the Spring of 2003, Pendleton Parkway blossomed richly. (City of Green River/ Roger Moellendorf photo)

PENDLETON PARKWAY: In 2002, after receiving a petition signed by local residents, the Green River Governing Body approved the renaming of the Riverview islands to Pendleton Parkway. This was to honor former Mayor Bonnie Pendleton who was instrumental in promoting Green River's beautification efforts, one of which was the islands separating traffic on Riverview Drive.

In the Spring of 2003, Pendleton Parkway blossomed richly. (City of Green River/Roger Moellendorf photo)

Donald G. Van Matre Jr.
1987-1990

DONALD G. VAN MATRE JR.

Donald G. Van Matre, Jr. was born in Rock Springs, Wyoming, on June 13, 1942. He was raised and educated in Eden Valley, Wyoming, attending Green River High School his junior and senior years.

Mr. Van Matre received his Bachelor's Degree in Business Administration from Idaho State University and his Master's Degree in Education from Hampton Institute, Virginia.

Mr. Van Matre served 20 years of active service with the U.S. Army Aviation Branch and is a graduate of the Command and General Staff College, Fort Leavenworth, Kansas. He retired as a Lieutenant Colonel.

Mr. Van Matre served as Mayor from 1987 through 1990.

AS MAYOR: With a decrease in revenues during his administration, Mayor Van Matre pushed for "Doing As Much With Less."

Street reconstruction activity did continue, as well as the continuation of the beautification of Flaming Gorge Way.

FMC Park was annexed into the City, plus the City took over operation of the Water Distribution System.

Green River celebrated Wyoming's centennial in 1990 with special planned events and parades. Union Pacific locomotive No. 8444 made an appearance to help with the festivities. (*The Green River Star* photo)

GEORGE A. ECKMAN

George A. Eckman
1991-1994

George Eckman was born in Baltimore, Maryland, October 22, 1948. He grew up in a rural/suburban area near Catonsville, Maryland. He earned an Associate Degree in Education at Catonsville Community College and a Bachelor's Degree in History at Towson State University.

Mr. Eckman was actively involved in the political and social transformations of the 1960s, gaining a deep appreciation of the complexities of modern society and its impacts on contemporary life.

Mr. Eckman taught history and science at public school level in Maryland, West Virginia and in New Mexico.

During the early 1970s, he traveled extensively in this country, Mexico and Canada, wandering and experiencing life in the "University of America."

He moved to Wyoming in 1974 and initially lived in the desert near the ghost town of Bryan. He obtained employment at a local trona mine.

He began involvement in state and local political affairs in 1982 and became active in the state Democratic party.

Mr. Eckman began his service with the City on the Planning and Zoning Revision Commission and the Board of Adjustment. He served on the Green River City Council from 1986 through 1990.

He was elected Mayor in 1990 and began his term in January of 1991.

The Green River Vol-unteer Fire Depart-ment moved into its new station at the corner of Shoshone and Hitching Post in October, 1994. (City of Green River photo)

AS MAYOR: Mr. Eckman assisted in the revision of the Zoning Ordinance, the development of parks and greening the city, initiating development of the Greenbelt/River Corridor project, road and sewer rehabilitation, construction of a new fire station, and promotion of increased citizen involvement in "their" community.

TRONA BRIDGE: On Saturday, September 17, 1994, during Mayor Eckman's term, the Trona Bridge was erected at Expedition Island as a Greenbelt Project.

Major funding of the bridge was made possible by FMC Corporation, General Chemical, Rhone-Poulenc, Solvay Minerals and Tg Soda Ash, with each donating $50,000.

The bridge was built by CME Engineering and Construction, and they donated the soil engineering work necessary for the bridge embankment design, thus saving $37,000. With help from the Wyoming Congressional delegation, a $10,000 grant was received from the U.S. Forest Service's Timber Bridge Initiative Program.

The bridge links Expedition Island to Riverside Park, thus providing a pedestrian link between the north and south sides of the city of Green River.

Ribbon-Cutting Ceremony on December 8, 1994: Representatives of groups responsible for the construction of the bridge gathered for a ribbon-cutting ceremony as Greenbelt Task Force President John Freeman addressed the crowd at Expedition Island. From left are Mayor Eckman, Solvay representative Rick Casey (obscured), FMC's Tom Coverdale, Tg's Robert Harris, Rhone-Poulenc's Mike Duffy, General Chemical's Keith Clark, Key Bank's Greg Price, Greenbelt Chairman Richard Watson. CME's Eric Christensen and Ron Tucker are featured on the following page. (City of Green River photo)

NORMAN C. STARK

Norm Stark was born on January 15, 1942 in Winterport, Maine. As a teenager, he came to Wyoming where he lived and worked on a cattle ranch on the Encampment River. In 1960 he graduated from Encampment High School. He attended the University of Wyoming, graduating with a Bachelor of Science Degree in secondary education. He taught math at Monroe Junior High in Green River from

Norman C. Stark
1995-2002

1964 to 1977.

In August of 1977, Mayor Dick Waggener appointed Mr. Stark as the first full-time Clerk/Treasurer for the City of Green River. He developed a modern computerized Finance Department and received the first GFOA (Governmental Financial Officers Association) Distinguished Budget Award in the state. Mr. Stark was a charter member of the Wyoming Clerks and Treasurers Association and served as treasurer and vice president.

Since coming to Green River in 1964, Mr. Stark served on numerous boards and commissions including the United Way, Southwest Counseling, Sweetwater Pride, Mansface Terrace Housing, Golden Hour Senior Citizens, GR Chamber of Commerce, Sweetwater County Tripartite, and the GR Prevention Coalition.

Many turned out at Noon on Saturday, October 11, 2003, for the dedication of the John Wesley Powell statue on the corner in front of the Sweetwater County Historical Museum. The statue commemorates Major John Wesley Powell's trips down the Green and Colorado Rivers in 1869 and 1871 departing from Green River. (Sweetwater County Historical Museum photo.)

Mr. Stark enjoys his family, traveling, reading and most kinds of exercise. He has run in over ten marathons including the Boston Marathon in 1984. He also had the honor to represent Green River by carrying the Olympic torch during the torch relay as it crossed the country for the 1984 Los Angeles Summer Games.

Mr. Stark was elected Mayor on November 8, 1994 and took office on January 2, 1995. He served the citizens in that office until January 7, 2003.

AS MAYOR: As Mayor, Mr. Stark was very involved in helping the youth of Green River. This included working with the youth, the City Council and City staff to bring about one of the first skate parks in the state. The youth raised money, made presentations to the Governing Body, and helped to construct the park, Area 51, which was located in Roosevelt Park. Other youth activities and accomplishments were the Mayor's Youth Council, Teen Court, Work Restitution, and work toward a Youth Center.

Many infrastructure improvements were accomplished during Mr. Stark's eight years as Mayor. Over 30 miles of streets and improvements in the appearance of the City horse corrals were completed.

The Whitewater Park's U-drops were created in the river and several miles of Greenbelt pathway were added along with the John Wesley Powell Statue.

The College Business Park was created, Council meetings began being televised on Channel 13, and joint meetings were held with the Rock Springs Council and the County Commissioners. A highlight was hosting the Wyoming Association of Municipalities Convention in 2001.

Mr. Stark and his wife, Shirley, volunteer in the community and spend time working with the Work Restitution youth at the Forest Service garden along Uinta Drive.

Mr. Stark thanks the City Councils with whom he worked for their foresight and visioning in completing many goals and objectives for the City.

WHITEWATER PARK:

Late in the year 2000, Green River's Greenbelt Task Force and Parks and Recreation Director Roger Moellendorf, presented a proposal to turn a small section of the Green River into a whitewater river course for kayaking. In 2001, Green River's governing body supported the construction of a Whitewater Park in the Green River near Expedition Island.

After months of designing and planning, months waiting for permits, and weeks of construction, the Whitewater Park was complete and ready for use during the summer of 2002. It provided whitewater experiences for kayakers, canoeists, innertubers, and rafters. The north channel of the river between Evers and Expedition Island parks was transformed into an attractive slalom course.

In 2003, the Park urged visitors to experience a whitewater blast at the Electrocutioner, Powell's Plunge and Castle Falls U-drops. The Park has become a constant attraction during the summer months for water sports enthusiasts from near and far.

While Norm Stark was mayor, the Green River Whitewater Park was created in the river by Expedition Island. A kayak enthusiast and his dog were two of the many enjoying the water of the Green River during the summer of 2003. (*The Green River Star* photo by Ann Jantz)

DAVID GOMEZ

David Gomez
2003-

David Gomez was born in Rock Springs, Wyoming, on March 19, 1952. At the time of his becoming Mayor, he had lived in Green River for 49.5 years out of the 50 years he had lived in Wyoming.

Mr. Gomez is one of seven children, five boys and two girls. His mother, Helen Gold, had married Joe E. Gomez.

Mr. Gomez married Becky Sue Beck on November 27, 1976. They have three children, Jeiremy, Nathaniel, and Kristian. He worked as a miner/roofbolter for Texas Gulf west of Green River and later began his own business, Crystal Clean Inc.

Mr. Gomez attended the University of Wyoming and has been an active member of the Knights of Columbus, Eagles, Search and Rescue, and the International Graphonalysis Society. He is certified in handwriting and enjoys camping, hunting, and spending time with his family.

Mr. Gomez was elected Mayor of the City of Green River on November 5, 2002 and took office January 6, 2003.

AS MAYOR: Mr. Gomez believes the most important issue facing Green River is finding ways to keep the citizens and children of Green River in Green River by establishing new businesses and maintaining the businesses currently in Green River.

Mayor Gomez reported that many new things were happening because of the efforts of an energetic and high-spirited council. Pictured are Mayor David Gomez and Council Members Henry Rood, Angelo Kallas, Ted York, Ken Ball, Pete Rust and Randy Walker. (City of Green River photo)

INDEX

F

G

T

U

V

W

Y

Z

CPSIA information can be obtained
at www.ICGtesting.com
Printed in the USA
FSHW011019210120
66319FS